Professionals

Software Development

with J...

a – Level 2

005.133

K. Mary Reid

Jenny Lawson

www.heinemann.co.uk
✓ Free online support
✓ Useful weblinks
✓ 24 hour online ordering

01865 888058

Heinemann
Inspiring generations

Heinemann Educational Publishers
Halley Court, Jordan Hill, Oxford OX2 8EJ
Part of Harcourt Education

Heinemann is the registered trademark of
Harcourt Education Limited

First published 2004

09 08 07 06 05 04
10 9 8 7 6 5 4 3 2 1

British Library Cataloguing in Publication Data is available
from the British Library on request.

ISBN 0 435 47150 3

Typeset by 🗡 Tek-Art, Croydon, Surrey

Original illustrations © Harcourt Education Limited, 2004

Cover design by Wooden Ark
Design by Wooden Ark
Printed in the UK by Bath Press Ltd
Cover photo: © Harcourt Index/Corbis

Acknowledgements
Every effort has been made to contact copyright holders of material reproduced
in this book. Any omissions will be rectified in subsequent printings if notice is
given to the publishers.

Screenshots reprinted by permission from Microsoft Corporation
Screenshot on page 241 reproduced with permission from Tesco

Websites
Please note that the examples of websites suggested in this book were up to
date at the time of writing. It is essential for tutors to preview each site before
using it to ensure that the URL is still accurate and the content is appropriate. We
suggest that tutors bookmark useful sites and consider enabling students to
access them through the school or college intranet.

Tel: 01865 888058 www.heinemann.co.uk

Contents

Introduction

The City & Guilds Level 2 Diploma for IT Practitioners is a collection of two related qualifications:

◆ Diploma for IT Practitioners (ICT Systems Support)
◆ Diploma for IT Practitioners (Software Development)

There are three books in this series, designed to meet the needs of these City & Guilds qualifications:

◆ Systems Support – Level 2
◆ Software Development with Visual Basic – Level 2
◆ Software Development with Java – Level 2

Units in this book

This book contains material to cover one core unit (205 *Create software components with Java*), Unit 206 (*Test software components*) and two other units from the bank of nine units (208 *Website design* and 209 *Create designs for software components*). It therefore provides enough units to complete the award for the Diploma for IT Practitioners (Software Development).

The source code for all the Java files plus other useful information and links can be found at www.neal.tzo.com/java.

	Systems Support – Level 2	Software Development with Visual Basic - Level 2	Software Development with Java – Level 2
Core units	401 Maintain equipment and systems	201 Create software components using 'C'	201 Create software components using 'C'
		202 Create software components using 'C++'	202 Create software components using 'C++'
		203 Create software components using Pascal	203 Create software components using Pascal
	402 Customer support provision	204 Create software components using Visual Basic	204 Create software components using Visual Basic
		205 Create software components using Java	205 Create software components using Java
		206 Test software components	206 Test software components
Optional units	403 Install and configure equipment and operating systems	207 Operating systems	207 Operating systems

	Systems Support – Level 2	Software Development with Visual Basic - Level 2	Software Development with Java – Level 2
	404 Install, configure and maintain software	208 Website design	208 Website design
	405 Systems testing		
	406 System monitoring and operation	209 Create designs for software components	209 Create designs for software components
	407 Repair centre procedure		
	408 Networking		

Assessment

Assessment is carried out by City & Guilds.

For all units, you will be expected to complete at least one timed class-based assignment which is set by the examination body. These assignments assess practical activities in the core units, and underpinning knowledge as well as practical activities for the optional units.

In addition, there are examinations which are designed to test knowledge and understanding of each core unit. These tests are 40-item multiple-choice questions, delivered on-line.

As with City and Guilds E-Quals awards, if you don't pass an examination or an assignment, you are welcome to make another attempt, at a new examination paper and/or a new assignment.

Create designs for software components

The chapters in this unit contain information about how to implement software features in both the Visual Basic and Java programming languages. You should refer to unit 2 for full details of how to write programs in one of these languages. The subject of program testing is part of this unit, but it is covered fully in unit 3.

Outcomes

- Describe the common features of high-level programming languages
- Specify data types and data structures
- Develop a software component design specification
- Validate the completed design specification

1 Describe the common features of high-level programming languages

Writing all but the simplest of computer programs is a complex process that requires planning. When building a house, the first step is for an architect to produce a detailed design. In the same way, when creating software the first step also involves designs.

A **program** is a set of instructions that tells the computer what to do. Whatever function you want a computer to perform, all you have to do is write the program.

A program is a little like a recipe for cooking a meal. A recipe lists, in detail, the steps you must follow to make the meal. Recipes are written in English, to be understood by humans, and they assume a level of common sense from the cook.

Computers, on the other hand, do not have common sense. They require a very precise set of instructions. The microprocessor or chip at the heart of a computer can understand instructions only in the form of binary codes (made up of 1s and 0s). But binary codes are very difficult for humans to understand, so all modern programming is done using **symbolic languages** with English-like statements, known as high-level programming languages. Over the years, many different high-level programming languages have been developed, each with its own set of features. Some of the best known are listed in Table 1.1.

Table 1.1 *High-level programming languages*	
Language	**Features**
C++	Low-level technical programming
Cobol	Traditionally used for business applications (stands for COmmon Business Orientated Language)
Fortran	Traditionally used for complex scientific programming (stands for FORmula TRANslation)
Java	Designed for Internet programming
Pascal	Often used for teaching programming
Visual Basic	Easy-to-use Windows programming language, developed by Microsoft

Table 1.2 shows a very simple program written in two different languages, Basic and Pascal.

Table 1.2 *Sample programs*

Basic	Pascal

Dim num1 as integer
Dim num2 as integer
Dim answer as integer
Print "Calculator Program"
Print "Enter first number"
Input num1
Print "Enter second number"
Input num2
answer = num1 + num2
Print "The answer is ", answer
	program simcalc(input, output);
	uses crt;
	var
	  num1 : integer;
	  num2 : integer;
	  answer : integer;
	begin
	  writeln ('Calculator Program');
	  writeln ('Enter first number');
	  readln (num1);
	  writeln ('Enter second number');
	  readln (num2);
	  answer := num1 + num2;
	  writeln ('Answer is ', answer);
	  delay (5000)
	end.

Once the program has been written using the high-level language, a piece of software known as a **compiler** is used to convert the high-level language into the binary instruction codes that the computer's microprocessor can understand.

Although there are many different high-level programming languages, they all share similar main features. However, there are many detailed differences between computer languages. This means that an expert in one language would not be able to use another without retraining.

1.1 Syntax and keywords

Programs are made up of **instructions** or **statements**. Each statement is written on a line on its own, using a text editor which is normally part of the programming IDE (integrated development environment), which also includes a compiler and other tools. The rules governing how these instructions are written are called the **syntax**. Each high-level language has its own syntax. If the syntax rules are broken when the program is written, when the compiler attempts to convert the instructions into binary codes, it will produce an error, telling you that it cannot convert the program into binary because you have made a syntax error. Figure 1.1 shows an example.

Program listing

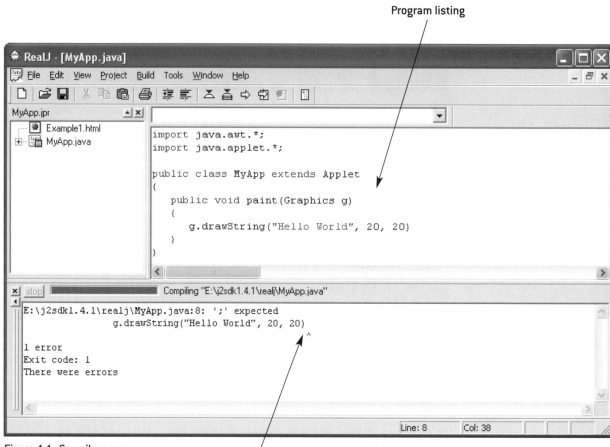

Figure 1.1 Compiler error

Compiler error listing
(a semi-colon is missing)

Program statements are made up of a **keyword** – that is, the actual instruction – and one or more **parameters** or **arguments** which qualify the keyword. For example, in the Basic programming language, if you want to display the words 'Hello World', the instruction would be:

```
Print "Hello World"
```

In this case, *Print* is the keyword and Hello World (placed between double quotes in the code) is the parameter which qualifies the keyword, showing what is to be printed. Programming languages have several hundred keywords, and part of learning how to use any language involves learning what the keywords are used for and the exact syntax of how they are used.

Part of the syntax of any language is the spelling of the keyword. So, for example, if you spell the Print keyword incorrectly (perhaps Pritn instead of Print) you have made a syntax error; the statement would be rejected by the compiler and it would issue an error message such as 'unrecognised keyword'.

The same statement in the Java language looks a little different:

```
System.out.print("Hello World");
```

Java has a rather more complex syntax than Basic. It is **case-sensitive**, which means that not only must you spell the keywords correctly, but the capitalization must be correct too – so both *System.Out.Print* and *system.out.print* would be incorrect.

Also, Java, C++ and Pascal require that you add a semi-colon at the end of each statement to show where one statement ends and the next begins. Omitting it will produce syntax errors when the program is compiled. COBOL, on the other hand, requires a full stop at the end of each statement. Basic does not use any punctuation at the end of each statement. Instead the lines are numbered, although if you want to put two statements on the same line you can do this, separating them with a colon.

PRACTICAL TASK 1.1

What programming language skills are most in demand in the job market? It is important that you develop your own skills in an area where you are most likely to get a job.

1 Carry out your own survey on which programming languages are most in demand. Go to some computing job websites (such as www.computing.co.uk/careers or www.totaljobs.com – select IT and Internet) and search for Java, Basic, C++ and other programming languages. How many jobs can you find for each language?

2 Make a list of the most popular languages and skills.

1.2 Comments

Although programs are intended to be understood by computers, it is important that humans can understand them too. Programmers often need to modify or correct programs, so it is good practice to include comments in your programs.

What does it mean?

Comments are plain English explanations of what parts of the program do. These comments are ignored by the compiler.

It is not necessary to add comments to every statement in the program. But comments should be added as often as required to explain what the statements that follow mean. The more complex the program, the greater the need for detailed comments.

So that the compiler knows where the comments are, they are preceded by a special character. In Basic, this a single quotation mark (') (or the keyword *rem*), while in Java and C++ it is two slashes (//). Table 1.3 shows two examples.

Table 1.3 *Sample programs with comments included*

Basic	Pascal

Rem Declare variables
Dim num1 as integer
Dim num2 as integer
Dim answer as integer
Print "Calculator Program"
Print "Enter first number"
Rem Accept first number
Input num1
Print "Enter second number"
Rem Accept second number
Input num2
Rem Add two numbers together
answer = num1 + num2
Rem Display the answer
Print "The answer is ", answer
	program simcalc(input, output);
	uses crt;
	// declare variables
	var
	  num1 : integer;
	  num2 : integer;
	  answer : integer;
	begin
	  writeln ('Calculator Program');
	  writeln ('Enter first number');
	  // accept first number
	  readln (num1);
	  writeln ('Enter second number');
	  // accept second number
	  readln (num2);
	  // add two numbers togther
	  answer := num1 + num2;
	  // display the answers
	  writeln ('Answer is ', answer);
	  // wait before closing window
	  delay (5000)
	end.

Comments should also be added at the beginning of the program stating who wrote the program, along with a brief description of its purpose and the date when it was last modified.

1.3 Variables and constants

Programs need to be able to store data.

◆ That data may be input from the user of the program or it may be the result of a calculation.

◆ The data may vary or it may be constant.

Programs store data that varies using what are called **variables**, and these are areas of the computer's memory allocated to the program. Variables have three attributes:

◆ a name

◆ a data type

◆ a value.

To refer to the variable, a **name** is given to it. The name is chosen by the programmer.

◆ All programming languages require variables to start with an alphabetic character.

◆ No programming language allows variable names to contain spaces.

◆ The variable cannot have the same name as one of that language's keywords. This is because each language has a list of so-called **reserved words**, which cannot be used as variable or constant names or as program or procedure names.

So, for example, *Print*, *22* and *my variable* would not be valid variable names (why not?), but *x* and *myvariable* would be valid. It is good practice to give a variable a name that tells something about its purpose. So, a variable used to store the score in a computer game might be called *score*.

The **data type** determines the data that can be stored in the variable. For example, a variable that holds someone's name will need to have a *text* data type, while a variable that holds their age will have an *integer* (that is, whole number) data type. Different languages allow different data types and give them different names, although all languages allow for **text**, **integer number** and **real number** data types. (A 'real number' is a number with a decimal point in it.)

The **value** is assigned during the program execution, and may depend on a number of things, such as user input. The value stored in a variable varies – hence the name 'variable'.

As well as allocating memory storage for values that vary, many programs need to store fixed values, or **constants**. For example, a program that needs to store the maximum score in an exam or the mathematical value of pi (3.14176...) would store these values in a constant, which – unlike a variable – does not change during the execution of the program.

Before either variables or constants can be used, they must be **declared**. The syntax of declaring variables depends on the programming language. For example, with the Basic language, to declare an integer variable called *mynumber* the instruction uses the *Dim* keyword:

```
Dim mynumber as Integer
```

What does it mean?

*An **integer** is a whole number, such as 3 or 25, without a fractional part. When declaring a variable in Basic, the **Dim** keyword is used to indicate that this is a variable declaration.*

With Java, declaring variables is a little simpler:

```
int mynumber;
```

Assigning a value into a variable is done using the **assignment operator**, the equals sign (=). So, to assign a value to the mynumber variable, using Basic, the statement would be:

```
mynumber = 2
```

In Java it would be:

```
mynumber = 2;
```

These assignments put the number 2 in the *memory area* called mynumber.

Constants also need to be declared. In Basic, the statement would be:

```
Const Pi = 3.14176
```

In Java (*float* is the data type for real numbers) the statement would be:

```
Final float Pi = 3.14176
```

Go out and try!

Find out how variables are created in Basic, Java and another language of your choice. Find out what data types these languages support, and what ranges of values can be stored in the different data types.

1.4 Arithmetic operators

Having assigned values to variables, it is often useful to carry out arithmetic using the usual four operators, as listed in Table 1.4.

Table 1.4 *Arithmetic operators*	
Operation	**Operator**
Addition	+
Subtraction	−
Multiplication	*
Division	/

Arithmetic operators can be used with actual numbers, or with values contained in variables or constants. So, in the Basic version of the example program shown in Table 1.2 (page 3), the instruction:

```
answer = num1 + num2
```

took the values contained in the variables *num1* and *num2*, added them together and placed the result in the variable called *answer*. The instruction:

```
answer = num1 * 2
```

would multiply the value in num1 by 2.

Parentheses allow you to change the order of precedence – that is, the order in which the different arithmetic operations are normally carried out. For example, you might imagine the calculation:

10 + 5 * 2

would give the result 30, but operators are *not* evaluated from left to right. Multiplication is done before addition, so the result would be 20 – with 5 multiplied by 2 first (giving 10), and then the 10 is added to give 20.

What does it mean?

Parentheses are rounded brackets, like this ( ). Calculations within parentheses are done first.

There is a simple mnemonic to help you remember the order of mathematical precedence, which is 'BODMAS'. This stands for:

◆ **B**rackets
◆ **P**owers **O**f
◆ **D**ivision
◆ **M**ultiplication } working from left to right
◆ **A**ddition
◆ **S**ubtraction } working from left to right

So anything in brackets is done first, followed by division and multiplication, and then any addition and subtraction as necessary.

To get the result of 30 in the earlier example, the expression would need to be written as:

(10 + 5) * 2

To raise a number to the power of a certain value, the **^ operator** is used. For example, the formula to find the area of a circle is:

$a = \pi r^2$

Therefore the following instruction, using two variables called *radius* and *area*, would implement this formula:

area = 3.14 * radius ^ 2

The **modulus operator** in Basic is *Mod*, and in Java it is %. So for example, in Java, 8 % 3 has the result 2.

What does it mean?

The modulus is the remainder left over after division. For example, 13 divided by 4 is 3 remainder 1 – so 1 is the modulus in that case.

What results will these formulae produce?

112 – 4 * 5

2(12 – 4) * 5

315 / 2

415 % 2

53.14 * 6 ^ 2

1.5 Program constructs

Programming languages provide a wide range of functions, with hundreds of keywords. Different programming languages, as already mentioned, have different syntax for writing instructions using these keywords. However, all programming languages provide instructions that control the program flow. These instructions allow blocks of code (i.e. a number of instructions which carry out a particular task) to be executed in different ways. The different ways block of code can be executed can be broadly divided into:

◆ sequence

◆ selection

◆ iteration.

These terms are sometimes called **program constructs** or **program control structures**, because programs are constructed out of blocks of code that are executed in one of these three ways.

Sequence is when the program statements are followed one after the other. An example might be doing a calculation or accepting some input from the user.

Selection is where a choice is made as to which set of instructions to carry out next. The choice is made based on a criterion such as an option the user has selected. In most programming languages, selection is done using the *if* keyword.

Generally, selection constructs take the form:

```
If (condition) then
   (
   statements to be executed if the condition is true
   )
else
   (
   statements to be executed if the condition is false
   )
end of selection construct
```

The exact syntax of the construct depends on the language in use.

Go out and try!

Find out what syntax is used in Java, Basic and one other language for creating if...else constructs.

Iteration is where instructions are repeated either a certain number of times or until some condition is met. An iteration construct is sometimes called a **loop**.

What does it mean?

*A **loop** is a part of a program that is repeated. For example, if you want a program that prints out a times-table from 1 to 12, the most efficient way to write the program would be with a section of code that repeats (loops) 12 times.*

Iteration can be implemented in a program in a number of different ways. In a *fixed* iteration construct, the loop is repeated a fixed number of times and is often implemented using the *For* keyword. However, there are situations in programming where the statements need to repeat until some condition is met, rather than a fixed number of times. This is often implemented using the *While* keyword, which takes the general form:

```
While (condition)
    (
    statements to be repeated while the condition is true
    )
```

With this type of loop, the condition is tested on entry into the loop. So, if it is not true at the start of the loop, the statements inside the loop will not be executed at all. A slightly different version of this loop has the condition at the exit point of the loop, which takes the form:

```
Repeat
    (
    statements to be repeated
    )
until (condition)
```

In this case, the statements within the loop will always be executed at least once because the condition is not tested until the end of the loop.

Check your understanding

Find out what different types of loops can be used in Java, Basic and one other language. In each case, find out what the syntax is for each type of loop.

Procedures

A common technique for dealing with complex programming problems (such as controlling a space rocket or producing a computer game) is to divide the problem up into sections. To start with, these can be large sections covering broad areas. Then, further detail can be added bit by bit to each of the sections until a detailed solution has been designed. Program design takes the same approach. Faced with a complex program to design and write, where do you start?

The first step is to divide the program up into sections, which in programming terminology are called **procedures** and **functions**. Within each procedure, the next step in the 'divide and conquer technique' of problem-solving is to identify which of the programming constructs are needed, and in which combination, to achieve the required functionality.

PRACTICAL TASK 1.2

Think of a task you are familiar with, such as completing a piece of course work. Break the task down into sections which involve different activities (just as you would break a programming task down into procedures), such as finding relevant library books. For each section (procedure), further subdivide the section and decide for each subsection what parts need doing in sequence (such as typing up the course work), making selections (finding suitable books) and repetition (refining and proof-reading your final document).

1.6 Relational and logical operators

Selection and some iteration constructs rely on a condition to decide how to proceed. This condition takes the form of a test, which needs to evaluate true or false, and is known as a **Boolean condition**. Here are some examples of Boolean conditions:

◆ Is this person over 18?

◆ Are there any seats free on the plane?

◆ Has a student achieved 80% attendance?

Boolean conditions use relational operators, such as equal to, greater than and less than. Table 1.5 shows the relational operators with their equivalent symbols for both Basic and Java.

More complex relational conditions can be put together using the logical operators, as listed in Table 1.6.

Table 1.5 _Relational operators_

Relational condition	Java operator	Basic operator
Equal to	==	=
Not equal to	!=	<>
Less than	<	<
Greater than	>	>
Greater than or equal to	>=	>=
Less than or equal to	<=	<=

Table 1.6 _Logical operators_

Logical condition	Java operator	Basic operator
AND	==	=
OR	!=	<>
NOT	<	<

What does it mean?

**Boolean** logic was developed by an English mathematician call George Boole, hence the name. Boolean logic is actually very simple and involves combining conditions with the AND, OR and NOT operators. For example, a condition such as 'male AND over 30' would select all people who are both men and over 30. The condition 'male OR over 30' would select people who were either men or over 30 (i.e. including all men of any age and women over 30).

Logical operators allow relational operators to be combined:

◆ Is this person over 18 AND under 60? – In this case, both conditions must be true for the expression to evaluate to true.

◆ Are there any seats free on the plane OR is there another flight the same day? – Here, either condition can be true.

In real-life applications, multiple combinations of conditions like these can introduce a considerable degree of complexity. In these situations, **decision tables** are sometimes used to identify the different conditions and associated actions.

What does it mean?

A **decision table** is used to model complex series of conditions and the actions that are taken in each situation. Many real-life applications have complex conditions. For example, issuing a bus pass may depend upon a number of conditions, such as the age of the applicant, where the person lives and whether he or she has a recent photograph. Decision tables are described on page 30.

Check your understanding

Write an *If* instruction (using the language of your choice) that will carry out one action if the value contained in a variable called *personsAge* is over 18 and under 60, and another action if it is not.

1.7 Structured programming

The concept of breaking a large and complex program into separate procedures has already been briefly introduced. Creating a program using this so-called structured approach has a number of advantages:

◆ Structuring a program in this way is an effective way of dealing with complexity.

◆ Since the same function is often required a number of times within the program (for example, when validating user input such as a date), creating a separate procedure to carry out this task avoids duplicating code and may create general-purpose procedures that can be re-used in other programs.

◆ In a large programming project, which may employ many programmers, by dividing the program up into procedures, each programmer can work independently on one or more procedures.

When program control is passed to a procedure from the main program, the main program can pass parameters to the procedure which the procedure then uses in its processing. For example, if a procedure is written to validate a date input by the user, the main program will pass the date the user entered. Once the procedure has carried out its task, it can return a value to the calling program. In the example of the data validation procedure, the procedure could return a Boolean value set to 'true' if the date was valid and 'false' if it was not valid.

1.8 Naming conventions

Just as adding comments to programs is considered good practice, so using consistent, meaningful names for variables, procedures and files is also good practice and helps to make programs more understandable. Remember that you cannot use any of the language keywords as variable or procedure names, nor can you have spaces in variable names. Where you want to use a meaningful variable name made of several words, just join them together leaving out the spaces, as in *dateOfBirth*. Note that it is a widely used convention to start variables' names with a lower-case character and, where it is made up of several words, each of those has an initial capital.

In a Windows programming environment, as well as naming variables, the window components such as text boxes, command buttons and list boxes also need names. This can easily lead to confusion! For example, you might have a text box used to enter someone's surname and decide to call the text box 'surname'. The value entered into this text box may need to be transferred to a variable, but what name do you choose for this variable? You cannot call both the variable and the text box the same name. It is therefore good practice to precede window component names with something that identifies not only that they are window components but also what type of component they are. Text boxes, for example, can be preceded with 'txt', so the name for the surname text box would be *txtSurname*. Table 1.7 shows suggested prefixes for the most common window components.

Table 1.7 **Component name prefixes**

Component	Suggested prefix
Command button	cmd
Text box	txt
List box	lst
Label	lbl
Check box	chk

Chapter summary

This chapter has covered all the practical activities listed under the first outcome in the specification, including:

◆ the main features of programming languages

◆ the use of arithmetic operators

◆ the program constructs of sequence, selection and iteration

◆ relational and logic operators

◆ structured programming

◆ naming conventions.

2 Specify data types and data structures

The concepts of variables and data types have already been introduced (see page 6). This chapter looks in more detail at different data types and introduces some more advanced topics such as arrays and file handling.

2.1 Data types

In general, a variable or constant can hold data of only one particular type. There are two fundamental data types – numbers and text – but many variations of these types exist, which, for example, hold numbers of different sizes. Table 1.8 describes the common data types in more detail.

Table 1.8 *Data types*

Data type	Allows for	Example	Java declaration	Visual Basic declaration
Integer	Whole numbers	5	Int age;	Dim age as integer
Floating point	Numbers with a decimal point	5.5	Float price	Dim price as single
Character	Single characters	m	Char gender	Dim gender as string
String	Strings of characters	John	String name	Dim name as string

Most languages provide different versions of the same data type to store different ranges of numbers. For example, the *Integer* data type in Visual Basic can only store numbers in the range −32,768 through to +32,767, while the *Long* data type can store numbers in the range approximately −2 million through to +2 million. The difference is due to the amount of memory used to store the variable – Integer uses 2 bytes (16 bits) whereas Long uses 4 bytes. Both Visual Basic and Java provide a floating-point data type called *Double* that can store very large numbers, which might be used in scientific calculations.

2.2 String manipulation

Most programming languages provide a number of built-in string manipulation functions. Some of the Java and Basic string manipulation functions are listed in Table 1.9.

There is a wide range of applications where string manipulation may be required. An example is the processing and validation of postcodes or other codes which contain combinations of alphabetic and numeric characters. The first four characters of a postcode contain a code which identifies the area of the country to which the postcode belongs, while the final three characters identify the street. In a program that sorts mail, the first step would probably

Table 1.9 *String manipulation functions*

Description	Basic function	Basic example	Java function	Java example, where string str contains 'Hello'
Returns the length of a string	Len	Len("hello") returns 5	length	str.length() returns 5
Converts a string to upper case	UCase	UCase("hello") returns "HELLO"	toUpper	str.toUpper() returns "HELLO"
Converts a string to lower case	LCase	LCase("HELLO") returns "hello"	toLower	str.toLower() returns "hello"
Returns a number of characters from the middle of a string	Mid	Mid("Hello", 2, 3) returns "ell"	substring	str.substring(1, 3) returns "ell"

Note that in Visual Basic the Mid function counts the characters in a string from 1, but the Java function substring counts from 0.

be to divide the mail into areas of the country. So, if the postcode were contained in a variable called *postcode*, the following instruction would move the area part of the postcode into a separate variable called *area*:

```
area = postcode.substring(0,2)
```

PRACTICAL TASK 1.3

What do the following Basic string functions return?

1 UCase("basic")

2 Len("what's for tea?")

3 Mid("String manipulation", 6,5)

2.3 Passing parameters and return values

Procedures are commonly passed one or more variables as parameters to process, and they then return a value when they have finished their task. Procedures, of course, have a name, and the general form of calling a procedure is as follows:

Procedure_name(parameter1, parameter 2, etc.)

The previous section on string manipulation introduced some built-in functions, provided as part of the programming language, which are passed parameters and which return values. Programmers can, of course, write their own functions or procedures. So, for example, if a procedure is required to validate a date, it might be called *vDate* and it is passed three integer variables, called *day*, *month* and *year*. Having validated the date, the procedure returns an integer which indicates whether the date was valid – or, if it was not valid, where the problem lies. In this example, the return value is placed in a variable called *isValid*:

```
isValid = vDate(day, month, year)
```

The scope of variables

One question that arises when designing procedures is whether the variables that exist in the main program can be accessed by the procedures (known as the scope of variables).

The answer is that it depends on how the main program variables are declared. If they are declared as **global variables**, then they can be accessed and used by the main program and all the procedures. If they are declared as **local variables**, then they cannot be accessed in that way.

What does it mean?

The **scope** of a variable refers to the extent to which the variable is available within the program. In a program that is spilt into different procedures, variables within the main program may or may not be available within the procedures.

Variables that are available is both the main program and the procedures are know as **global** variables, while those which are not are known as **local** variables.

It is generally accepted that global variables are not a good idea and should be avoided if possible. The problem with them is that it is easy to make mistakes and misuse them. This is especially the case if several programmers are working on the same program. One programmer may use a global variable in a procedure for one thing while another programmer may use it in a slightly different way. Another reason is that global variables make maintaining large programs difficult. For example, it may be decided that a particular global variable needs to be changed from an integer to the real data type (see page 7). This would mean that all the procedures using the global variable would need to be changed.

Data hiding

Using only local variables within procedures is sometimes called data hiding, because all the data (variables) are hidden within the procedure. The only way data can be put into and taken out of the procedure is by using the parameters that are passed and the return value, and this is called the **public interface** of the procedure.

In the example of the date validation procedure, the variables used as parameters for the procedure contain the values which are passed to the procedures for processing. This is known as passing parameters **by value**. In some circumstances, the parameters passed do not contain the values themselves; instead they are a **pointer** to the actual value. A pointer contains the memory address of the variable or object that is being passed. This is known as passing parameters **by reference**. An example of this can be found in Windows programming where objects such as a command button are created and then passed as parameters to the procedure which adds them to the current window. In this case, the procedure is not passed a simple variable containing a value, but is being passed the name of an object, the name being a way to refer to the object itself.

The concept of passing parameters by reference is often a difficult one to grasp. An analogy can be drawn with a treasure hunt. You may be led to look under a stone, and under the stone you might find the treasure itself (by value) or you might find a clue which tells you where to look for the treasure (by reference).

2.4 Arrays

Mostly, variables are used to store a single value. However, there are situations when variables are needed to store a number of related items. For example, consider a program that records and processes the number of hours of sunshine each day in a week. Seven variables could be created, one for each day of the week, such as (in Basic):

```
Dim sunshine1, sunshine2, sunshine3, sunshine4, sunshine5,
                              sunshine6, sunshine7 as single
```

The problem with this approach is that when the program does any processing with this data it needs to process each variable separately, rather than use a loop to process them. For example, if the program needs to print out each variable it would need seven separate Print statements.

The solution to this problem is to use an array. An array is a special type of variable that can store a collection of items all of the same data type. Arrays are declared in a similar way to normal variables, except that the number of **elements** in the array (that is the number of items it can store) must be indicated. So the array needed to store the number of hours of sunshine in a week would be declared, in Basic, like this:

```
Dim sunshine(6) as single
```

Array elements are numbered (or *indexed* to use the proper term) from 0. So sunshine(6) produces a seven-element array – sunshine(0) through to sunshine(6).

All the array elements can now be printed using a loop; for example:

```
For i = 0 To 6
Print sunshine(i)
Next i
```

Here the loop counter (the variable *i*) is used as a **subscript** to access each element of the array.

> ### What does it mean?
>
> *A **subscript** is a number that is used to access an individual element of an array.*

The data in an array sometimes needs to be searched or sorted. Searching through an array for a particular value, such as the largest or smallest, involves looping through the array to find the required value, using a *For* loop. For example, suppose the program for recording sunshine hours needs to find the day with the highest number of hours. This Basic code shown provides the required value and stores it in a variable called *Highest*:

```
Highest = sunshine(0)
For i = 1 To 6
   If sunshine(i) > Highest Then
      Highest = sunshine(i)
   End if
Next i
```

Sorting involves putting the items in an array in some order, such as ascending numeric order. There are many sort algorithms available, and the topic of designing efficient sort routines is a subject within itself.

> ### What does it mean?
>
> *A **sort algorithm** is a method or technique for sorting a number of items into some kind of order (usually ascending or descending numerical order).*

A simple, but not particularly efficient, sorting algorithm, called the **bubble sort**, is described here. With this type of sort, the program uses a loop to check each element in the array to see whether it has a higher value than the next element. If it has, it swaps the values in the two elements.

The bubble sort is best explained by an example. Suppose the array shown in Figure 1.2 is to be sorted into ascending order.

Array element	0	1	2	3	4	5	6
Value	9	7	8	3	6	5	2

Figure 1.2 Starting array

The loop would first compare elements 0 and 1, and – noting that they are in the wrong sequence – it would swap them. Then it would compare elements 1 and 2 – they would be out of sequence too, so they would be swapped; and so on. Figure 1.3 shows the results of the first loop through the array with the swapped values shaded.

Array element	0	1	2	3	4	5	6
Start values	9	7	8	3	6	5	2
Loop 1	7	9	8	3	6	5	2
Loop 2	7	8	9	3	6	5	2
Loop 3	7	8	3	9	6	5	2
Loop 4	7	8	3	6	9	5	2
Loop 5	7	8	3	6	5	9	2
Loop 6	7	8	3	6	5	2	9

Figure 1.3 First loop

As can be seen, at the end of the first loop through the array the highest value (9) is in the correct place, but the rest of the array is not sorted. The loop must be executed for as many times as there are items in the array, using another loop.

The sample Basic code below would sort the array holding the number of sunshine hours:

```
For j = 0 To 6
   For i = 0 To 5
   If sunshine(i + 1) > sunshine(i) Then
      temp = sunshine(i)
      sunshine(i) = sunshine(i + 1)
      sunshine(i + 1) = temp
   End If
   Next i
Next j
```

Sorting is a very common data-processing function, and efficiency is important because the more efficient the sort, the quicker it can be done. While speed may not be an issue with just seven data items, real-life data-processing sorts may involve tens of thousands if not millions of data items. The bubble sort code shown above would prove particularly inefficient if that data was already partially sorted with perhaps just one or two items out of sequence. This is because it goes on looping through the array even when no swaps are required.

This could be avoided by using a variable as a **flag**. A flag is an indicator used to tell whether an event has occurred or not. The flag could be set to 0 at the beginning of the inner loop, and set to 1 if a swap is needed. At the end of the loop, the flag could be inspected to see whether it was still zero. If it was, this would indicate that no swaps had taken place, so the array must now be sorted in order and no further iterations through the outer loop are required.

Go out and try!

As mentioned earlier, there are many other – more efficient – sorting routines. Some of these are highly complex. Two relatively straightforward ones that you can investigate are the *insertion sort* and the *merge sort*.

2.5 File manipulation

Variables provide storage for data while the program is running, but once the program ends all the data held in variables is lost. For permanent storage, data must be written to a file saved on the computer's disk.

Data written to **files** must be structured in some way. For example, suppose a program is written to record details of students enrolled on a course. The students' details are written to a file, and the data for each student is held in a **record**. The individual items of data recorded for each student, such as name, date of birth and address, are held in **fields**. Each record contains a complete set of fields. This example is illustrated in Figure 1.4.

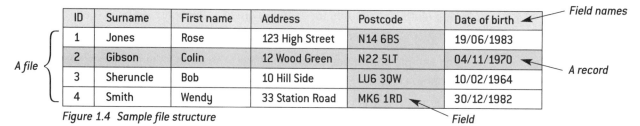

Figure 1.4 Sample file structure

Serial files

The simplest type of file is a serial file. With this type, records are written to the file as they arise naturally, and so may be in no particular order. While this makes writing records to the file simple, finding a particular record within a serial file can be very inefficient. Since the records are in no particular order, each record must be read one at a time until the required one is found. This may work reasonably quickly for files with just a few hundred records, but it would be impossibly slow for larger files.

Sequential files

In a sequential file, the records are written in a particular order, based on one of the fields – which is known as the **key field**. The key field should uniquely identify each record on the file, so the field chosen is often a code such as an account number or product code. Before a series of records can be written to a sequential file, they must be sorted into key order – hence the importance of sorting routines.

Using sequential files presents a number of issues. Finding a particular record in the file could be done by simply reading through the file one record at a time until the required one is found, as with a serial file. However, as the records are in key order there is a more efficient way.

PRACTICAL TASK 1.4

Imagine a file used to store details of all the music CDs in your collection. What fields would the file need? What would you use as a key field?

Imagine a sequential file of outstanding orders that has 200 records. The order numbers (the key field) on the file run from 110 to 550 and order number 250 is the one that is required. The quickest way to find the required record would be to read the record at the middle of the file (record number 100) and check what order number that record has. Since the records are in order number order, if the record in the middle of the file has an order number greater than 250, then the required record must lie in the lower half of the file; while if the middle record has an order number less than 250, the record must lie in the upper half. Let us assume that the middle record has an order number of 325, so the required record is in the lower half. The next step is to read the middle record in the lower half of the file – record number 50 – and check the order number of that record. The same logic applies to this record: if its order number is over 250, the required record is in the lower half of this section of the file; if not then the required record must be in the upper half. This routine is followed until the actual record is found, each time halving the number of records under consideration.

Inserting new records

Another issue with sequential files is inserting new records. If the record(s) to be inserted have key values higher than any of the existing records, then there is no problem because the record can be inserted at the end of the file. However, many applications will require that new records with key values within the range of existing values be inserted. In these situations, complex processing is involved to allow space to be made in the file to allow the new record to be inserted in the correct place among the existing records.

Using sequential files places a considerable burden on the programmer, requiring complex programs to be written to deal with finding, inserting and deleting records. For this reason almost all modern applications use a database management system (such as Microsoft's *Access*) which deals with all these issues. Database management systems (DBMSs) provide a programming interface using a special database language called SQL.

What does it mean?

SQL (structured query language) allows programs to be written that issue a procedure call to the database management software, sending an SQL statement as a parameter.

Database management systems and the SQL language are a complex topic, on which whole books have been written. They are beyond the scope of this unit.

PRACTICAL TASK 1.5

Find out about a database management system such as *Access*, *mySQL* or *Oracle*. Could you store your CD collection database using these systems? Will they allow you to search for matching records using only the key files, or can you search on any fields? Do you need to know SQL to use these database management systems? Can programs be written to interface with these systems?

2.6 Binary and ASCII

Computers store and process all data and instructions as binary codes – that is, numbers that contain 1s and 0s only. In the decimal number system, each digit in a number (from the right) represents an increase in magnitude of ten. So, for example, the number 234 represents:

◆ 4 ones

◆ 3 tens

◆ 2 hundreds.

In a binary number, each digit (from the right) represents an increase in magnitude of two. So a binary number such as 10011 represents:

◆ **1** one

◆ **1** two

◆ **0** fours

◆ **0** eights

◆ **1** sixteen.

You can easily convert this number to decimal by adding up the one, two and sixteen, which gives 19.

Converting a decimal number to binary involves repeatedly dividing the number by two:

```
19 divided by two gives:
9 remainder 1
    9 divided by 2 gives:
    4 remainder 1
        4 divided by 2 gives:
        2 remainder 0
            2 divided by 2 gives:
            1 remainder 0
                1 divided by 2 gives
                0 remainder 1
```

Then read the remainders off *from the bottom*, which gives: 10011.

The decimal numbers 1 to 10 and their binary equivalents are shown in Table 1.10.

Table 1.10 **Decimal table**				
Binary				**Decimal**
$8 = 2^3$	$4 = 2^2$	$2 = 2^1$	$1 = 2^0$	
0	0	0	1	1
0	0	1	0	2
0	0	1	1	3
0	1	0	0	4
0	1	0	1	5
0	1	1	0	6
0	1	1	1	7
1	0	0	0	8
1	0	0	1	9
1	0	1	0	10

Check your understanding

1 Convert 101100 from binary into decimal.

2 Convert 93 from decimal into binary.

All the characters you can print or display, plus many more control characters, are encoded into groups of seven binary numbers using **ASCII codes** (pronounced *askey*). The complete set of ASCII character codes is shown in Table 1.11. So, for example, the ASCII code for the letter 'a' is 97, while the code for 'z' is 122. The upper-case characters have different codes, so the code for 'A' is 65.

When comparisons between character values are done (using an If instruction, for example), the comparisons are done using the ASCII values. This means that when validating user input the program will need to test for both the upper-case and lower-case characters, since they will not be considered as the same.

You can print out the ASCII code of any character using the *Asc* function in Basic. The instruction:

```
Print Asc("z")
```

will print 122.

Table 1.11 ASCII table

Binary pattern	ASCII code	Hex code	Character	Binary pattern	ASCII code	Hex code	Character	Binary pattern	ASCII code	Hex code	Character
00000000	0	00	Null	00101011	43	2B	+	01010110	86	56	V
00000001	1	01	SOH	00101100	44	2C	,	01010111	87	57	W
00000010	2	02	STX	00101101	45	2D	-	01011000	88	58	X
00000011	3	03	ETX	00101110	46	2E	.	01011001	89	59	Y
00000100	4	04	EOT	00101111	47	2F	/	01011010	90	5A	Z
00000101	5	05	ENQ	00110000	48	30	0	01011011	91	5B	[
00000110	6	06	ACK	00110001	49	31	1	01011100	92	5C	\
00000111	7	07	BEL	00110010	50	32	2	01011101	93	5D	]
00001000	8	08	BS	00110011	51	33	3	01011110	94	5E	^
00001001	9	09	HT	00110100	52	34	4	01011111	95	5F	_
00001010	10	0A	LF	00110101	53	35	5	01100000	96	60	`
00001011	11	0B	VT	00110110	54	36	6	01100001	97	61	a
00001100	12	0C	FF	00110111	55	37	7	01100010	98	62	b
00001101	13	0D	CR	00111000	56	38	8	01100011	99	63	c
00001110	14	0E	SO	00111001	57	39	9	01100100	100	64	d
00001111	15	0F	SI	00111010	58	3A	:	01100101	101	65	e
00010000	16	10	DLE	00111011	59	3B	;	01100110	102	66	f
00010001	17	11	DC1	00111100	60	3C	<	01100111	103	67	g
00010010	18	12	DC2	00111101	61	3D	=	01101000	104	68	h
00010011	19	13	DC3	00111110	62	3E	>	01101001	105	69	i
00010100	20	14	DC4	00111111	63	3F	?	01101010	106	6A	j
00010101	21	15	NAK	01000000	64	40	@	01101011	107	6B	k
00010110	22	16	SYN	01000001	65	41	A	01101100	108	6C	l
00010111	23	17	ETB	01000010	66	42	B	01101101	109	6D	m
00011000	24	18	CAN	01000011	67	43	C	01101110	110	6E	n
00011001	25	19	EM	01000100	68	44	D	01101111	111	6F	o
00011010	26	1A	SUB	01000101	69	45	E	01110000	112	70	p
00011011	27	1B	ESC	01000110	70	46	F	01110001	113	71	q
00011100	28	1C	FS	01000111	71	47	G	01110010	114	72	r
00011101	29	1D	GS	01001000	72	48	H	01110011	115	73	s
00011110	30	1E	RS	01001001	73	49	I	01110100	116	74	t
00011111	31	1F	US	01001010	74	4A	J	01110101	117	75	u
00100000	32	20	space	01001011	75	4B	K	01110110	118	76	v
00100001	33	21	!	01001100	76	4C	L	01110111	119	77	w
00100010	34	22	"	01001101	77	4D	M	01111000	120	78	x
00100011	35	23	#	01001110	78	4E	N	01111001	121	79	y
00100100	36	24	$	01001111	79	4F	O	01111010	122	7A	z
00100101	37	25	%	01010000	80	50	P	01111011	123	7B	{
00100110	38	26	&	01010001	81	51	Q	01111100	124	7C	ı
00100111	39	27	'	01010010	82	52	R	01111101	125	7D	}
00101000	40	28	(	01010011	83	53	S	01111110	126	7E	~
00101001	41	29	)	01010100	84	54	T	01111111	127	7F	del
00101010	42	2A	*	01010101	85	55	U				

Numbers 0 to 9 have an ASCII code, the code for 0 is 48, 1 is 49, etc. However, representing numbers as ASCII code is treating them as text, rather than numbers with which you can do arithmetic. For example, if you enter the Basic instruction:

    Print "1" + "2"

it will print 12 – that is, the text string "1" joined together (or *concatenated* to use the correct term) with the text string "2". If you enter:

    Print 1 + 2

you will be given the result 3, which is the numbers 1 and 2 added.

What does it mean? *Concatenate is a technical term which means to link or join together. When you concatenate two strings (such as 'cat' and 'dog'), they are linked together in a single string, to become 'catdog'). Both Java and Visual Basic use the + sign to concatenate strings.*

Therefore, while characters can be stored on a computer only as binary numbers using the ASCII encoding scheme, numbers can be represented either by their binary equivalent or as their ASCII value. So, the number 5 can be represented as its binary equivalent, 101, or as its ASCII value 53, which in binary is 0110101.

Chapter summary

This chapter has covered all the practical activities listed under the second outcome in the specification, including:

◆ identifying the basic data types
◆ string manipulation methods
◆ local and global variables
◆ the use of arrays
◆ file manipulation
◆ binary and ACSII representation of numbers.

3 Develop a software component design specification

Before a program can be written, a design must be produced. Structured programming design techniques involve two main steps:

1 Modularise the program. As already mentioned, this involves breaking the program down into smaller parts, or procedures, each of which performs a particular task.

2 Design how each of the modules will work.

The procedures of the program can be graphically illustrated using a **structure chart**. This is a diagram showing the overall structure of the program, how it will be split into different procedures, and how the procedures will interact.

A number of different design techniques are used to identify how the procedures themselves will work. Two techniques will be described here in detail.

◆ **Decision tables** are useful where there are a lot of different options to choose from and you want to identify what happens in each circumstance.

◆ **Program design languages**, such as flowcharts and pseudo-code, are more detailed techniques, often used in the later stages of the design process.

In addition, the input, output and storage requirements of the program must be identified, and suitable file layouts, input screens and output report formats must be designed.

3.1 Structure charts

Structure charts are simple diagrams that identify how the program will be spilt into procedures, what order the procedures will be called in, what parameters will be passed to each procedure, and what values will be returned. The chart is drawn with a box containing the name of the main program at the top. Each of the different procedures is shown in a box below, connected to the main program by a line. An arrow is drawn pointing into each procedure box showing the parameter to be passed to the procedure. Another arrow is drawn pointing back into the main program box showing the value to be returned by the procedure. This is shown in Figure 1.5.

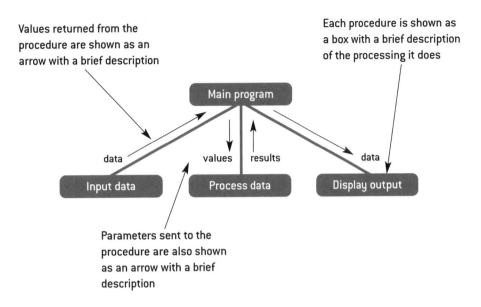

Values returned from the procedure are shown as an arrow with a brief description

Each procedure is shown as a box with a brief description of the processing it does

Parameters sent to the procedure are also shown as an arrow with a brief description

Figure 1.5 Sample structure chart

CASE STUDY

Northgate College

Northgate College requires a program that will accept a student's details before they are recorded on a database. The program needs to validate the student's date of birth and postcode, and return a code to indicate whether the validation has been successful – or if not, what the error was. The program could be divided into three procedures: a date validation procedure, a postcode validation procedure, and a procedure to display the meaning of an error code returned by either of the two other procedures. The structure chart for this arrangement is shown in Figure 1.6.

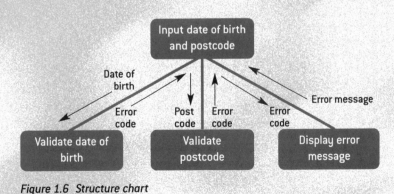

Figure 1.6 Structure chart

PRACTICAL TASK 1.6

You are planning to write a program to allow you to search for CDs on your CD collection database by their catalogue numbers. The program needs to accept a catalogue number, check that it is in the correct format (e.g. numeric), and then search for a matching catalogue number on the file. It then has to return the CD details if found, and an error code if not. Draw the structure chart for this program.

3.2 Decision tables

Another design tool that is useful where the processing in a program includes a range of true or false values is a decision table. A decision table has two parts – **conditions** and **actions**. All the possible combinations of conditions are listed at the top of the table. For example, consider an application which plans the food deliveries for a supermarket. Part of the program decides what type of lorry the food will be sent by. This choice is based on two conditions:

1 Is the food perishable?

2 Is the journey over 3 hours?

The top part of the decision table for this application therefore lists the four possible combinations, shown in Figure 1.7.

Conditions	Rule 1	Rule 2	Rule 3	Rule 4
Perishable food?	Y	Y	N	N
Journey over 3 hours?	Y	N	Y	N
Actions				
Normal lorry		X	X	X
Refrigerated lorry	X			

Figure 1.7 Decision table

The actions (i.e. what to do in each condition) are listed in the lower part of the table. In the supermarket delivery example, there are two possible actions – using a refrigerated lorry or using a normal lorry. If the food is perishable and the journey time is more than 3 hours, a refrigerated lorry is used; in all other cases a normal lorry is used. Therefore, the lower (actions) part of the decision table shows which type of lorry is used for each rule.

Decision tables make it easy to see that all the different possibilities have been covered, and they also help to design the code for the rules. The top half of the table makes up the If conditions, while the lower part shows what to do in each situation.

CASE STUDY

Ezee Klaim

Ezee Klaim is an insurance company. The company requires a program for insurance claims handling. The various rules that apply to how claims are authorised are shown in a decision table (Figure 1.8).

Note the pattern of Ys and Ns when the table is extended from two conditions to three conditions.

◆ Draw up a decision table describing a series of rules that apply in a situation you are familiar with – for example, the rules regarding bus pass applications, coursework hand-in rules, eligibility for allowances or benefits, and so on.

Data	Claims handling rule numbers							
Rules	1	2	3	4	5	6	7	8
Policy valid?	Y	Y	Y	Y	N	N	N	N
Claim below £10k?	Y	Y	N	N	Y	Y	N	N
No claims in last 6 months?	Y	N	Y	N	Y	N	Y	N
Actions								
Authorise	X							
Send inspector		X	X					
Refer to manager				X				
Refuse					X	X	X	X

Figure 1.8 Insurance claims handling decision table

Check your understanding

Northgate College

Northgate College has rules about how much students must pay to do a course.

◆ Overseas students must pay the full college fees.

◆ Home students receiving Jobseeker's Allowance (JSA) do not pay anything.

◆ Home students not on JSA and over the age of 21 pay 50% of the full fee.

◆ Home students not on JSA and under 21 pay 25% of the full fee.

Draw up a decision table for these rules.

3.3 Program design language

The design process having been started with the structure chart, a program design language then provides a way to add much more detail to the design for each procedure. There are a number of different program design languages that can be used. Two are described here: flowcharts, and pseudo-code or structured English.

Flowcharts

As the name suggests, a flowchart is a diagram showing the steps that must be taken to carry out some task. (Flowcharts can be used to design all sorts of processes, not just programming ones.) A flowchart is a good tool to use at the early stages of understanding how a particular procedure will work as it produces an easy-to-follow graphical representation of the processing involved.

Using a flowchart, the different programming constructs (sequence, selection and iteration) required to complete the required task within a particular procedure can be identified.

Flowcharts use a variety of symbols, linked by arrows to indicate the type of step involved at each stage. A sample flowchart is shown in Figure 1.9, which shows the steps for bubble sorting an array.

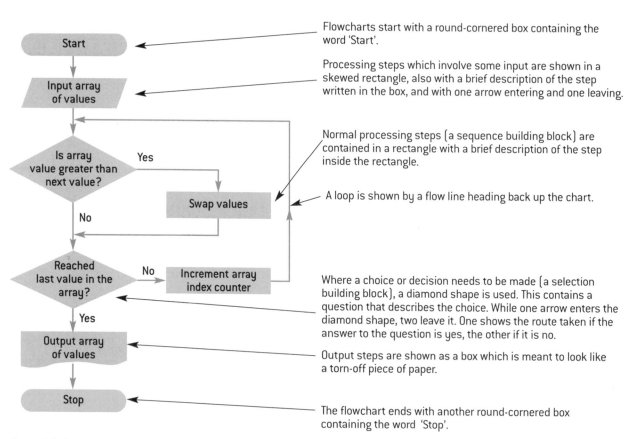

Flowcharts start with a round-cornered box containing the word 'Start'.

Processing steps which involve some input are shown in a skewed rectangle, also with a brief description of the step written in the box, and with one arrow entering and one leaving.

Normal processing steps (a sequence building block) are contained in a rectangle with a brief description of the step inside the rectangle.

A loop is shown by a flow line heading back up the chart.

Where a choice or decision needs to be made (a selection building block), a diamond shape is used. This contains a question that describes the choice. While one arrow enters the diamond shape, two leave it. One shows the route taken if the answer to the question is yes, the other if it is no.

Output steps are shown as a box which is meant to look like a torn-off piece of paper.

The flowchart ends with another round-cornered box containing the word 'Stop'.

Figure 1.9 Sample flow chart

Flowcharts are a good introduction to program design methods. However, they are not good for complex problems because the flowcharts themselves can become complex and difficult to follow. Furthermore, although they give a good idea of the general processing tasks required, they do not bear a particularly close resemblance to the code that will eventually be written.

CASE STUDY

Northgate College

A flowchart showing the process of validating a student's date of birth is shown in Figure 1.10.

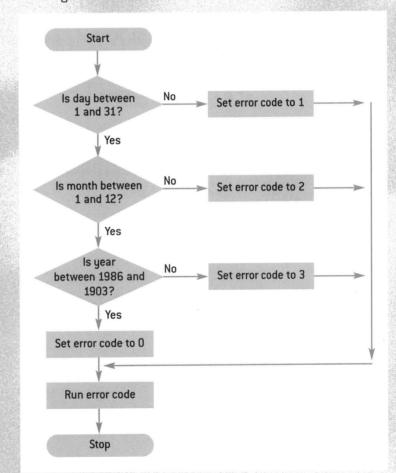

Figure 1.10 Data validation flowchart

◆ Draw a flowchart for the Ezee Klaim insurance claims-handling decision table example shown earlier in Figure 1.8.

Pseudo-code or structured English

Pseudo-code (sometimes called structured English) is a 'half-way house' between written English and programming code. It is sometimes used as the final stage in designing the processing involved, and allows a detailed design of the programming code to be produced without worrying too much about the exact syntax of the language. Pseudo-code uses typical program instructions and common programming keywords to implement control structures, such as:

◆ *If* to implement selection
◆ *Do while* and *Repeat until* to implement iteration.

There are no standards for pseudo-code, so common sense and a knowledge of programming languages are required. Instructions should include active verbs such as read, calculate or update, rather than vague phases or words like 'process'.

CASE STUDY

Ezee Klaim

The decision table for Ezee Klaim's claims-handling procedure (Figure 1.8) could be further developed by writing the pseudo-code:

```
If Valid = 'no' Then
    Print 'Reject'
Else
    If claimValue > 10 Then
        If noClaims = 'yes' Then
            Print 'Send inspector'
        Else
            Print 'Call manager'
    End If
Else
    If noClaims = 'no' Then
        Print 'Send inspector'
    Else
        Print 'Authorise'
End If
```

◆ Draw up the pseudo-code for the Northgate College decision table you created earlier.

PRACTICAL TASK 1.7

Write the pseudo-code for the date validation routine shown in the flowchart shown earlier in Figure 1.10.

3.4 File layouts

The way files need to be organised into records and fields has already been discussed (see page 22). The exact details of this arrangement must be designed and recorded using a table (sometimes called a **data dictionary**) which shows the fields contained in each record, the name of the field, its length and the type of data it stores.

Check your understanding

You decide to write a simple program – called My Contacts – that will be used to record contact details of your friends and relations. The file used to store the data could have a layout as shown in Figure 1.11. What field would you use as the key field?

Field name	Length	Data type
First_name	20	Alphabetic
Surname	20	Alphabetic
Home_phone	15	Numeric
Mobile_phone	15	Numeric
E-mail_address	15	Alphanumeric
Birth_date	8	Date (dd/mm/yy)
Address	20	Alphabetic
Town	20	Alphabetic
Postcode	7	Alphanumeric

Figure 1.11 File layout

PRACTICAL TASK 1.8

Create a file layout for the 'students file' of Northgate College.

3.5 Screen layouts

Most of the design methods looked at so far concentrate on the internal working of the program. The data to be input into the program will probably have been identified, but now it is time to design how the input screens will look to the user, and how the input data will be validated.

Data validation

Validation of data is important. You must make sure that only correct data is accepted, because incorrect data may cause problems when you try to process it. For example, a text value input when a numeric one is expected may cause the program to crash. Incorrect data such as a wrong postcode or invalid date of birth is useless. Two main types of validation check can be done.

◆ A **range check** checks that numeric data is within a valid range of values. Date checking is an example of this. Month numbers, for example, must be in the range 1 to 12. Any value outside the range is invalid and should be rejected.

◆ A **type check** tests input to ensure it is the correct data type. A person's surname, for example, must contain only alphabetic characters, while a quantity of items purchased must be numeric.

Check digits

Code numbers such as account numbers or ID numbers need to be correct. But unlike with data such as people's names, mistakes are not easily seen. To reduce errors, these code numbers sometimes have a check digit included.

A check digit is a value that is calculated from the other numbers in the code number. When the code number is input, the check digit is recalculated and compared with the number that is input. If the calculated check digit is different from the one that the user has input, then an input error must have been made. Many commonly used code numbers have check digits – credit card numbers, supermarket bar codes and ISBN numbers are examples.

Every book has an ISBN (International Standard Book Number), which is ten digits long plus a final check digit (or letter X, standing for 10). The ISBN number of the *BTEC First for IT Practitioners* course book is 0-435-45469-5, so the check digit is 5. To calculate an ISBN check digit, two steps are required.

◆ The first nine digits of the ISBN are multiplied by weighted values which correspond to the digit's position. So the first number (from the left) is multiplied by 1, the second by 2 and so on. All these values are then added together.

◆ The resulting value is divided by 11, and the check digit is *the remainder*.

So, using the ISBN for the book mentioned above, the check digit is calculated as follows:

$$0 \times 1 = 0$$
$$4 \times 2 = 8$$
$$3 \times 3 = 9$$
$$5 \times 4 = 20$$
$$4 \times 5 = 20$$
$$5 \times 6 = 30$$
$$6 \times 7 = 42$$
$$6 \times 8 = 48$$
$$9 \times 9 = 81$$

On adding these together we obtain a total of 258. When divided by 11 this leaves a remainder of 5 – which is therefore the check digit required.

Check your understanding

1   What check digit should be added to this ISBN number: 0-131-90190-?

2   A user has entered an ISBN number as 0-19-861200-3. Recalculate the check digit to find out whether the number has been input correctly.

Screen design

The layout of the contents of a screen is important because it forms the main user interface. If a screen is not labelled correctly or clearly, or is inconsistent or illogical in the order of the fields, users may find the program confusing and difficult to use. If the screen layout is messy, and contains spelling errors, users may come to the conclusion that the software is of poor quality.

Screen designs consist of three main parts:

◆ the screen layout showing the position of the various controls such as labels, input boxes and buttons

◆ the input data table, showing what data is input to each input box and how it is validated

◆ a table showing the error messages to be displayed if the validation of input data is unsuccessful.

The screen layout can be hand-sketched, or drawn using a graphics program, or laid out using a form design tool, such as that included in Visual Basic. Screen layouts must be clearly labelled, with the various controls placed in a neat and consistent way, with proper horizontal spacings and vertical alignment. The controls should be in a logical order; that is, they should be in the order the user is most likely to use them, from the top of the screen to the bottom.

CASE STUDY

Northgate College

The screen layout for the Northgate College student records system is shown in Figure 1.12.

The input data table for this screen is shown in Figure 1.13. Note that because this data is to be recorded on a file, the information about the field name, type and length will be the same as shown in the file layout.

The validation error code, along with the messages displayed, is shown in Figure 1.14.

Student records

First name [   ]   Surname [   ]

Address [   ]   Date of birth [   ]

Town [   ]   Gender [   ]

Postcode [   ]   Course code [   ]

[OK]   [Cancel]

Figure 1.12 Student records input screen

Field	Field type	Field length	Validation
Surname	Alphabetic	20	Must be entered
First name	Alphabetic	20	Must be entered
Address	Alphabetic	20	Must be entered
Town	Alphabetic	20	Must be entered
Postcode	Alphanumeric	8	Must be in the format: AA99-9AA
Date of birth	Date (dd/mm/yy)	8	Must be a valid date
Gender	Alphabetic	1	Must be M or F
Course code	Numeric	4	Range 0001 to 1750

Figure 1.13 Input data

Error code	Error message
0	No error (no message displayed)
1	"Surname missing"
2	"First name missing"
3	"Address missing"
4	"Town missing"
5	"Postcode missing or invalid"
6	"Date of birth missing or invalid"
7	"Gender must be M or F"
8	"Course code missing or invalid"

Figure 1.14 The meanings of error codes

◆ What other information about the design for the screen would be useful?

Check your understanding

Create a data input screen layout for the My Contacts program data file, shown earlier in Figure 1.11.

When designing data input screens you must try to think of all the possible error conditions that could occur. Validation of the input data using range and type checks have already been mentioned. These are important and should prevent your program crashing because data input is of the wrong type. Also, they can help prevent invalid data getting into the system. Remember, too, that certain *combinations* of input data may be invalid. For example, imagine a program that allows users to order a new car on-line. If a user selects the convertible (open-top) version of a car, he or she should not be allowed to choose a sunroof as one of the optional extras!

Error conditions

Error conditions that cause a program to crash unexpectedly are clearly important to avoid. The main sources of these types of error are described below.

- **Invalid data type.** An example is trying to put a text value into a variable that has a numeric data type. Type checks should be used to prevent this type of error.

- **Arithmetic errors.** Certain types of calculation are invalid and will cause the program to crash, such as an attempt to divide a number by zero. Range checks should be used on input data to ensure zero values cannot be used in calculations using division.

- **Index number errors.** If a program attempts to access an array index that is greater than the size of the array, then the program will crash. For example, if a program has a ten-element array and a loop within the program attempts to access the eleventh element, the program will crash. Loops need to be carefully inspected and tested to ensure there are no circumstances in which this kind of error can occur.

- **File error.** If the program reads or writes to files, there are a number error conditions that can occur. The file may have been deleted or moved, the disk may be full, or some other kind of disk input/output (I/O) error may occur. The program must also never attempt to read records beyond the end of the file. Some of these types of error may be beyond the control of the programmer, so when carrying out file I/O tests, it is wise to use the error detection methods built into many programming languages to catch unexpected errors. Visual Basic has the 'on error goto' construct, while Java has 'try … catch'.

Making sure a program is as error-free as possible is the purpose of program testing, covered in detail in the section on testing (see page 48).

3.6 Print layouts

Much of what has already been said about screen layout design applies also to printed reports. These, too, must be clear, neat, consistent and logical, with informative titles. Printed reports often include lines of information listed down the page. This information often needs to be listed in a particular order and perhaps grouped in some way. The field names of the data to be printed must be either drawn from the fields in the file layout or generated at print time.

CASE STUDY

Northgate College

A printed report that lists all the students, grouped by course number and sorted alphabetically within the course by surname, is required by the students record system. The layout for the report is shown in Figure 1.15.

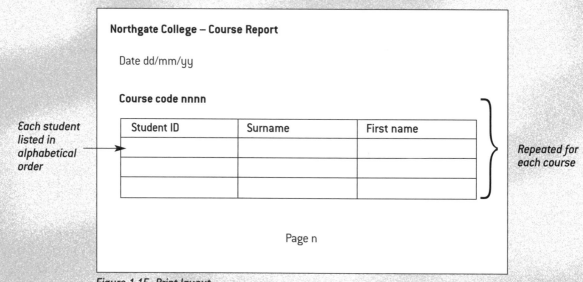

Figure 1.15 Print layout

◆ What other information about the design for the report would be useful?

3.7 A worked example

This section shows how the various tools described in the previous sections can be used to design a simple system. The system to be designed is a payroll system used to calculate monthly salaries based on rates of pay and hours worked.

Structure charts

The initial stage in the design is to decide what main functions the program will have. Information about this may well come from the people who will use the program – and will be detailed in the program specification. This program will have three main functions.

1 Add new or modify existing employee details.

2 Add details about hours worked.

3 Print salary slips.

These functions can be described in a simple structure chart as shown in Figure 1.16.

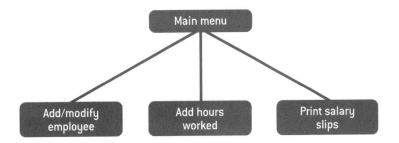

Figure 1.16 Structure chart for the payroll program

Detailed structure charts will be produced here only for the 'Add hours worked' and 'Print salary slips' modules.

A structure chart for the *Add hours worked* procedure is shown in Figure 1.17, in which there are three modules:

◆ *Find employee.* This module will have passed to it the employee's ID as a parameter, and it will search the data file containing the employee's details. It will return the employee's name (if found) or an error code (if not found).

◆ *Input details of hours worked.* This module will accept and validate the number of hours worked by the employee and the week number that the hours apply to.

◆ *Write hours worked to file.* This module will write the employee's ID and hours worked to the hours-worked data file. It will return a result code to indicate whether it was successful.

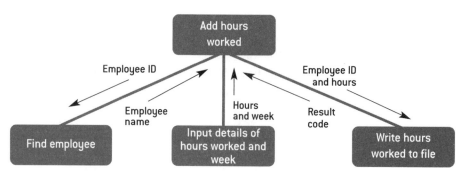

Figure 1.17 *Structure chart for the procedure to add hours worked*

It now becomes clear that *two* data files will be needed: an employee file and an hours-worked file. The layouts for these files will be defined later.

The structure chart for the *Print salary slips* procedure is shown in Figure 1.18. This procedure also has three modules:

◆ *Find employees and hours worked*. This module has passed to it the week number for which payslips are to be produced. It then searches through the hours-worked files to find records relating to this week. When it finds matching records, it will place them in an array and return that array to the main program when it reaches the end of the file. A *two-dimensional array* will be needed, containing the employee ID and the hours worked.

◆ *Calculate salary*. This module has passed to it the array created by the previous module and calculates the money due to each employee based on the hours worked. This data is placed in another array which is returned to the main program.

◆ *Print salary slips.* This module takes the two arrays created by the previous two modules (containing the employee details, hours worked and salary due) and formats the data into a printed payslip.

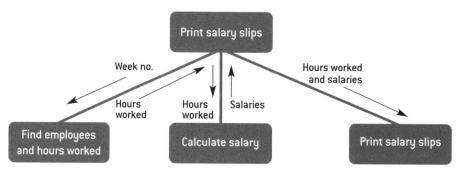

Figure 1.18 *Structure chart for the procedure to print wage slips*

Detailed designs

Now that the structure diagrams have identified the overall structure of the program, detailed designs should be produced for each module that has been identified. In this worked example, detailed designs will be produced only for the *Find employee* and *Calculate salary* modules.

First let us tackle the design for the *Find employee* module. When an employee's hours worked are being entered, the employee's ID number is used to identify the person. The purpose of this module is to check that the ID is valid and is the correct one. Having completed a validation check on the ID (more about that later), the program needs to loop through all the records in the employee file, checking to see whether a match can be found for the ID number that has been passed to the program. If no match can be found, then an error code is returned. If a match *is* found, the employee's name is copied from the file and returned to the main program. The flowchart for the program is shown in Figure 1.19.

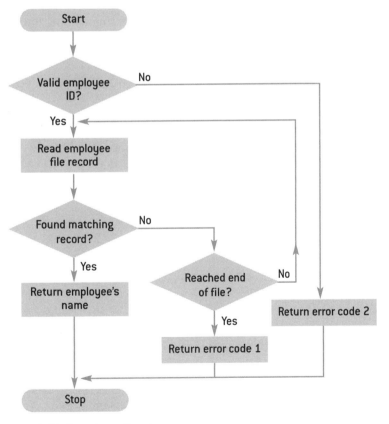

1.19 Find-employee flowchart

Next, the *Calculate salary* module has to take the number of hours worked and calculate how much to pay the employee. This company has two rules about salary calculations.

◆ If the employee is a supervisor, he or she is paid £9 per hour regardless of how many hours worked.

◆ If the employee is not a supervisor, he or she is paid £7 per hour. However, if the person works more than 35 hours in the week, he or she is paid £7.40 per hour.

These rules are summarised in the decision table shown in Figure 1.20.

Conditions	Rule 1	Rule 2	Rule 3	Rule 4
Supervisor?	Y	Y	N	N
Over 35 hours worked?	Y	N	Y	N
Actions				
£7 per hour				X
£7.40 per hour			X	
£9.00 per hour	X	X		

Figure 1.20 Calculate wage decision table

The flowchart which implements the rules shown in the decision table is shown in Figure 1.21.

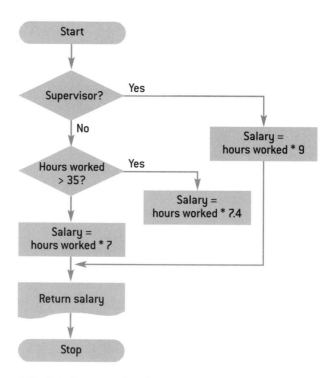

1.21 Calculate wage flowchart

File layouts

File layouts for the employee and hours-worked files are shown in Figure 1.22.

Employee

Field name	Datatype	Length
Employee_ID	Integer	6
First_name	String	25
Surname	String	25
Address_1	String	25
Address_2	String	25
Town	String	25
Postcode	String	7
Home_phone	String	12
Bank_AC_no	Integer	20
Supervisor	Boolean	-

Hours-worked

Field name	Data type	Length
Empolyee_ID	Integer	6
Week_number	Integer	2
Hours_worked	Integer	3

Figure 1.22 File layouts

Input and output specifications

An **input specification** will be produced here for only the 'Add hours worked' procedure. From the structure chart (Figure 1.17) it can be seen that this procedure is made up of three sub-procedures. However, a single input screen can be used to input details of the employees' IDs for whom the hours are to be added, the week number and the actual hours worked. The screen form layout is shown in Figure 1.23.

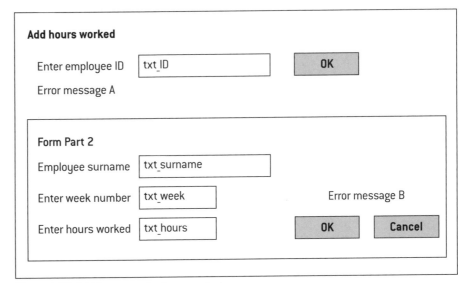

Figure 1.23 Add-hours-worked screen design

This is a two-part form. An employee's ID is entered in the first part and the OK button is clicked. If a valid employee ID is entered and that employee exists on the employee file, then the second part of the form appears, with the employee's surname shown in the *txt_surname* text box. Figure 1.24 lists the fields on the form and the validation rules applied.

Field name	Type	Validation
txt_ID	Input	Numeric, 6 digits
txt_surname	Ouput	-
txt_week	Input	Numeric, range 1 to 52
txt_hours	Input	Numeric, range 1 to 120

Figure 1.24 Fields on the form

There are two error message fields, detailed in Figure 1.25. Error message A is used to display any errors relating to an employee's ID, while error message B is used to display errors relating to the week number or hours worked.

Error message A	
Code	Message displayed
0	(no error)
1	Non-numeric employee ID
2	Employee ID not 6 digits
3	Employee ID not on file
Error message B	
0	(no error)
1	Non-numeric week number
2	Week number must be in range 1 to 52
3	Non-numeric hours worked
4	Hours worked must be in the range 1 to 120

Figure 1.25 Error messages

An output specification (print layout) will now be produced for the salary slips. These are simple printed sheets that are given to employees to show how much they are being paid and how it was calculated. The layout of the sheet is shown in Figure 1.26.

```
Salary slip
Date: dd/mm/yy


First name                    '          Family name


┌─────────────────┬─────────────────┬─────────────────┐
│ Hours worked    │ Hourly rate     │ Total salary    │
├─────────────────┼─────────────────┼─────────────────┤
│ n.n             │ £n.nn           │ £nnn.nn         │
└─────────────────┴─────────────────┴─────────────────┘
```

Figure 1.26 Print layout for wage slips

PRACTICAL TASK 1.9

Complete the design for this system.

Chapter summary

This chapter has covered all the practical activities listed under the third outcome in the specification, including:

◆ structure charts

◆ decision tables

◆ flowcharts and pseudo-code

◆ data validation

◆ error conditions.

4 Validate the completed design specification

Having completed the design for the program, there are two important steps to be take before the program is actually written.

4.1 Verify the design

The design must be verified against the specification. The program specification lists what the users of the program want. It tells the designer what the program will do, what features it will have, what data it will accept or reject, and what calculations it will carry out. The program designer should use the specification as a type of guide book for writing the program.

However, sometimes the designer may forget or misinterpret some features listed in the specification and the design produced may not match the specification as closely as it should. Therefore, once the design is complete the designer (or if possible someone who has not worked on the design – since it is sometimes difficult to spot one's own mistakes) should go through the specification line by line checking that all the features and functions required have been covered in the design and that the design is *complete*.

As well as checking that the design conforms fully with the specification, it is also important to check that the design is *consistent*. **Consistency** covers a wide range of areas. It includes, for example, making sure that a sensible naming convention is used, making sure screen layouts have a uniform design, and ensuring that the design from the high-level structure diagrams through to the low-level pseudo-code is consistent – and in particular that there are no functions mentioned in the structure diagram for which no lower-level design exists.

4.2 Testing

Testing is a vital (though often unpopular!) part of software development. The users of the software would not be very impressed if the program produced the wrong answers, nor would they be happy if the program kept crashing. Testing is the process of checking that all the functions of the program work as they should and give the correct results. The definitions of terms like 'work as they should' and 'correct results' need to come from the original program specification that was agreed by the users and the developers before the program was written.

As well as checking that the program works correctly when used correctly, the software developer also needs to check that the program is robust and can withstand being used incorrectly to a great extent without crashing. The reason why this is important is because the users of the program are unlikely to be computer experts. They may misunderstand how the program is supposed to be used, they may also make mistakes when using the program – pressing keys or clicking buttons in error or making inappropriate entries in a text box.

The final testing of the program cannot be fully completed until the program is written. However, at this stage two aspects of the testing can be done.

1 **Test data** can be prepared.

2 **Dry-run testing** can be used to test the logic of the design.

Test data

Test data is input data that will be used to find out whether the program deals with it correctly. This involves choosing some input values and then manually working out what output the program *should* produce with these chosen inputs (the *expected outputs*). The program is then run using these input values and the expected outputs are compared with the actual ones produced by the program. If there is a difference between the expected and actual outputs, then the program has failed the test and will need to be modified so that the actual and expected values match.

The choice of input values is important. A range of values needs to be chosen in each of the following categories.

◆ **Normal values** are what would normally be expected as an input value.

◆ **Boundary values** would, in the case of a numeric input, be the highest possible value and the smallest possible value (i.e. the values on the boundary). In the case of a text value they might be a very large number of characters or very few. For example, in a text box where someone's name is to be entered, two extreme values might be 'Ng' and 'Fotherington-Thomas'.

◆ **Abnormal values** are invalid entries. Examples are 32/10/02 for a date, 205 for someone's age, or a text value where a numeric one is expected.

The test data with the chosen input values and the expected results is *recorded*, usually in some type of table – with an empty column for the actual results of the tests to be recorded once the program has been written.

Dry-run testing

Dry-run testing is used to check the logic of the design. It is particularly appropriate where the logic is complex, such as in nested If statements, or within loops. It involves working through the low-level design documents, such as pseudo-code, using imaginary input values, and keeping track, using a pen and paper, of the values that will be recorded in the variables the design uses.

Chapter summary

This chapter has briefly covered the practical activities listed under the fourth outcome in the specification (validate the completed design specification). A more detailed explanation of this topic can be found in unit 3 on testing.

Unit 2

Create software components using Java

This unit covers the knowledge and skills required to create applets using the Java programming language. The unit has four learning outcomes in the specification. In order to approach the material in a logical sequence, they have been covered in the order shown below. The final learning outcome of this unit – *Test a software component and produce printed output* – is covered fully in unit 3 of this book.

This unit finishes with the creation of *two full programs*.

Outcomes

◆ Manage the development environment

◆ Create code for a specified software component

◆ Use components to create a graphical user interface (GUI)

◆ Test a software component and produce printed output –
   see *unit 3*.

51

1 Manage the development environment

Computers can understand instructions only when they are in **machine code**. Machine code consists of binary numbers. So, for example, the *Add* instruction might be 10010001.

It is, of course, very difficult for humans to write programs in machine code, so almost all modern programming is done using so-called **high-level languages,** such as Visual Basic, C++ and Java. Programs in these languages are written with English-like statements, but this **source code** still needs to be converted into machine code before the computer can run it.

The traditional software development process involves first writing a program using the English-like syntax (with a grammatical structure) of the language in use, and then using a piece of software called a **compiler** to convert the program into machine code (often called **object code**). This object code is then linked together with other pieces of program code – such as standard functions for input/output (I/O) or mathematics – to produce the **executable program**.

The compiling process, as well as converting the program to object code, involves checking the **syntax** of the program. Since it is very common to make syntax errors when writing a program, it often takes several attempts before the program compiles without errors.

Java programs are compiled in a similar way to that described above. However, Java is a platform-independent language, which means it will work on a variety of different computers (PCs, Apple Macs, UNIX machines, etc.). Therefore, the Java compiler produces special instructions called **Java byte code**, which is not machine code. To run Java code on a computer, you need a piece of software called a **Java virtual machine** (JVM) which converts the Java byte code into real machine code. Therefore, to run the same code on a PC and an Apple Mac, all you need is a different JVM.

Java is designed for the World Wide Web. All common browsers, such as Microsoft's *Internet Explorer* and Netscape's *Navigator*, can have a JVM added as a plug-in.

1.1 Accessing the development environment

We will be using the Sun Java development toolkit, which has the benefit of being free. But it does not include an IDE (integrated development environment – editor, compiler, etc. built into one program), so our programs will be written in the traditional way using a text editor (e.g. Windows *Notepad*), and then compiled using a separate compiler. Before you can compile and run any of the examples in this book, you must install the Sun

Java development toolkit (SDK). This can be downloaded from the Sun website – http://java.sun.com/j2se/1.4.2/download.html.There are also commercial Java IDEs available, such as Microsoft *J++* and Borland *Jbuilder*.

Java programs can be written which work in a number of different environments, the simplest of which is text-based MS-DOS programs. Windows-based Java programs can also be written which work as standalone applications or as applets that work within an Internet browser. Initially, a simple Java applet will be written here. Then, in order to introduce the basic concepts of Java programming, some simple programs will be written that are DOS-based. These programs will introduce the basic building blocks of program writing:

◆ sequence

◆ selection

◆ repetition.

Once you have grasped these basic programming concepts, Windows programs and more complex applets will be written. That is really what Java was created for.

1.2 Creating a source code file

Tradition dictates that the first program students write in any language is the 'Hello World' program. This simply displays the message 'Hello World'. Figure 2.1 shows the code for what we have called the HelloApp program. It was written using the text editor *Notepad*.

```
HelloApp.java - Notepad
File  Edit  Format  View  Help
import java.awt.*;
import java.applet.*;

public class HelloApp extends Applet
{
        public void paint(Graphics g)
        {
                g.drawString("Hello World", 20, 20);
        }
}
```

Figure 2.1 The HelloApp extension

Note that Java is **case-sensitive**. You must use upper case (capitals) exactly as shown in the example (except within the quotation marks), so *String* and *string* are two different things – only one of which is correct! Typing instructions in the wrong case will cause compiler errors.

The **indentation** shown in the program code is good practice but is not essential. Pressing the Tab key will indent the line for you.

At this stage you should concentrate on understanding how to use the Java development environment, so no explanation of the program code is given here – that will come later.

Having typed the program code using *Notepad*, the program must be saved. Call it HelloApp.java in the C:/j2sdk1.4.1/bin folder. This file is known as the **source file**.

1.3 Compile a source code file

Having saved the file, open a MS-DOS command prompt window and change the prompt to the \j2sdk1.4.1\bin folder as noted above. Now type:

```
Javac HelloApp.java
```

Javac is the name of the Java compiler. If you have typed the program correctly, you will just be returned to the command prompt, which means that the program compiled without errors. The compiler will produce a binary file from the source file – called a bytecode or **class file** – with the name *HelloApp.class*. This is the file that will be loaded into the Internet browser. However, before moving to the next step, the problem of compiler errors needs to be addressed!

1.4 Resolving syntax errors

Java, like all programming languages, has strict rules about how instructions are written (the rules are called the language **syntax**). The fact that typing instructions in the wrong case will cause compiler errors has already been mentioned, and many other typing errors will cause compiler errors. If you do make a mistake – for example, if you omitted the semi-colon (;) at the end of the line g.drawString("Hello World", 20, 20); – then you will see an error message as shown in Figure 2.2.

```
cx  Command Prompt

E:\j2sdk1.4.1\bin>javac HelloApp.java
HelloApp.java:8: ';' expected
                g.drawString("Hello World", 20, 20)
                                                    ^
1 error

E:\j2sdk1.4.1\bin>_
```

Figure 2.2 Notification of a compiler error

If this happens, go back to *Notepad* and correct the error. Re-save the file, then return to the command prompt and try again. You can leave the file open in *Notepad* while you do this, but you must remember to save it each time you modify it.

1.5 Creating an HTML file

Before the HelloApp program can be run, an HTML file must be created which will load the HelloApp.class file into an Internet browser. HTML is the language in which simple web pages are created. Writing HTML code is a subject in itself, so only a very simple HTML file will be created here which simply contains a reference to the applet class file.

The HTML file can be typed in *Notepad* in much the same way as the Java source file was, and saved with the '.html' file extension. It must be saved in the same C:\J2sdk1.4.1\bin folder as the Java files. The HTML code is:

```
<html>
<body>
<applet code="HelloApp.class" width=150 height=100>
</applet>
</body>
</html>
```

This line refers to the applet:

```
<applet code="HelloApp.class" width=150 height=100>
```

and it simply tells the browser to load the HelloApp.class file into a window that is 150 pixels in width and 100 pixels in height.

1.6 Running the applet

There are two ways in which you can now run the applet. Probably the simplest method is to use the Appletviewer program that comes with the Sun Java toolkit. At the command prompt (in the C:\j2sdk1.4.1\bin folder), type:

```
appletviewer hello.html
```

Press Enter and the applet will run in its own window, as shown in Figure 2.3.

Figure 2.3 Applet running using the Appletviewer

An alternative method is to load the HTML file into an Internet browser. In *Internet Explorer*, you can simply use the *Open menu* command under the *File* menu, and browse to the HelloApp.html file.

1.7 Exiting the development environment

There is no special way of exiting the DOS-based Sun Java development environment. Make sure you have saved the source file in *Notepad* before you attempt to compile it. To close the applet viewer and the command prompt window, just click the close ('X') buttons in the top right corners of their respective windows. If you are using a commercial IDE, then exit it by choosing the *Exit* option under the *File* menu.

Chapter summary

This chapter has covered:

◆ using the Sun Java SDK

◆ creating Java source files using *Notepad*

◆ compiling source files and dealing with compiler errors

◆ creating an HTML file containing a reference to a Java applet

◆ running a Java applet using the applet viewer and an Internet browser

◆ exiting the development environment.

---

2 Create code for a specified software component

Java applets are designed for the Windows programming environment, which involves a certain amount of complexity. In order to grasp the basics of Java programming without getting involved in the complexity of Windows, programming applets will be put aside for the moment and a number of very simple DOS-based Java programs will be written. The 'Hello World' Java application looks rather different from the applet. The code for the program is:

```
public class hello
{
    public static void main(String args[])
    {
    System.out.println ("Hello World");
    }
}
```

PRACTICAL TASK 2.1

Type the program in *Notepad* (or whatever text editor you use) and then save it in the C/:j2sdk1.4.1/bin folder, calling it hello.java. Having saved the file, open a command prompt window, change to the \j2sdk1.4.1\bin folder, and compile hello.java in the same way as you did with the applet – by typing:

```
Javac hello.java
```

Once you have the program successfully compiled, you can run it using the JVM. To do this, type (at the command prompt):

```
Java hello
```

You should see the output shown in Figure 2.4.

```
Command Prompt

E:\j2sdk1.4.1\bin>javac hello.java

E:\j2sdk1.4.1\bin>java hello
Hello World

E:\j2sdk1.4.1\bin>_
```

Figure 2.4 Running the hello application

2.1 Classes

The first line of the program introduces the concept of classes:

```
class hello
```

Java is an **object-orientated programming (OOP) language**. OOP programs are written in units called classes, and everything within the class is contained in a set of curly braces like this { }.

Note that the curly braces are always in pairs! Missing out the ending curly braces will cause compiler errors.

Also note that the *class name* (hello, in this case) and the *name of the file* must match, so this program must be called hello.java.

The next line reads:

```
public static void main(String args[])
```

All the programs you write to start with will have this line.

2.2 Attributes and methods

Classes have two aspects: attributes and methods.

◆ The data that belong to a class are called **attributes**.

◆ The things a class can do are called **methods**.

The hello class does not contain any attributes, but it does contain a method – the main method – which is what this line defines. The meaning of the public, static void and (String args[ ]) will become clear later.

Applications in Java must always have a main method. Everything within the main method is contained within curly braces.

The only instruction in the program is the line:

```
System.out.println ("Hello World");
```

It prints whatever is placed inside the round brackets. Note that every Java instruction ends in a semi-colon, and missing out the semi-colons will cause compiler errors.

PRACTICAL TASK 2.2

Write a program that displays this message:
Hello Alan
I've written another program.

2.3 Comments

As well as instructions, you should also add comments to the programs you write. Comments are plain-English explanations of what part of the program does, and these comments are ignored by the compiler. It is good practice to include comments in your programs because they can help others to understand what the program does. You must include a double slash (//) before any lines in your programs that are comments; otherwise, the compiler will think they are program instructions and this will cause errors.

2.4 Variables and constants

For programs to be useful, they need to store data. Think of a simple hand-held calculator. For it to work, it needs to store the numbers you input. In addition, many calculators have a memory function that allows them to remember the result of a previous calculation. The programs also need a way to store data in the computer's memory. Programs do this by creating (or declaring) named areas in the memory, called **variables**. Variables have three attributes: a name, a data type and a value.

The **name** is given by the programmer. Variable names in Java must meet a number of criteria. They must not already be a name used in the Java language (such as *void* or *class* – these are known as **reserved words**). There can be no spaces in the name, and it must not contain any mathematical symbols. The name *can* start with a letter, an underscore or a dollar sign.

The **data type** is also decided by the programmer. It determines the type of data that can be stored in the variable. The data type is set when the variable is created, and it cannot be changed by the program or by the user. Also, the programmer must ensure that only data of the correct type is stored in that variable.

A variety of data types can be used in Java programs. Those used most often are:

◆ int – which is used for storing integers (whole numbers such as 4, 8, 245)
◆ float – which is used for storing real numbers (i.e. with a decimal part, such as 1.5 and 27.543)
◆ double – which is used for storing very large real numbers
◆ char – which is used for storing characters (such as 'y' and 'a')
◆ boolean – which is used for storing a value of true or false.

The **value** is what is stored in the variable. This varies depending on a number of things, such as user input – hence the name 'variable'.

The name and data type are set when a variable is declared in a Java program. The value in the variable can be assigned within the program, or it may come from user input. A variable used to store the score in a computer game might be declared like this:

```
int score;
```

Here, *score* is the name of the variable and *int* is the data type. To assign a value to this variable, the equals sign (known as the **assignment operator**) is used:

```
score = 0;
```

A variable can be thought of as a named area or box in the computer's memory, as shown in Figure 2.5.

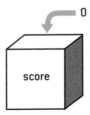

Figure 2.5 Putting a variable into the computer's memory

As well as assigning values to variables, you can also use variables on the right-hand side of an expression. In this case, the value contained in the variable is used. As an example, consider this simple Java program:

```
public class var_eg
{
    public static void main(String args[])
    {
    int x;
    int y;
    x = 2;
    y = x * 4;
    System.out.println (y);
    }
}
```

The asterisk (*) is the Java arithmetical operator for multiplication, so the expression $y = x * 4$ takes the value in x (previously the value of 2 was assigned to x), multiplies it by 2, and places the result in the variable y.

What does it mean?

*An **expression** is a way of writing a mathematical calculation, a type of mathematical shorthand. So an expression like:*

$$y = x * 4$$

means 'take whatever value is contained in the variable x, multiply it by 4, and place the resulting value in the variable y'. More details of the arithmetic operators and writing expressions can be found in unit 1, on page 8.

If it were possible to look into the memory locations used by the variables while the program was running, you would see what is shown in Figure 2.6.

	x	y
int x;		
int y;		
x = 2;	2	
y = x * 4;	2	8
System.out.println (y);	2	8

Figure 2.6 Looking inside the memory locations

In the program shown earlier, the last line:

```
System.out.println (y);
```

will print out the value contained in the variable y. You can add some informative text to this output using the plus symbol (+) to make it more understandable to the program's user:

```
System.out.println ("The answer is "+ y);
```

Note here the need to add a *space* before the last quotation mark – otherwise, the value in y will be printed directly after the word 'is', with no space between.

Java, in common with most programming languages, has a full range of arithmetic operators, and parentheses (brackets) can be used to modify the order of mathematical precedence. See pages 8 and 9 in unit 1 for more information on mathematical operators and precedence rules.

PRACTICAL TASK 2.3

1 Copy the last program discussed above. Then compile it and check that it works.

2 Modify the program so that, after it has printed the value of *y*, it multiplies it by 4 again and prints the new result.

3 Add informative text to the program.

4 Add a comment to the program.

There are situations when a value that does not change is required within a program. Examples are the mathematical value of pi (about 3.14176) or a conversion between feet and metres. These types of value should be named and declared as **constants** rather than as variables. Constants are declared in a very similar way to variables, except that the keyword *final* precedes the declaration, like this:

```
final double PII = 3.14176
```

It is a convention in Java that constants are given names in upper-case letters (hence PII).

What does it mean?

Constants are rather like variables, with one important difference. The value in a constant is set when it is declared and it cannot change. In fact, if you attempt to change the value in a constant you will get an error message when you compile the program.

2.5 Accepting input from the user

So far, the programs that have been written do calculations (such as y = x * 4;) and produce output using the *println* instruction. To be really useful, programs need to accept input from the person using them.

As mentioned earlier, Java is really designed for use within web pages in a Windows environment. For this reason, the people who developed the Java language did not think it necessary to provide a simple method to accept text from the keyboard in a DOS environment. The programming code required to do this is quite complex, so a simple class has been provided, called *Kbinput*, which will help you concentrate on the fundamental principles of programming and leave the complexity until later.

Kbinput is not a standard part of Java – you need to download it from the website www.neal.tzo.com/java. You must place it in the \j2sdk1.4.1\bin folder. The Kbinput class has a variety of methods that allow it to accept different types of data. The first one we will use is the *Kbinput.getnumber* method which allows input of an integer.

The program shown next is a version of the multiplication program. Instead of the value of the variable *x* being set in the program, it is entered by the user:

```
public class input_eg
{
    public static void main(String args[])
    throws java.io.IOException
    {
    int x;
    int y;
    System.out.println ("Enter a whole number");
    x = Kbinput.getnumber();
    y = x * 4;
    System.out.println (x + " multipled by 4 is " + y);
    }
}
```

There are two lines in this program that need explanation. First, the rather strange-looking instruction:

```
throws java.io.IOException
```

is required by the compiler when the program accepts input from the keyboard, and it prevents problems if there is an error. You need not worry about it too much at this stage – we will return to it later! The other line is:

```
x = Kbinput.getnumber();
```

This uses the getnumber( ) method of the Kbinput class to accept an integer value from the keyboard and place it in the variable *x*.

PRACTICAL TASK 2.4

1 Compile and run the program input_eg. You will find that it asks you for a whole number, which you need to enter from the keyboard. It then multiplies that number by 4 and prints the result. The value in the variable *x* now varies each time the program is run, depending on the input from the user.

2 Your program will multiply the number entered by the user only by 4. A general-purpose multiplication program could be developed from this if the user were able to input another number and these two numbers were multiplied together. Attempt to write such a program, remembering that you will need another variable.

2.6 Selection constructs

The instructions in the programs written so far have all to be executed one after another, in sequence. However, there are many circumstances when programs need to make choices and take different courses of action. For example, many computer games allow the player to choose different levels of difficulty. Based on the user's choice of level, the program then selects a different speed to run at, or introduces more obstacles, or whatever, depending on the type of game.

The 'if' instruction

In Java (as in many programming languages), selection is achieved using the *if* instruction. The instruction takes this form:

```
if (condition)
    {
    instructions to be followed if condition is true
    }
```

The condition is some kind of test which can have a true or false outcome (known as a Boolean condition – more information is in unit 1, on page 12). So, for example, in the computer game mentioned above, if the user's choice of level was held in an integer variable called *level*, then the 'if' instruction might look like this:

```
if (level ==1)
    {
    instructions to be followed if condition is true
    }
```

The instructions within the curly braces are executed only if the condition is true. If the condition is false, then the instructions within the braces are not executed and the next instruction to be executed is the next one after the ending curly brace.

Note that the Java operator meaning 'equal to' is *two* equals signs (==). This is because a single equals sign works as an assignment operator, so 'level = 1' would set the value in the variable level to 1, rather than comparing the value in the variable with 1. The instruction:

```
if (level =1)
```

will result in a compiler error.

The next example program demonstrates the use of the 'if' instruction. It asks the user to enter two integers. The user then enters a '+' to add the two numbers or a '-' to subtract them:

```
public class simcalc
{
   public static void main(String args[])
   throws java.io.IOException
   {
   int num1;
   int num2;
   int answer = 0;
   char opcode;
   System.out.println ("Calculator Program");
   System.out.println ("Enter first number");
   num1 = Kbinput.getnumber();
   System.out.println ("Enter second number");
   num2 = Kbinput.getnumber();
   System.out.println ("Enter + for add or - for subtract");
   opcode = Kbinput.getchar();
   if (opcode == '+')
      {
      answer = num1 + num2;
      }
   if (opcode == '-')
      {
      answer = num1 - num2;
      }
   System.out.println ("Answer is " + answer);
   }
}
```

Note that a variable called *opcode* is used to store the user's '+' or '-', so the data type of this variable is *character* (char). To input a character, the *getchar* method of the Kbinput class is used, rather than the *getnumber* method used for integers. Therefore, the instruction to input this character is:

```
opcode = Kbinput.getchar();
```

PRACTICAL TASK 2.5

Produce a modified version of the program simcalc that can do multiplication and division too. What happens with this program if you make an invalid entry, such as '?' for the mathematical operator?

The full list of **relational operators** you can use in Java is shown is Table 2.1.

Java operator	Meaning
==	Equal to
!=	Not equal to
<	Less than
>	Greater than
>=	Greater than or equal to
<=	Less than or equal to

Table 2.1 **Java comparison operators**

The 'if...else' instruction

In the way the 'if' instruction has been used so far, there is no specific action taken if the condition is false. In contrast, the 'if...else' instruction is used when some action is required also if the condition is false. Such an instruction is preceded by the *else* instruction, as follows:

```
if (condition)
    {
    instructions to be followed if condition is true
    }
else
    {
    instructions to be followed if condition is false
    }
```

The next example program demonstrates the use of the *if...else* instruction:

```
public class age
{
    public static void main(String args[])
    throws java.io.IOException
    {
    int age;
    System.out.println ("Enter your age");
    age = Kbinput.getnumber();
    if (age > 16)
        {
        System.out.println ("You are old enough to drive.");
        }
    else
        {
        System.out.println ("You are too young to drive.");
        }
    }
}
```

The instructions inside the curly brackets of an 'if or else' statement can themselves be yet more 'if or else' instructions. These are known as **nested if** statements. For example, the last program above can be modified to show that people who are aged 16 can drive on a provisional licence:

```
public class age
{
    public static void main(String args[])
    throws java.io.IOException
    {
    int age;
    System.out.println ("Enter your age");
    age = Kbinput.getnumber();
    if (age > 16)
        {
        System.out.println ("You are old enough to drive.");
        }
    else
        {
        if (age == 16)
            {
            System.out.println ("You can drive as a learner.");
            }
        else
            {
            System.out.println ("You are too young to drive.");
            }
        }
    }
}
```

Nested ifs can become very complex, so **decision tables** are often used to design them. Decision tables are described in detail in unit 1 (page 30).

> ## What does it mean?
>
> *The term **nested** refers to program constructs such as selection statements which are within an already existing construct of the same type. So, for example, an 'if or else' construct that was contained within a section of code that was already part of an 'if or else' construct would be considered as a nested if.*

The switch instruction

An alternative to using nested ifs is the *switch* instruction. Using *switch* produces much neater code that is easier to read. However, *switch* can be used only when testing for specific values in a variable, not ranges (such as >16).

The next program below is a variation on the simple calculator written earlier. This version does addition, subtraction and multiplication. It also checks that the user makes a valid entry for the *opcode* variable, which the previous version just ignored:

```
public class simcalc_switch
{
    public static void main(String args[])
    throws java.io.IOException
    {
    int num1;
    int num2;
    int answer = 0;
    char opcode;
    System.out.println ("Calculator Program");
    System.out.println ("Enter first number");
    num1 = Kbinput.getnumber();
    System.out.println ("Enter second number");
    num2 = Kbinput.getnumber();
    System.out.println ("+ for add, - for subtract, * for multiply");
    opcode = Kbinput.getchar();
    switch (opcode)
        {
        case '+' : answer = num1 + num2; break;
        case '-' : answer = num1 - num2; break;
        case '*' : answer = num1 * num2; break;
        default: System.out.println("Invalid entry");
        }
    System.out.println ("Answer is " + answer);
    }
}
```

The switch statement starts with the instruction:

```
switch(opcode)
```

Here, opcode is the variable that will be tested. Then, within the curly braces, there is a list of the possible values in that variable, preceded by the instruction *case* and followed by the instructions to be followed if the variable does indeed contain that value; for example:

```
case '+' : answer = num1 + num2; break;
```

The *break* instruction makes the program skip the rest of the switch statement if the test is true.

The *default* instruction at the end lists the instruction to be followed if none of the above cases is true, so:

```
default: System.out.println("Invalid entry");
```

will display the message 'Invalid entry' if the user does not enter +, - or *.

PRACTICAL TASK 2.6

Write a program using the *switch* instruction that will display the classroom number in which each tutor group will have their lessons. There are three tutor groups, numbered 1, 2 and 3. Group 1 meet in room A5, group 2 in B10 and group 3 in W105. The program should ask you to enter the tutor group number and then display the room number. It should display an appropriate error message if a number other than 1, 2 or 3 is entered.

2.7 Iteration constructs

So far we have looked at using sequence and selection in Java. The third and final form of program control is **iteration**. This involves repeating instructions a certain number of times or until some condition is met, in what is called a **loop**. There are a variety of instructions used in Java to create loops. The first one to investigate is the **for** loop. A 'for' loop is used to repeat a section of code a certain number of times.

The 'for' loop

Consider a program that would display the six-times table (that is, 1 * 6 = 6, 2 * 6 = 12 and so on up to 12 * 6 = 72). We could write such a program using the sequence programming method, like this:

```
answer = 6 * 1;
System.out.println ("6 times 1 is " + answer);
answer = 6 * 2;
System.out.println ("6 times 2 is " + answer);
. . .
System.out.println ("6 times 12 is " + answer);
```

However, it would be much more efficient and require less code to use a '**for**' **loop**. A 'for' loop has a **counter**, which is an integer variable that keeps track of how many times the loop has been executed.

What does it mean?

*An **integer variable** is a variable that is declared with a data type of integer.*

At the start of the 'for' loop, the counter is used in three conditions, like this:

for (*start_condition; while_condition; action condition*)

The *start* condition sets the initial value of the counter, usually 0 or 1. The *while* condition is used to control when the loop ends, since the loop continues only while this condition is true. The *action* condition controls how the counter is changed each time around the loop (normally by having 1 added to it). So, for the times-table program, the *for* instruction would look like this:

```
for (i = 1; i <= 12, i ++)
```

The loop counter used here is an integer variable called *i*, which traditionally is the name given to 'for' loop counters. The action condition 'i++' is Java shorthand for '*i = i + 1*'. The complete program is:

```
public class times
{
    public static void main(String args[])
    {
    int i;
    int answer;
    for (i = 1; i <= 12; i++)
      {
      answer = i * 6;
      System.out.println (i + " times 6 is " + answer);
      }
    }
}
```

Note that the loop counter variable can be used within the code of the loop, although you must not change the value of the loop counter.

PRACTICAL TASK 2.7

Modify the times-table program so that, rather than just producing the six-times table, it asks the user to enter a number and then displays the times-table for that number.

The 'while' loop

In some situations, a loop is required which, rather than looping for a fixed number of times (as the 'for' loop does), continues until some condition is met. In these situations, a **while loop** is used – the loop continues while some condition is true. One situation where 'while' loops can be used is in validating user input, with the loop continuing while the user makes invalid inputs.

Earlier, a games program was discussed which asked the user to select the level at which he or she wanted to play the game. Suppose that three levels were available – 1, 2 and 3. The next section of code shows how a 'while' loop could be used to reject invalid inputs:

```
System.out.println ("Choose your level: 1, 2 or 3")
level = Kbinput.getnumber();
while (level > 4)
    {
    System.out.println ("Invalid entry: choose 1, 2 or 3")
    level = Kbinput.getnumber();
    }
```

In this case, the instruction within the pair of curly brackets will be executed while the condition is true (level > 3). Note that, if the user enters a valid number the first time, the code within the while loop will not be executed at all.

However, this validation routine is not foolproof! What if the user enters 0, or even −1 as the level? Both these entries are less that 4, so the 'while' condition is not met. The loop condition needs to test whether the value in the *level* variable is >4 or <0. **Logical operators** such as OR and AND are represented by symbols in Java, as shown in Table 2.2.

Table 2.2 *Logical operators*

Logical operator	Java symbol
AND	&&
OR	||
NOT	!

What does it mean?

*Logical operators allow you to combine conditions which evaluate to true or false. So the condition level >4 OR level <0 will evaluate to **true** if the variable level contains a value which is greater than 4 or greater than 0. Logical operators are explained in more detail in unit 1, on page 12.*

Therefore, the 'while' condition required above to catch values both above 4 and below 1 is:

```
while (level > 4 || level < 1)
```

PRACTICAL TASK 2.8

Modify the times-table program you wrote in Practical task 2.7 so that the user can request times-tables only in the range 1 to 12.

The 'do...while' loop

The third type of loop, the **do...while loop**, is similar in many ways to the 'while' loop. However, one important difference is that the loop condition is tested at the end of the loop rather than at the beginning. This means that the loop is always executed at least once. In the input validation loop for the game program level, if the user made the correct input the first time, then the code in the 'while' loop would not be executed at all. There are some situations where you need the code in the loop to be executed at least once.

Consider the simple calculator written earlier (see page 64), which adds or subtracts one set of numbers and then exits. It would be much more useful if, having completed one calculation, it then asked the user whether another calculation is required or whether the program should close. The modified code for this version of the program is:

```
public class simcalc3
{
    public static void main(String args[])
    throws java.io.IOException
    {
    int num1;
    int num2;
    int answer = 0;
    char opcode;
    char reply;
    System.out.println ("Calculator Program");
    do
        {
        System.out.println ("Enter first number");
        num1 = Kbinput.getnumber();
        System.out.println ("Enter second number");
        num2 = Kbinput.getnumber();
        System.out.println ("Enter + for add or - for subtract");
        opcode = Kbinput.getchar();
        if (opcode == '+')
            {
            answer = num1 + num2;
            }
        if (opcode == '-')
            {
            answer = num1 - num2;
            }
        System.out.println ("Answer is " + answer);
        System.out.println ("Type X to exit, or C to continue");
        reply = Kbinput.getchar();
        }
    while (reply != 'X');
    }
}
```

In this version, the main part of the program has been placed in a 'do...while' loop. When the first calculation has been done, the program asks the user to enter an X to exit or a C to continue. This response is placed in a variable called *reply*. The 'while' loop condition, at the end of the loop, tests the value in the *reply* variable and, while it is not equal to X, the loop continues.

In the calculator program simcalc3, although the instructions tell the user to 'Type X to exit, or C to continue', only the X is tested for. Thus the user can enter any character to continue the program. Modify the program using a 'while' loop to validate this input so that only X or C can be input by the user.

Indentation

In the programs written so far, the code has been indented (tabbed in from the left-hand margin) within both selection and iteration constructs. Such indentation makes the code easier to read because it shows clearly where the constructs start and finish. These programs will work fine without the indentations, but its use is considered good practice and is highly recommended.

2.8 Arrays

So far the variables have been used to store a single value each. However, there are situations when it is useful to have a variable that can store a whole series of related values – using an **array**. For example, suppose a program is required that will provide lottery numbers, using the random number method (which is *Math.random()*). The lottery requires six numbers between 1 and 49, and they can be stored in six integer variables such as:

```
int lotto1;
int lotto2;
int lotto3;
...
```

However, a much more sensible solution would be to declare a six-element array, which is done like this:

```
int lotto[] = new int[6];
```

This creates a six-element array, lotto[0] through to lotto[5]. The real benefit of arrays is the index number. This identifies the individual elements of the array, and it can be a variable such as the counter in a 'for' loop. The program to generate the six lottery numbers makes use of this feature:

```
public class lotto
{
    public static void main(String args[])
    throws java.io.IOException
    {
    int lotto[] = new int[6];
    int i;
```

```
System.out.println ("lottery numbers");
for (i = 0; i < 6; i++)
    {
    lotto[i] = 1 + (int)(48 * Math.random());
    System.out.println ("Your number " + (i + 1) + " is " +
                                                  lotto[i]);

    }
  }
}
```

A 'for' loop is used to produce the six numbers and place them in the array. The instruction that creates the number is:

```
lotto[i] = 1 + (int)(48 * Math.random());
```

This needs a little explaining. Math.random() produces a value of the data type *double* between 0 and 1. Multiplying this value by 48 gives a value between 0 and 48, while adding 1 to it gives a value between 1 and 49 (unless this step was done the number 0 would occasionally appear, which is not valid for the lottery). This double value must be converted to an integer, since only whole numbers are valid. It is converted to an integer simply by placing (int) in front of the expression (known as **type casting**).

What does it mean?

Type casting is the technical term for converting data from one data type to another.

PRACTICAL TASK 2.10

Type in the lottery program and try it out. Run it a number of times and see whether you can spot any problems with the numbers it produces.

Occasionally, the program lotto will produce duplicate numbers, whereas six *different* numbers are needed for the lottery. To work properly every time, as each number is produced the program needs to scan back through the numbers it has already produced to see whether there are any duplicates. If there are, another number needs to be produced. Here is the code for the modified program:

```
import java.lang.*;
public class lotto2
{
    public static void main(String args[])
    throws java.io.IOException
    {
    int lotto[] = new int[6];
    int j;
    int i;
```

```
int answer = 0;
char opcode;
char reply;
System.out.println ("Lottery numbers");
for (i = 0; i < 6; i++)
   {
   lotto[i] = 1 + (int)(48 * Math.random());
   for (j = 0; j < i; j++)
      {
      while (lotto[i] == lotto[j])
         {
         System.out.println("Duplicate found");
         lotto[i] = 1 + (int)(48 * Math.random());
         }
      }
   System.out.println ("Your number " + (i + 1) + " is " +
                                          lotto[i]);
   }
}
}
```

This program has an additional loop, inside the main loop, which uses a *while* instruction to produce another number if a duplicate is found. The program prints the message 'Duplicate found', just so that you can see that the duplicate detection code is really working.

2.9 The 'break' instruction

A 'for' loop is used where the loop is to be executed a certain number of times. However, there are some circumstances where a program may need to exit the loop before it is complete. In these situations, the **break** instruction is used to end the loop, and it is normally combined with an *if* instruction which tests for some condition.

Consider the next simple program, which fills a six-element array with random numbers and then searches through the array for the first number that is greater than 50:

```
import java.lang.*;
public class breakEG
{
   public static void main(String args[])
   throws java.io.IOException
   {
   int myarray[] = new int[6];
   int j;
   int i;
   System.out.println ("Break example");
   for (i = 0; i < 6; i++)
```

```
            {
            myarray[i] = (int)(99 * Math.random());
            System.out.println ("Array index " + i + " is " + myarray[i]);
            }
        for (j = 0; j < 6; j++)
            {
            if (myarray[j] > 50)
                {
                break;
                }
            }
        System.out.println ("First number greater that 50 is at index "
                                                                + j);

        }
    }
```

In this program, rather than loop through the array even if the value has been found, a *break* instruction is used to stop the 'for' loop as soon as a value over 50 is found. This leaves the loop counter containing the index number of the array element which contains the value that the program was searching for.

PRACTICAL TASK 2.11

The last program has a flaw. What happens if none of the array elements contains a value over 50? How can you correct this problem?

2.10 Object orientation

The basic program building blocks – sequence, selection and iteration – have now been explained. It is time to look at the concept of **object orientation** (OO), which is fundamental to the design and development of more complex Java programs.

Why use OO methods?

Over the years since the first computer programs were written, software has become increasingly complex and developers have tackled increasingly large and complex systems. Many techniques have been devised to design and develop these systems, but many systems have still suffered from problems such as late delivery, faults and failing to meet users' needs.

OO methods provide a relatively new approach to software development that promises to produce software that is easier to develop, maintain and reuse.

The software development methods used in the past involved dividing a program into various functions which carry out a particular task. However, the data that these functions used was shared between the different functions.

This led to unreliable programs that were difficult to maintain, and were not easily reusable. For example, if you discovered that a change was needed to one of the items of data used in the system (perhaps the data type needed to change from integer to double), then you would need to find all of the functions that used that data item and modify them all so they used the modified item.

Object orientation involves linking the data and the function together in the basic OO building block of the **object**.

Objects

Software objects are based on real-world things in the application area that the software is being written for.

◆ In a library system, the objects might include books, members and loans.
◆ In a mail order system, objects might include customers, orders and products.

Objects generally represent either physical things, like customers and books, or conceptual things like an order or a loan.

Closely related to the concept of the object is the **class**. A class is like an object factory or a **template** for the objects of that class. For example, in the class *cars*, objects of that class might be my Renault, the Queen's Rolls Royce and my neighbour's Rover. These are all **instances** of the class.

The structure of a class

Classes have data associated with them, called **attributes**.

◆ A customer object would have attributes such as name, address, telephone number and so on.
◆ A book object would have attributes such as title, author, ISBN, publisher, etc.

What does it mean?

Attributes are the data that belongs to the class, the things that describe the class.

Classes also have functions, called **methods**. Methods are things that the class can do.

◆ A customer class might have a 'change of address' method.
◆ A book class in a library system might have a 'go on loan' method.

What does it mean?

Methods are the functions of a class, the things that the class can do.

A class defines the attributes and methods, and all objects of that class have the same attributes and methods.

Classes can be described by using a **class diagram**. This lists the name of the class, the attributes and the methods. Figure 2.7 shows the class diagram for the *Student* class. This simple class has just two attributes (name and marks), and three methods (set name, show marks and update marks).

Student
StudentName
StudentMarks
setName
showMarks
updateMarks

Figure 2.7 *Class diagram*

An OO system is made up of objects (created using the class as a template) which work together by one object requesting a service from another (using the methods of that class). This process of requesting services is known as **message passing**. For example, if we also imagine a *Teacher* class, then an object of the *Teacher* class might pass a message to the *Student* class asking it to invoke its *showMarks* method, and the *Student* object would return the mark.

What does it mean?

Message passing is the technical name for the process by which one class gets another class to do something by calling one of its methods.

It is important to understand that the only way in which other objects can gain access to the attributes of a class is by the methods of that class. This is one of the key differences between the earlier approaches to program design – where data is passed between functions – and the OO approach in which data is contained within the object and is accessible only by the object's methods. This concept is known as **encapsulation**.

What does it mean?

Encapsulation is the technical name for the way in which the attributes (data) and the methods (functions) of a class are packaged together within the class, and the data of the class can be accessed only via the methods.

A class's methods have names (like *updateMarks* in the student example) and are either passed a value or return a value (or both). The *updateMarks* method would be passed a value (that is, the marks to be added to that student's total) and the *showMarks* method would return a value (the student's current total marks).

It is, of course, possible to write your own classes and create objects using them. However, to start with, it is helpful to look at a ready-made class that comes as part of the Java language. The **String class** is used to create and process string objects. A string is a sequence of characters, so "hello", "KR02 STX" and "cats and dogs" are all strings. Some programming languages allow the creation of string variables, in the same way that you can create integer or real variables for numbers. Java, on the other hand, uses the String class.

The String class has a number of methods, some of which are shown in Table 2.3.

Table 2.3 **Methods of the String class**			
Method name	**What is does**	**Value passed to method**	**Value returned from method**
length	Returns the length of the string passed to it	None	Length of string, int data type
toUpperCase	Returns the string converted to upper case	None	A string object
toLowerCase	Returns the string converted to lower case	None	A string object
substring	Returns a section of the string. Two integers are passed to the method which indicate the starting and ending points of the section	Two integers	A string object

To write a program that uses the String class, the first step is to create a string object. This is known as **creating an instance** of the class. This is done using a special method of the class called the **constructor**. The constructor is used like this:

```
String myString = new String();
```

This instruction creates a new string object called *myString*. When the program has assigned a value to this string, then the methods can be used. So, to display the length of the string, this instruction could be used:

```
System.out.println("String is " + myString.length() + " characters
                                                        long");
```

Here is a complete program, showing how the methods listed above can be used:

```
class usingString
{
    public static void main(String[] args)
    {
    String myString = new String();
    myString = "how much is that doggie in the window";
    System.out.println("String is " + myString.length() +
                                    " characters long");
    System.out.println("In upper case: " + myString.toUpperCase());
    System.out.println("In lower case: " + myString.toLowerCase());
    System.out.println("Characters 6 to 8 are " + myString.
                                    substring(5,8));
    }
}
```

When this program is run, it produces the output shown in Figure 2.8.

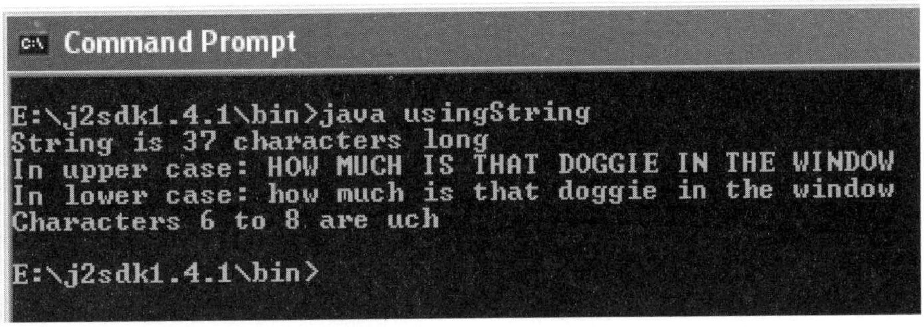

Figure 2.8 An example of usingString

Notice that, in line with the object-oriented philosophy, as users of the string class you need know nothing of the internal workings of the class; the methods of the class provide the public interface.

There is actually a quicker way to create a string object. The instruction:

```
String myString = new String();
```

can be shortened to:

```
String myString;
```

This makes it look the same as creating an integer or other variable, which is why it was not initially used, as an object is in fact being created. However, now that this point has been made, the shorter version will be used here.

Method declaration

Having looked at how an existing standard class can be utilised, consider how a simple class can be created by returning to the *Student* class mentioned earlier. This has two methods as described in Table 2.4.

Table 2.4 Methods of the Student class

Method name	What is does	Value passed to method (arguments)	Value returned from method
updateMarks	Adds mark to student's current marks	Mark to be added (int)	None
showMarks	Returns student's current marks	None	Student's current marks

A class diagram for this class, drawn to the **UML (universal modelling language) standard**, is shown in Figure 2.9.

Student
StudentNumber : int
StudentMarks : int
Student(int)
updateMarks(int)
showMarks() : int

Figure 2.9 UML class diagram for the Student class

The code to implement the *Student* class is (notice the comments):

```
class Student
{
    private int studentNumber;
    private int studentMarks;

    // constructor
    public Student(int numberIn)
    {
    studentNumber = numberIn;
    studentMarks = 0;
    }

    // update marks method
    public void updateMarks(int markIn)
    {
    studentMarks = studentMarks + markIn;
    }

    // show marks method
    public int showMarks()
    {
    return studentMarks;
    }
}
```

Let us look at each part, starting with the attributes of the class:

```
private int studentNumber;
private int studentMarks;
```

These two integer variables store the student's number and the student's mark. They are both declared **private**, so that they cannot be accessed from outside the class except by the class methods. Next look at the constructor:

```
// constructor
public Student(int numberIn)
{
studentNumber = numberIn;
studentMarks = 0;
}
```

The constructor takes that name of the class. It is declared **public** because this, and all methods of the class, need to be accessible from the programs that will use the methods. The constructor is passed an integer value which is the student's number. Values passed to methods in this way are known as **arguments** or **parameters**.

What does it mean?

Parameters or *arguments* are data that is sent to a method. The method carries out its processing using this data.

Now look at the *updateMarks* method:

```
// update marks method
public void updateMarks(int markIn)
{
studentMarks = studentMarks + markIn;
}
```

This method is passed an integer value which is the mark to be added to the student's running total – hence the (int markIn) following the method name. This method does not return any value to the class that calls it, so the method name is preceded by the word '**void**'. Figure 2.10 shows an annotated version of the code.

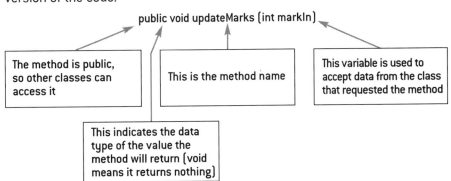

public void updateMarks (int markIn)

| The method is public, so other classes can access it | This is the method name | This variable is used to accept data from the class that requested the method |

This indicates the data type of the value the method will return (void means it returns nothing)

Figure 2.10 *Use of void with a method*

The code of the method is contained within curly braces and is very simple. It takes the value passed to it by the class that requested it (in the variable *markIn*) and adds it to the total student marks (in the variable *studentMarks*).

Finally, look at the *showMarks* method:

```
// show marks method
public int showMarks()
{
return studentMarks;
}
```

Once again, the method is *public* but, unlike with the *updateMarks* method, this one does not accept any input from the requesting class – although it does return an integer value: the student's current mark. Therefore, the method name is preceded by 'int' (to show that it returns an integer value) and followed by an empty set of round brackets (showing that it does not accept any input value).

A class like this does not run on its own. A program must be written that will try out the methods that have been created. Such a program – StudentTester.java – is shown below:

```
class StudentTester
{
    public static void main (String[] args)
    throws java.io.IOException
    {
    int studentNo;
    int markIn;
    int numberOut;
    char reply;
    System.out.println ("Please enter the student number");
    markIn = Kbinput.getnumber();
    Student newStudent = new Student(markIn);
    do
        {
        System.out.println ("Enter marks");
        markIn = Kbinput.getnumber();
        newStudent.updateMarks(markIn);
        numberOut = newStudent.showMarks();
        System.out.println ("Marks = " + numberOut);
        System.out.println ("Type X to exit or C to continue");
        reply = Kbinput.getchar();
        }
    while (reply != 'X');
    }
}
```

Typical output from this program is shown in Figure 2.11.

```
C:\ Command Prompt

E:\j2sdk1.4.1\bin>java StudentTester
Please enter the student number
12345
Enter marks
4
Marks = 4
Type X to exit, or C to continue
C
Enter marks
3
Marks = 7
Type X to exit, or C to continue
X

E:\j2sdk1.4.1\bin>_
```

Figure 2.11 Typical program output

More about implementing classes

There are a couple of other points worth bearing in mind about implementing classes. The first is that class methods may have more than one parameter passed to them. The *Student* class used so far creates a student with a number, but no name. There is no reason why the constructor cannot be modified to deal with a name as well. An additional private attribute will be needed to hold the student's name, and the constructor will need to be modified, as follows (modifications are show in **bold**):

```
class Student
{
    private int studentNumber;
    private String studentName;
    private int studentMarks;

    // constructor
    public Student(int numberIn, String nameIn)
    {
    studentNumber = numberIn;
    studentName = nameIn;
    studentMarks = 0;
    }
}
```

PRACTICAL TASK 2.12

Add a method to the Student class, called *showName*, which returns the student's name.

The second point about creating objects from classes is that there is, of course, no restriction on creating more than one instance of the same class. The program shown next is a development of the StudentTester program – it now creates two objects of the *Student* class: one called *firstStudent* and the other called *secondStudent*. The program uses the modified version of the *Student* class, which includes the student's name, as described above, and the *showName* method you wrote for Practical task 2.12:

```
class StudentTester
{
    public static void main (String[] args)
    throws java.io.IOException
    {
    int studentNo;
    String studentName;
    int markIn;
    int numberOut = 0;
    char reply;
    int whichone;

    // details of first student
    System.out.println ("Please enter the first student number");
    markIn = Kbinput.getnumber();
    System.out.println("Please enter first student name");
    studentName = Kbinput.getstring();

    // create student instance
    Student firstStudent = new Student(markIn, studentName);

    // details of second student
    System.out.println ("Please enter the second student number");
    markIn = Kbinput.getnumber();
    System.out.println("Please enter second student name");
    studentName = Kbinput.getstring();

    // create student instance
    Student secondStudent = new Student(markIn, studentName);
    do
        {
        System.out.println ("Enter 1 for first student, 2 for second");
        whichone = Kbinput.getnumber();
        System.out.println ("Enter marks");
        markIn = Kbinput.getnumber();
        if (whichone == 1)
            {
            firstStudent.updateMarks(markIn);
            numberOut = firstStudent.showMarks();
            studentName = firstStudent.showName();
```

```
            }
        if (whichone == 2)
            {
            secondStudent.updateMarks(markIn);
            numberOut = secondStudent.showMarks();
            studentName = secondStudent.showName();
            }
        System.out.println ("Marks for " + studentName + " are " +
                                                        numberOut);
        System.out.println ("Type X to exit or C to continue");
        reply = Kbinput.getchar();
        }
        while (reply != 'X');
    }
}
```

Inheritance

One of the goals of the object-orientated approach to software development is to make software more easily reusable. In the past, software written for one purpose was not easy to reuse for a similar (but not identical) purpose because the modifications necessary to make it suitable for the new purpose were difficult and involved making changes to the original code. Object-orientated programming avoids this problem using what is called **inheritance**.

The concept of inheritance is easily understood in relation to real-world objects. For example, earlier the idea of the *cars* class was introduced. The *cars* class might have attributes such as colour, maximum speed, price, etc. It might also have methods such as *startEngine* and *increaseSpeed*. What if a class for motorcycles were also needed? While this class would share many attributes and methods with the *cars* class, there would be some differences. A motorcycle class would not need an attribute for the number of doors, but a car class might, for example. The answer to this problem is to define a class, perhaps called *motorvehicles*, which has all the attributes and methods common to all motor vehicles. This class is then extended by other classes which inherit the basic set of attributes and methods from the *motorvehicle* class but add their own relevant attributes and methods. The inheritance relationship between classes is shown in Figure 2.12.

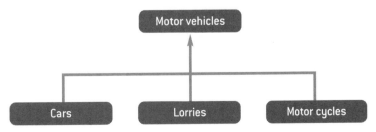

Figure 2.12 The inheritance relationship between classes

Inheritance relationships are sometimes called 'is-a-kind-of' relationships, so a motorcycle is a kind of motor vehicle. Also, classes such as *motorvehicles* are know as **super classes**, while those that extend the super class, such as the *cars* class, are know as **sub-classes**.

To demonstrate how inheritance is implemented in Java, the *Student* class will again be used. Imagine that we want to deal with both full-time and part-time students in the program. For the sake of simplicity, assume that the only attribute part-time students require that full-time ones do not is the day of the week they attend college. Two additional methods will be required, one to set the day they attend and the other to return the day they currently attend. The *Student* class (the super class) will therefore be extended by the *PartTimeStudent* class (the sub-class). The UML class diagram, setting out the inheritance relationship, is shown in Figure 2.13.

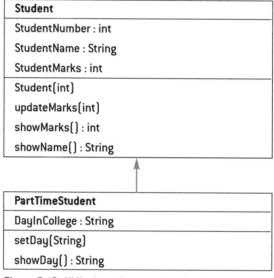

Figure 2.13 *UML class diagram showing the inheritance relationship*

In keeping with the object-oriented philosophy, the *PartTimeStudent* class should be implemented without interfering with the original *Student* class. The internal workings of the super class do not need to be known or understood; all that is required is an understanding of the super class's methods.

The code for the *PartTimeStudent* class is shown below, with an explanation of the key points following it:

```
class PartTimeStudent extends Student
{
    private String dayInCollege;
```

```
// constructor
public PartTimeStudent(int numberIn, String nameIn)
{
super(numberIn, nameIn);
}

// setDay method
public void setDay(String day)
{
dayInCollege = day;
}

// showDay method
public String showDay()
{
return dayInCollege;
}
}
```

The first point to notice is the first line of the class:

```
class PartTimeStudent extends Student
```

This tells us that the class extends the *Student* class. The class has one attribute, which holds the day that the student attends college:

```
private String dayInCollege;
```

The constructor needs a little explaining. The parameters passed to the constructor are the same as those passed to the *Student* class and, in fact, all this constructor does is call the constructor of the super class (Student) using the 'super' instruction. In this way, the *PartTimeStudent* class adds functionality to (extends) the *Student* class without interfering with the code.

The methods of the class should need little explaining as they simply set and return the value of the *dayInCollege* attribute.

As with the *Student* class, a program is needed to test out the methods of the *PartTimeStudent* class, such as the program PTStudentTester.java:

```
class PTStudentTester
{
    public static void main (String[] args)
    throws java.io.IOException
    {
    int studentNo;
    String studentName;
    String day;
    int markIn;
    int numberOut = 0;
    char reply;
    int choice;
```

```
// details of part-time student
System.out.println ("Please enter student number");
markIn = Kbinput.getnumber();
System.out.println("Please enter student name");
studentName = Kbinput.getstring();
System.out.println("Please enter day in college");
day = Kbinput.getstring();

// create part-time student instance
PartTimeStudent newStudent = new PartTimeStudent(markIn,
                                         studentName);
newStudent.setDay(day);
do
   {
   System.out.println ("Enter 1 to update marks, 2 to change
                                              day");

   choice = Kbinput.getnumber();
   if (choice == 1)
      {
      System.out.println ("Enter marks");
      markIn = Kbinput.getnumber();
      newStudent.updateMarks(markIn);
      }
   if (choice == 2)
      {
      System.out.println("Enter new day");
      day = Kbinput.getstring();
      newStudent.setDay(day);
      }
   numberOut = newStudent.showMarks();
   day = newStudent.showDay();
   System.out.println ("Marks = " + numberOut);
   System.out.println ("Day in college is " + day);
   System.out.println ("Type X to exit, or C to continue");
   reply = Kbinput.getchar();
   }
while (reply != 'X');
   }
}
```

This program is based on the StudentTester.java program written previously although, in this version, the user is given the option of either recording marks or changing the student's day of attendance.

PRACTICAL TASK 2.13

Create a *bankacc* class. The UML design diagram for the class is shown in Figure 2.14. Write a program that uses all methods of the class, allowing the user to create an account, deposit money, withdraw money and check the balance.

bankacc
Balance : double
getBalance() : double
withdraw(double)
deposit(double)

Figure 2.14 UML diagram for the bankacc class

Chapter summary

This chapter has covered:
◆ creating classes
◆ use of comments
◆ variables, constants and data types
◆ selection constructs (if...else, switch)
◆ iteration constructs (for, while, do...while)
◆ indenting code to improve readability
◆ arrays
◆ the break instruction
◆ object orientation, including attributes and methods, and the concept of encapsulation
◆ manipulating string objects
◆ creating user-defined classes
◆ creating an inheritance hierarchy using 'extends'.

3 Use components to create a graphical user interface (GUI)

Now that the basic concepts of Java programming have been covered, it is time to move on to writing Java programs for the Windows environment. To start with, you will learn more about Java applications, which will run using the Java development toolkit built in JVM (Java Virtual Machine). Later, you will return to creating Java applets designed to run within a web browser. To support Windows programming, Java uses the Abstract Window Toolkit (AWT).

What does it mean?

The **Abstract Windows Toolkit (AWT)** is built into the Java programming language and includes all of the classes needed to create Windows objects, such as buttons and text boxes.

The AWT classes are based on an inheritance structure, as shown in Figure 2.15. Note that the *Container* class is sub-classed to provide *Window* and *Panel* sub-classes, and these themselves are further sub-classed.

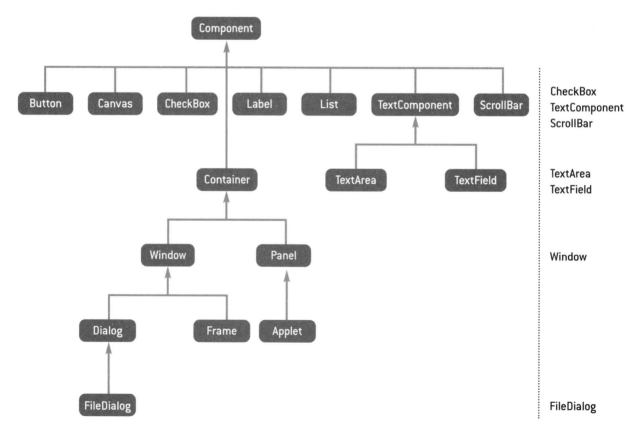

Figure 2.15 Classes of the AWT

3.1 Introduction to Windows programming

The first program written here follows the general structure with which you should be familiar, in that two programs are written.

◆ The first is a class which draws a circle with the words "Hello World" in it.

◆ The second is a 'tester' program that creates a Windows frame and then uses an object of the first class to put something in the frame (i.e. the circle and the words).

This approach will prove particularly useful when you have to write programs to run within a web browser or applet viewer, since very little modification will be needed.

The class which draws the circle and words, WinHello.Java, is shown in the code in Figure 2.16.

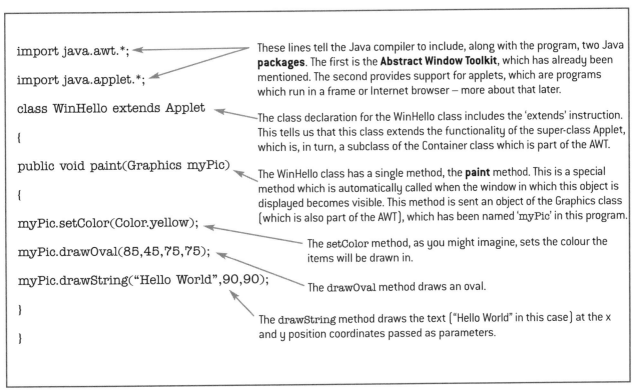

```
import java.awt.*;

import java.applet.*;

class WinHello extends Applet

{

public void paint(Graphics myPic)

{

myPic.setColor(Color.yellow);

myPic.drawOval(85,45,75,75);

myPic.drawString("Hello World",90,90);

}

}
```

These lines tell the Java compiler to include, along with the program, two Java **packages**. The first is the **Abstract Window Toolkit**, which has already been mentioned. The second provides support for applets, which are programs which run in a frame or Internet browser – more about that later.

The class declaration for the WinHello class includes the 'extends' instruction. This tells us that this class extends the functionality of the super-class Applet, which is, in turn, a subclass of the Container class which is part of the AWT.

The WinHello class has a single method, the **paint** method. This is a special method which is automatically called when the window in which this object is displayed becomes visible. This method is sent an object of the Graphics class (which is also part of the AWT), which has been named 'myPic' in this program.

The setColor method, as you might imagine, sets the colour the items will be drawn in.

The drawOval method draws an oval.

The drawString method draws the text ("Hello World" in this case) at the x and y position coordinates passed as parameters.

Figure 2.16 The class that draws the circle and words in WinHello.java

The *drawOval* method has three parameters that set the location and size of the oval, in pixels, in the form:

```
drawOval(x-position, y-position, length, height)
```

Figure 2.17 shows how these parameters are interpreted.

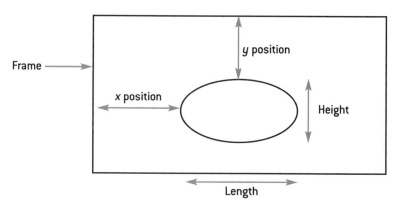

Figure 2.17 The drawOval method

Note that in this program, since the length and height are equal (75), a circle will be drawn.

The *drawString* method draws the text ("Hello World" in this case) at the *x* and *y* position coordinates passed as parameters.

The second program is the 'tester' program that creates a frame and then adds a *WinHello* object to it. The code for this program is explained in Figure 2.18. When this program is run, the output should look like that shown in Figure 2.19.

```
import java.awt.*;

class HelloTester

{

    public static void main (String[] args)

    {

    Frame frame = new Frame();          The Frame class is also part of the AWT, and this line creates a new
                                        Frame object called frame.

    WinHello myHello = new WinHello();  This line creates an object of the WinHello class called myHello.

    frame.setSize(250,200);             This instruction uses the setSize method of the frame object to
                                        set the size (in pixels) of the frame.
    frame.setBackground(Color.blue);
                                        The setBackground method sets the background colour for the frame.
    frame.add(myHello);
                                        The add method adds an object to the frame, in this case the
    frame.setVisible(true);             myHello object.

    }
                                        Finally, this line makes the frame visible.
}
```

Figure 2.18 The tester program

Figure 2.19 HelloTester running

Unfortunately, the frame class does not provide a method to close the window, which you would normally do by clicking the 'X' in the top right corner. You will therefore need to click back on the black DOS screen window where you ran the program from and press Ctrl + C to end the program.

PRACTICAL TASK 2.14

Modify the WinHello class so that it also includes the text "My first Windows program", below the circle, in red.

3.2 Implementing a listener to handle events

The simple WinHello class that has been written so far does not demonstrate how to deal with user input. Windows programming is often known as **event-driven** programming because you must write code to deal with user events, such as the user clicking a button with the mouse.

To demonstrate how this can be done, a modified version of the WinHello class will be created. This version has two buttons; clicking them displays either the 'Hello World' message or a 'Goodbye' message, as in Figure 2.20.

Implementing this version requires quite a number of changes to the WinHello program. The new program, *WinButtons*, is shown and explained in Figure 2.21, with the lines of code that have been added shown in bold.

Figure 2.20 Use of the WinButtons class

```
import java.awt.*;
import java.applet.*;
import java.awt.event.*;
class WinButtons extends Applet implements
                        ActionListener
{
    private boolean goodbye;
    private Button helloButton = new Button ("Say Hello");
    private Button goodbyeButton = new Button ("Say
                                        Goodbye");
    public WinButtons()
    {
    this.add(helloButton);
    this.add(goodbyeButton);
    goodbye = false;
    helloButton.addActionListener(this);
    goodbyeButton.addActionListener(this);
    }
    public void paint(Graphics myPic)
    {
    myPic.setColor(Color.yellow);
    myPic.drawOval(85,45,75,75);
    if (goodbye == false)
        {
        myPic.drawString("Hello World",90,90);
        }
    if (goodbye == true)
        {
        myPic.setColor(Color.red);
        myPic.drawString("Goodbye",100,90);
        }
    }
    public void actionPerformed(ActionEvent clickButton)
    {
    if (clickButton.getSource() == helloButton)
        {
        goodbye = false;
        repaint();
        }
    if (clickButton.getSource() == goodbyeButton)
        {
        goodbye = true;
        repaint();
        }
    }
}
```

Another Java package must be imported to deal with event handling.

The class header has had the words implements ActionListener added to it. ActionListener is a special interface class which has a method called actionPerformed (used later in the program).

Three new attributes have also been added. The goodbye attribute is used to indicate if the "Say Goodbye" button has been clicked. It is set to true if it has, and false if it has not. The other two attributes create objects of the Button class. The constructor of this class is passed the caption for the button as a parameter.

A new constructor has been added for the WinButtons class. The add method is used to add the two buttons; 'this' is used when a class method refers to the object itself. The add method is a method of the container class, of which the applet class is a subclass. Remember, this class extends the applet class, so all the methods of the super classes are available to it via inheritance.

The goodbye attribute is set to false so the "Hello World" message will initially appear.

These two lines add an actionListener for each of the buttons. This effectively waits for an event (i.e. the user clicks one of the buttons). Then, when one occurs, it is dealt with using the event handler in 'this' applet.

These lines simply draw a different message depending on whether the goodbye attribute is set to true or false.

This actionPerformed method is required by the ActionListener interface. When the mouse is clicked, this method is sent an ActionEvent object (called clickButton here) and this class has a getSource method which provides the name of the object that was clicked. By using this method within an if instruction, it is possible to tell which button was clicked and to set the goodbye attribute accordingly. The repaint method simply calls the paint method again so the circle and the message are drawn again, but the content of the message is dependent on the goodbye attribute as explained earlier.

Figure 2.21 Alterations to the WinHello program

As with the WinHello class, a tester program is required to add a WinButtons object to a frame. The same program can be used as before, except that a *WinButtons* object must be created, rather than a *WinHello* one.

3.3 Creating Java applets

The technique of using a 'tester' program to add the programs to a frame could be used for all the Java programs written. Programs written in this way, with a 'main' method, are known as **Java applications**. However, Java was written with the World Wide Web in mind, and Java applets can be run within an Internet browser program such as *Internet Explorer* or an applet viewer such as the one that comes with the Java SDK.

Converting the Windows programs written so far from applications to applets is quite simple. Two changes are needed:

1   The word 'public' needs to be added to the class header.

2   The constructor needs to be replaced with a special method called *init*, although all of the code that was in the constructor stays in the init method.

The *WinButtons* class, modified to run as an applet (and called WinButtonsApplet), is shown below, with the modifications in bold:

```
import java.awt.*;
import java.applet.*;
import java.awt.event.*;
public class WinButtonsApplet extends Applet implements
                                        ActionListener

{
    private boolean goodbye;
    private Button helloButton = new Button ("Say Hello");
    private Button goodbyeButton = new Button ("Say Goodbye");

    public void init()

    {
    this.add(helloButton);
    this.add(goodbyeButton);
    goodbye = false;
    helloButton.addActionListener(this);
    goodbyeButton.addActionListener(this);
    }
    public void paint(Graphics myPic)
    {
    myPic.setColor(Color.yellow);
    myPic.drawOval(85,45,75,75);
    if (goodbye == false)
        {
```

```
        myPic.drawString("Hello World", 90, 90);
        }
    if (goodbye == true)
        {
        myPic.setColor(Color.red);
        myPic.drawString("Goodbye", 100, 90);
        }
    }
    public void actionPerformed(ActionEvent clickButton)
    {
    if (clickButton.getSource() == helloButton)
        {
        goodbye = false;
        repaint();
        }
    if (clickButton.getSource() == goodbyeButton)
        {
        goodbye = true;
        repaint();
        }
    }
}
```

To run an applet, you need to embed it in an HTML web page. HTML is the code that web browsers understand. A very simple web page, which contains a reference to the applet WinButtonsApplet, can be created using the following HTML code:

```
<html>
<applet code="WinButtonsApplet" width=250 height=175>
</applet>
</html>
```

This code can be typed in a text editor such as *Notepad*, and then saved in a file ending with the extension.html. In the example below, the file is called applet.html. The WinButtonApplet.java program should then be compiled in the normal way using Javac, and the applet then viewed using the Appletviewer program, as shown in Figure 2.22.

```
Command Prompt - appletviewer applet.html

E:\j2sdk1.4.1\bin>javac WinButtonsApplet.java
E:\j2sdk1.4.1\bin>appletviewer applet.html
```

Figure 2.22 The command prompt to view the applet

The applet will then run as before, but this time in the Appletviewer – see Figure 2.23. Unlike the frame used previously, the Appletviewer can be closed by clicking the close button in the top right of the window.

Figure 2.23 WinButtonsApplet running

PRACTICAL TASK 2.15

Convert the program you wrote in Practical task 2.14 to an applet.

3.4 More Windows components

Most Windows programs require more than just buttons. To accept user data input, they need text boxes. The next applet demonstrates how to accept input from, and return output to, a text box. This simple applet has a single text box in which the user enters an integer and then clicks the button. This adds the number in the box to itself and displays the result in the same box (see Figure 2.24).

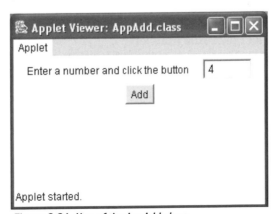

Figure 2.24 Use of the AppAdd class

First, the code for the AppAdd program is shown and explained in Figure 2.25. This program shares many features with the previous one. It has an *actionPerformed* method, for example, which deals with user events. There are some other differences which are explained in the code annotations.

```java
import java.awt.*;
import java.applet.*;
import java.awt.event.*;
import java.text.*;
public class AppAdd extends Applet implements
                         ActionListener
{
    private Label theLabel = new Label ("Enter a
                number and click the button");
    private TextField numberText = new TextField(5);
    private Button addButton = new Button ("Add");

    public void init()
    {
    this.add(theLabel);
    this.add(numberText);
    this.add(addButton);
    addButton.addActionListener(this);
    }

    public void actionPerformed(ActionEvent clickButton)
    {
    String numberIn = numberText.getText();
    int n;
    if (clickButton.getSource() == addButton)
        {
        n = Integer.parseInt(numberIn);
        n = n + n;
        numberIn = "" + n;
        numberText.setText(numberIn);

        }
    }
}
```

These three attributes define the label, text box and button that appear in the frame. The Button class has already been used in the previous program. The Label class creates a label and is passed the text to appear in the label as a parameter. The TextField class creates a text box, and a number is passed as a parameter which indicates the length of the box.

The constructor for this program should be familiar. It simply uses the add method to add the label, text box and button and then creates an action listener for the button.

The event handler will run if the 'Add' button is clicked. It takes the number that the user has typed into the text box, adds it to itself and then returns the result to the text box.

This String attribute is used to hold the text from the text box, which is retrieved using the getText method.

This integer attribute is used to hold the value once it has been converted to a number.

An if instruction is used to determine if the event was caused by clicking the 'Add' button.

To convert the String value from the text box into an integer, the parse.Int method is used:

The value in n is then added to itself and converted back to a String value.

This is then inserted back into the text box using the setText method.

Figure 2.25 The AppAdd program code

This applet needs to be embedded in an HTML file as before, and run using the Appletviewer or *Internet Explorer*. Example code for a suitable HTML file is shown below:

```
<html>
<applet code="AppAdd.class" width=300 height=150>
</applet>
</html>
```

PRACTICAL TASK 2.16

It is not too difficult to work out how to convert this simple example program into a simple calculator which will add two numbers that the user enters. Instead of just one text field, it requires three – one each for the numbers the user enters and another for the answer. Once you have made this version work, you can add buttons for multiply, divide and subtract as well.

3.5 Layout managers

So far, no mention has been made of how components such as text boxes and buttons can be laid out in the applet window. The positioning of such components is controlled by the **layout manager** in use.

Flow layout
. . . .

The default layout manager is called **FlowLayout**, which simply arranges the components in the applet windows as they are added, starting a new row when required. Other layout managers are available which give more control over the positioning of components. However, this section investigates how the flow layout manager works, before moving on to the other layout managers. To do this, a simple class will be created which adds a label and four buttons. The code for this applet is:

```
import java.awt.*;
import java.applet.*;
public class flow extends Applet
{
    private Label theLabel = new Label ("Flow Layout");
    private Button ButtonA = new Button ("A");
    private Button ButtonB = new Button ("B");
    private Button ButtonC = new Button ("C");
    private Button ButtonD = new Button ("D");

    public void init()
    {
```

```
            this.add(theLabel);
            this.add(ButtonA);
            this.add(ButtonB);
            this.add(ButtonC);
            this.add(ButtonD);
        }
    }
```

The HTML used to display this applet is:

```
<html>
<applet code="flow.class" width=150 height=150>
</applet>
</html>
```

The applet produces a display as shown in Figure 2.26.

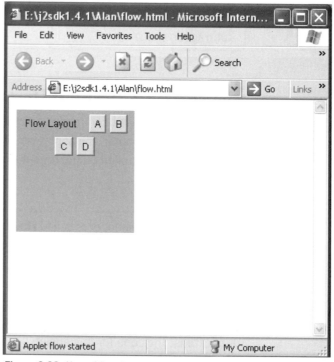

Figure 2.26 Use of flow layout

As you can see, the layout is not very neat! However, if the size of the applet window is increased from 150 pixels to, for example, 200, then all of the components will be displayed along the top line (try it).

Border layout

Another layout manager available is called **BorderLayout**. This divides the window into five regions called North, South, East, West and Center (see Figure 2.27).

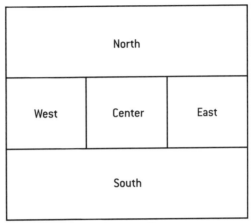

Figure 2.27 Border layout policy

The previous program can easily be modified (changes shown in bold) to use this layout manager, like this:

```
import java.awt.*;
import java.applet.*;
public class border_layout extends Applet
{
    private Label theLabel = new Label ("Border Layout");
    private Button ButtonA = new Button ("A");
    private Button ButtonB = new Button ("B");
    private Button ButtonC = new Button ("C");
    private Button ButtonD = new Button ("D");
    public void init()
    {
    setLayout(new BorderLayout());
    this.add("North", theLabel);
    this.add("West", ButtonA);
    this.add("Center", ButtonB);
    this.add("East", ButtonC);
    this.add("South", ButtonD);
    }
}
```

An additional instruction is needed:

```
setLayout(new BorderLayout());
```

This tells the program to use the border layout manager. Then as each component object is added, the region of the border must also be indicated. For example, the label is added to the North region using this instruction:

```
this.add("North", theLabel);
```

When this applet is run, using the same HTML as before, the result is rather different – see Figure 2.28.

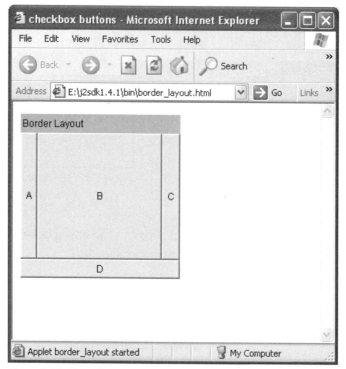

Figure 2.28 Use of border layout

Unlike with flow layout, the relative positions of the components will not alter if the size of the applet window is altered (try it).

Grid layout

Another layout manager, which gives even greater control over the positioning of various components, is **GridLayout**. This layout manager allows you to specify the number of rows and columns you require for the various components. The gap between them can also be specified. The example program, modified to use GridLayout, is:

```
import java.awt.*;
import java.applet.*;
public class grid_layout extends Applet
{
    private Label theLabel = new Label ("Grid Layout");
    private Button ButtonA = new Button ("A");
    private Button ButtonB = new Button ("B");
    private Button ButtonC = new Button ("C");
    private Button ButtonD = new Button ("D");
```

```
public void init()
{
setLayout(new GridLayout(3,3,10,10));
this.add(theLabel);
this.add(ButtonA);
this.add(ButtonB);
this.add(ButtonC);
this.add(ButtonD);
}
}
```

The instruction that sets the new layout manager now looks like this:

```
setLayout(new GridLayout(3,3,10,10));
```

This sets up a grid of three rows and three columns (the first number is the rows, the second the columns) with ten pixels between each. When you add components, they are added across the columns, then down the rows. The applet is shown running in Figure 2.29.

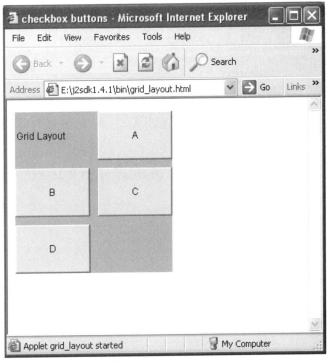

Figure 2.29 Use of grid layout

Using panels

As you can see, none of the layout managers provides a particularly neat looking applet window. However, you can divide the applet window into **panels**, each of which can use a different layout manager. A panel is a type of container which is used for organising components. With this technique, panel objects are created and then components are added to the panel. Then, the panel is added to the applet frame.

In the example shown and explained in Figure 2.30, two panels are created. TopPanel is used to add the label, using the default FlowLayout. ButtonPanel is used for the buttons which are added using a 2 × 2 grid layout.

```
import java.awt.*;
import java.applet.*;
public class panels extends Applet
{
    private Panel TopPanel = new Panel();          Each panel is created in the normal
    private Label theLabel = new Label ("Using Panels");   way, using a constructor.
    private Panel ButtonPanel = new Panel();
    private Button ButtonA = new Button ("A");
    private Button ButtonB = new Button ("B");
    private Button ButtonC = new Button ("C");
    private Button ButtonD = new Button ("D");

    public void init()
      {
      TopPanel.add(theLabel);
      this.add(TopPanel);
      ButtonPanel.setLayout(new GridLayout(2,2,10,10));    The layout is set for the panel.
      ButtonPanel.add(ButtonA);
      ButtonPanel.add(ButtonB);                            Then the components are added to
      ButtonPanel.add(ButtonC);                            the panel.
      ButtonPanel.add(ButtonD);
      this.add(ButtonPanel);                               Finally, the panel is added to the
      }                                                    applet window.
}
```

Figure 2.30 Code for panels

When the applet is run, using the same HTML as before, it gives a neater appearance than any of the layout managers provided by themselves, as shown in Figure 2.31.

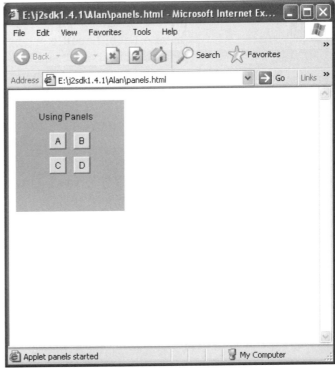

Figure 2.31 Use of panels

Experiment with using different layout policies and panels to modify the appearance of the simple calculator you wrote for Practical task 2.16.

3.6 More GUI components

So far, only text boxes and buttons have been used. There are, of course, many other GUI components.

Check boxes

Check boxes allow a user to select various options. Clicking the check box with the mouse places a tick in the box, indicating that the option has been selected.

The first program to demonstrate how check boxes can be used simply places a series of check boxes in the applet window. The processing of the user's selection will be explained later. The code of the program – which creates three check boxes, labelled 'Yes', 'No' and 'Maybe' – is:

```
import java..awt.*;
import java.applet.*;
public class checkbox extends Applet
{
```

```
private Label LabelYes = new Label("Yes");
private Checkbox CheckYes = new Checkbox ();
private Label LabelNo = new Label("No");
private Checkbox CheckNo = new Checkbox ();
private Label LabelMaybe = new Label("Maybe");
private Checkbox CheckMaybe = new Checkbox ();

public void init()
{
this.add(LabelYes);
this.add(CheckYes);
this.add(LabelNo);
this.add(CheckNo);
this.add(LabelMaybe);
this.add(CheckMaybe);
}
}
```

Check box objects are created and added to the applet window in the same way as the other components looked at so far. With a similar HTML file to that used previously, this applet will appear as shown in Figure 2.32 when it is run.

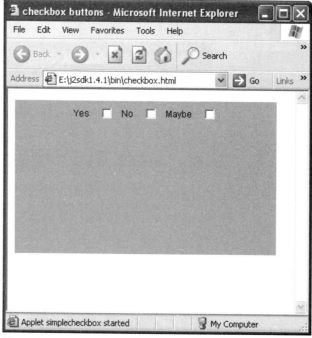

Figure 2.32 The Checkbox applet

Radio buttons

You will find that, if you try clicking the check boxes, you can select any combination of the boxes. This may suit some applications, but others may require that only one of the check boxes can be selected at a time. These types of check box are sometimes called **radio buttons**.

To create radio buttons, they must be assigned to a group. The example program, modified to create radio buttons, is shown and explained in Figure 2.33, with the modified lines highlighted.

```
compcode 35
import java.awt.*;
import java.applet.*;
public class checkbox extends Applet
{
    private Label LabelYes = new Label("Yes");
    private Checkbox CheckYes = new Checkbox ();
    private Label LabelNo = new Label("No");
    private Checkbox CheckNo = new Checkbox ();
    private Label LabelMaybe = new Label("Maybe");
    private Checkbox CheckMaybe = new Checkbox ();
    private CheckboxGroup decision = new CheckboxGroup();

    public void init()
    {
    CheckYes.setCheckboxGroup(decision);
    CheckNo.setCheckboxGroup(decision);
    CheckMaybe.setCheckboxGroup(decision);
    this.add(LabelYes);
    this.add(CheckYes);
    this.add(LabelNo);
    this.add(CheckNo);
    this.add(LabelMaybe);
    this.add(CheckMaybe);

    }
}
```

A CheckboxGroup called 'decision' is created.

Each of the check boxes that form part of the radio button set are added to the group.

Figure 2.33 *Code for radio buttons*

The applet is shown running in Figure 2.34. Note that the shape of the check boxes is different (circular rather that square) when they are part of a group.

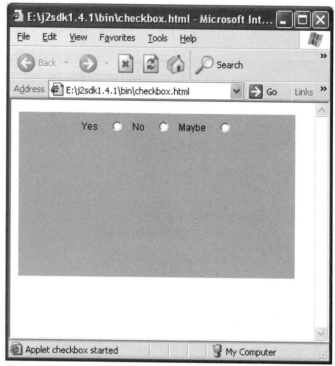

Figure 2.34 Use of radio buttons

Processing the user's check box selection is done using an *ActionListener*, as previously explained.

What does it mean?

An ActionListener is a section of code that deals with an event such as the program users clicking a button, or in this case making a selection from a check box.

The code for the modified program is shown below. A text box has been added to show the choice made, and a button to trigger the event. The lines that have been added are shown in bold:

```
import java.awt.*;
import java.applet.*;
import java.awt.event.*;
public class checkbox extends Applet implements ActionListener
{
    private Label theLabel = new Label("You choose");
    private TextField choice = new TextField(5);
    private Label LabelYes = new Label("Yes");
    private Checkbox CheckYes = new Checkbox ();
    private Label LabelNo = new Label("No");
    private Checkbox CheckNo = new Checkbox ();
    private Label LabelMaybe = new Label("Maybe");
    private Checkbox CheckMaybe = new Checkbox ();
    private CheckboxGroup decision = new CheckboxGroup();
    private Button okButton = new Button ("OK");
```

```
public void init()
{
CheckYes.setCheckboxGroup(decision);
CheckNo.setCheckboxGroup(decision);
CheckMaybe.setCheckboxGroup(decision);
this.add(theLabel);
this.add(choice);
this.add(LabelYes);
   this.add(CheckYes);
this.add(LabelNo);
this.add(CheckNo);
this.add(LabelMaybe);
this.add(CheckMaybe);
this.add(okButton);
okButton.addActionListener(this);
}

public void actionPerformed(ActionEvent makeChoice)
{
if (CheckYes.getState() == true)
   {
   choice.setText("Yes");
   }
else if(CheckNo.getState() == true)
   {
   choice.setText("No");
   }
else if(CheckMaybe.getState() == true)
   {
   choice.setText("Maybe");
   }
}
}
```

The check boxes are tested using the *getState()* method. This will return a value of 'true' if the check box has been selected, or 'false' if not selected. The applet is shown running in Figure 2.35. The user must first click one of the check boxes and then click the 'OK' button, which will then display the option chosen in the text box.

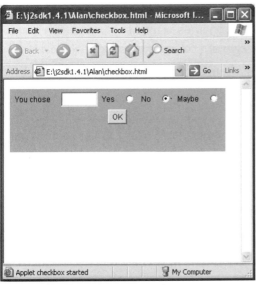

Figure 2.35 The radio button applet

List boxes

List boxes give the opportunity for the user to select from a list of items. To demonstrate their use, another simple applet will be written. This displays a list box with three items in it, as shown in Figure 2.36.

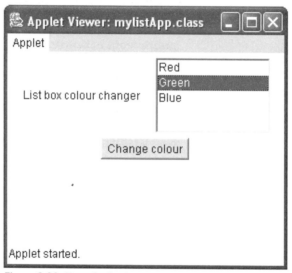

Figure 2.36 Use of a list box

When the user selects one of the colour names in the list box and then clicks the 'Change colour' button, the background colour of the applet window changes. The code for this applet is shown and explained in Figure 2.37.

Choice boxes

A choice box (sometimes called a **drop-down box**) is very similar to a list box, except that it displays only a single line, with a button to drop down the items in the list. The constructor for the *Choice* class does not take any parameters (unlike the constructor for the *List* class which takes the number of lines in the list), but it shares the same methods with the Choice class.

```
import java.awt.*;
import java.applet.*;
import java.awt.event.*;
public class mylistApp extends Applet implements ActionListener
{
    private Label theLabel = new Label("List box colour changer");
    private List myList = new List(4);
    private Button Change = new Button("Change colour");
    public void init()
    {
    this.add(theLabel);
    this.add(myList);
    myList.add("Red");
    myList.add("Green");
    myList.add("Blue");
    this.add(Change);
    Change.addActionListener(this);
    }
    public void actionPerformed(ActionEvent clickButton)
    {
    if (clickButton.getSource() == Change)
      {
      if (myList.getSelectedIndex() == 0)
        {
        setBackground(Color.red);
        }
      if (myList.getSelectedIndex() == 1)
        {
        setBackground(Color.green);
        }
      if (myList.getSelectedIndex() == 2)
        {
        setBackground(Color.blue);
        }
      }
    }
}
```

A list box object is created. The number passed as a parameter is the number of lines in the text box.

The list box is added to the applet, and its own add method is used to add items into the list box. If more items are added to the list than there are lines in the list, then scroll bars automatically appear in the list box.

The action listener for the 'Change colour' button uses a multiple if statement along with the getSelectedIndex method of the list class to identify which of the items in the list box was selected. Items in the list box are numbered from zero.

Figure 2.37 Code for list box colour change

PRACTICAL TASK 2.18

Convert the colour changer program to use a choice box rather than a list box. As the two classes are very similar, the only change needed is to the constructor.

Text area

The final GUI component covered in this section is the *TextArea* class. This provides a text box with multiple rows and columns. The number of rows and columns is set in the constructor, so:

```
private TextArea myText = new TextArea(3,8);
```

will provide a box with three rows and eight columns.

PRACTICAL TASK 2.19

Using the simple calculator you created in Practical task 2.16, add a text area that shows details of the calculations done, like a printing calculator. You will need to add a 'Clear' button to clear the contents of the text area.

3.7 Dialogues, frames and menus

A **dialogue** is a type of window that pops up so that the user can interact with the program in some way. Dialogue boxes are often brought on to the screen using menus. So, for example, if you select the *File* menu in Microsoft Word, and the *Open* option within that menu, the 'Open' dialogue box pops up on the screen. (The American spelling, dialog, is seen in many applications and is used in Java.)

Both *Dialog* and *Menu* classes can be added to a frame but not to a panel. Therefore, although Java applications can be created using dialogues and menus, applets cannot (at least not without using some additional features of Java which are beyond the scope of this book). So, for this section, Java applications must be written – and recall that this involves creating a 'tester' program rather than an HTML page to run the program.

Creating dialogues is quite complex. The code to create the dialogue object is placed in one Java source file, and the code for the frame is placed in another. An **association** needs to be created between the two objects. As before, a simple example will be used, which displays the window shown in Figure 2.38.

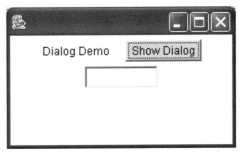

Figure 2.38 Using the usingDialog class (1)

When the 'Show Dialog' button is clicked, a dialogue box pops up – see Figure 2.39.

Figure 2.39 Using the usingDialog class (2)

If you enter a name into the text box and then click the 'OK' button, the dialogue will close and the name entered will appear in the text box on the previous window – see Figure 2.40.

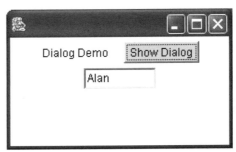

Figure 2.40 Using the usingDialog class (3)

Now the code will be explained, starting with the code for the Dialog class, which is called *myDialog*. The code is shown and explained in Figure 2.41.

```java
import java.awt.*;
import java.awt.event.*;
class myDialog extends Dialog implements
                      ActionListener
{
    private Label theLabel = new Label("Enter
                            Username");
    private TextField textIn = new TextField(8);
    private Button okButton = new Button("OK");
    private Component createdBy;

    public myDialog(Frame frameIn, Component
                    componentIn)
    {

        super(frameIn);
        createdBy = componentIn;
        setLayout(new FlowLayout());
        this.add(theLabel);
        this.add(textIn);
        this.add(okButton);
        okButton.addActionListener(this);
        setSize(200,200);
        setVisible(true);

    }
    public void actionPerformed(ActionEvent e)
    {
    createdBy.setName(textIn.getText());
    dispose();

    }
}
```

The class definition extends the Dialog class, as this in not a Panel or Applet.

This new attribute is used to hold a reference to the component (Panel object) that created the dialogue (remember, Component is the super class of the Java AWT, a Panel object is a sub class).

The constructor sends two parameters, a Frame object and a Component object. A Frame object is always required when a dialogue is created, since the dialogue must be associated with the frame that generates it. The component is a reference to the component that created the dialogue. The Frame object is used as a parameter to the Dialog constructor.

Since this class extends the Dialog class, the super keyword is used.

The attribute createdBy is assigned to the Component object.

This sets the layout the flow layout, since the default layout for Dialog objects is border layout.

The label, the text box and the button are added to the dialogue, and an action listener is added for the button. The size for the dialogue must be set and it must be made visible.

The ActionPerfomed method does not need to determine what caused the event since the button has the only action listener.

The dialogue needs to transfer the string in the textIn text field back to the component that created the dialogue. The attribute createdBy has been assigned to this component, but how does the string get into that component? In an object-orientated system, the functionality of an object is provided by the object's methods, so the object that created the dialogue needs a method (called setName) that allows the string to be passed back from the dialogue.

Finally, the dialogue needs to be closed, removing the dialogue from the screen, returning the user to the class which opened the dialogue in the first place.

Figure 2.41 Code for a dialogue box

Containers *are a* Graphics *class, a sub-class of the components of the Java AWT (see the inheritance diagram in Figure 2.15, on page 90). Containers are an abstract class – that is, you never create objects of the container class, only of the sub-classes which inherit its features. The two sub-classes of the container class are the* Panel *class and the* Window *class.*

Panels *are used in applets and they are basically boxes into which other components such as text areas and buttons can be placed.*

The Window *class is further sub-classed into* Frames *and* Dialogs. *Frames basically perform the same function for a Java application as panels do for an applet.*

Next, the code for the *showDialog* class will be described. Remember, this is the class with the button on it, which when clicked makes the dialogue appear. The code is shown and explained in Figure 2.42.

```java
import java.awt.*;
import java.awt.event.*;
class showDialog extends Panel implements ActionListener
{
    private String userName;
    private Label theLabel = new Label("Dialog Demo");
    private Button showButton = new Button("Show Dialog");
    private TextField theText = new TextField(8);
    Frame thisFrame;

    public showDialog(Frame frameIn)
    {
        thisFrame = frameIn;
        this.add (theLabel);
        this.add (showButton);
        this.add (theText);
        showButton.addActionListener(this);
    }
    public void setName(String nameIn)
    {
        userName = nameIn;
        theText.setText(userName);
    }
    public void actionPerformed(ActionEvent e)
    {
        new myDialog(thisFrame, this);
    }
}
```

This class extends the Panel class.

This class needs to know the location of the frame it will run in, since it has to pass this information to the dialogue, so an attribute is declared for this purpose.

The constructor sends the frame as a parameter and …

… the attribute is assigned to it.

This section of code creates a method for this class called setName which allows the text in the theText text field to be set by the dialogue.

The actionPerformed method creates a new myDialog object, sending it the reference to the Frame it is running in, in the form of the thisFrame attribute, and a reference to the Panel object (referred to as 'this').

Figure 2.42 Code for the showDialog class

The third source file required is the 'tester' program that creates the frame for the showDialog class to run in, called *showDialogTester*. The code for this is very similar to that used for other Java application tester programs. It is:

```
import java.awt.*;
public class showDialogTester
{
    public static void main(String[] args)
    {
    Frame myFrame = new Frame();
    showDialog myProg = new showDialog(myFrame);
    myFrame.setSize(250,150);
    myFrame.add(myProg);
    myFrame.setVisible(true);
    }
}
```

The constructor used for the dialogue in the myDialog class – *super(frameIn)* – creates a **non-modal** dialogue box, which means that the frame that created the dialogue is still active and the user could continue to interact with it. While this may be desired in some cases, it is more common for dialogue boxes to be **modal** – that is, the parent frame is not able to accept user interaction until the dialogue is closed.

What does it mean?

Modal and *non-modal* are standard Windows terminology for the way dialogue boxes behave.

The File...Open dialogue box found in many applications is a modal dialogue box. (In Microsoft Word, choose the File menu, then the Open option, and the File...Open dialogue box will appear.) You must close the File...Open dialogue box before you can return to the application that opened it.

However, some dialogue boxes are non-modal. In Microsoft Word, the Edit...Find dialogue box (Edit menu, Find option) is non-modal. You can return to the editing window in Word and continue typing while the Find dialogue box is still on the screen (but not active).

A modal dialogue can be created using a slightly different constructor. Rather than just taking one parameter (the reference to the parent frame), this constructor also takes a Boolean parameter. It is set to 'true' to create a modal dialogue or to 'false' for a non-modal one. So, to create a modal dialogue version of the myDialog class the instruction would be:

```
super(frameIn, true)
```

PRACTICAL TASK 2.20

Modify the myDialog class to make it modal.

The showDialog class displays the dialogue box when a button is clicked, but in many cases **menus** are used to bring dialogues on to the screen (and to perform many other functions too). Creating menus is not particularly complex, but it is important to understand some menu terminology. Figure 2.43 shows the new version of the showDialog class, called *showDialogWithMenu*. One of the menus has been dropped down.

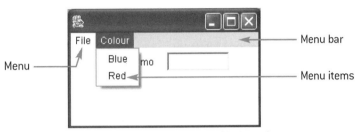

Figure 2.43 Use of the showDialogWithMenu class

To create menus like this, a menu bar, menus and menu items must be declared. Then the bar must be added to the frame, the menus added to the bar and the items added to the menus. The code for the showDialogWithMenu class is shown and explained in Figure 2.44.

```
import java.awt.*;
import java.awt.event.*;
class showDialogWithMenu extends Panel implements ActionListener
{
    private String userName;
    private Label theLabel = new Label("Menu Demo");
    private TextField theText = new TextField(8);
    private MenuBar myBar = new MenuBar();
    private Menu fileMenu = new Menu("File");
    private Menu colourMenu = new Menu("Colour");
    private MenuItem enterItem = new MenuItem("Enter username");
    private MenuItem blueItem = new MenuItem("Blue");
    private MenuItem redItem = new MenuItem("Red");
    Frame thisFrame;

    public showDialogWithMenu(Frame frameIn)
    {
        thisFrame = frameIn;
        thisFrame.setMenuBar(myBar);
```

These are the declarations for the bar, the menus and the menu items.

Within the constructor, the bar is added to the frame using the setMenuBar method of the Frame class.

```
      myBar.add(fileMenu);
      myBar.add(colourMenu);
      fileMenu.add(enterItem);
      colourMenu.add(blueItem);
      colourMenu.add(redItem);
      this.add (theLabel);
      this.add (theText);
      enterItem.addActionListener(this);
      blueItem.addActionListener(this);
      redItem.addActionListener(this);
   }
   public void setName(String nameIn)
   {
     userName = nameIn;
     theText.setText(userName);
   }
   public void actionPerformed(ActionEvent e)
   {
     if(e.getSource() == enterItem)
     {
        new myDialog(thisFrame, this);
     }
     if(e.getSource() == blueItem)
     {
        setBackground(Color.blue);
     }
     if(e.getSource() == redItem)
     {
        setBackground(Color.red);
     }
   }
}
```

Then the menus are added and the items added to the menus.

Action listeners are added for each of the menu items.

Different actions are performed for each of the menu items.

Figure 2.44 *Code for the showDialogWithMenu class*

This program uses the same myDialog class, and the only modification needed to the tester class is to change the name of the class constructor from showDialog to showDialogWithMenu.

3.8 Images, shapes and fonts

The *paint* method of the *Component* class has already been introduced. When a paint method is called (which happens automatically when the frame or panel becomes visible), an object of the *Graphics* class is sent to it. Graphics objects have lots of useful methods. The ones already used are setColor, drawstring, drawOval and repaint, but there are many more.

The *drawImage* method will place a graphic image in an applet window. The graphic image must first be loaded using the *getImage* method. This method take two parameters – the URL of the graphics file, and the name of the file. If the graphics file is being loaded from the same location as the HTML file that loads the applet, then the *getDocumentBase* method can be used to return the location of the file. Here is an example:

```
myImage = getImage(getDocumentBase(), "testImage.jpg");
```

In the example shown in Figure 2.45, a graphic image is displayed as a background to the applet window.

Figure 2.45 Graphic image used as a background

The code for this applet is:

```
import java.awt.*;
import java.applet.*;
public class imageApp extends Applet
{
```

```
private Image myImage;
public void paint(Graphics g)
{
myImage = getImage(getDocumentBase(), "testImage.jpg");
g.drawImage(myImage, 0, 0, this);
g.drawString("What a beautiful view", 20, 20);
}
}
```

The line that displays the image is:

```
g.drawImage(myImage, 0, 0, this);
```

The 0, 0 refers to the top left coordinates of the image – this refers to the applet in which the image is to be displayed.

This method simply displays as much of the graphic image in the applet window as will fit. However, by using a slightly different version of the method the image can be scaled to a particular size. To scale the image, two additional integer parameters are required, setting the horizontal and vertical size in pixels. So, for example, this instruction:

```
g.drawImage(myImage, 0, 0, 160, 200, this);
```

will scale the image to 160 pixels in width and 200 in height, as shown in Figure 2.46.

Figure 2.46 A scaled graphic image

The **setColor** method has been used before, with one of the preset colour names, such as:

    g.setColor(Color.green);

There are 13 preset colours: black, blue, cyan, darkGray, gray, green, lightGray, magenta, orange, pink, red, white and yellow. It is also possible to create new colours by creating colour attributes with parameters setting the individual levels of red, green and blue. The colour levels are numbered between 0 and 255. So, for example, 255,0,0 would give the pure colour red. To create a new colour, called brown, the code would be (assuming the graphics object was named g):

    Color brown = new Color(125, 75, 0);
    g.setColor(brown);

The **drawOval** method has also been used before, but there is also a *drawRect* method for drawing a rectangle, and versions that will draw filled shapes, *fillOval* and *fillRect*. There is also a *drawLine* method for drawing lines, and *drawArc* and *fillArc* methods for arcs. The parameters for all these methods are described below:

◆ drawLine(int x1, int y1, int x2, int y2) – with x1 = starting *x* coordinate, y1 = starting *y* coordinate, x2 = ending *x* coordinate, and y2 = ending *y* coordinate

◆ drawRect(int x, int y, int width, int height) – with x = *x* coordinate of top left corner, y = *y* coordinate of top left corner, width = width of rectangle, and height = height of rectangle

◆ fillRect – with the same parameters as drawRect, but the rectangle is filled with the current colour

◆ drawArc(int x, int y, int width, int height, int startAngle, int arcAngle) – with x and y = *x,y* coordinates of top left corner of the arc, startAngle = initial angle of the arc, and arcAngle = angular extent of the arc

◆ fillArc – with the same parameters as drawArc, but the arc is filled with the current colour

◆ fillOval(int x, int y, int width, int height).

An example of the way these graphics methods can be used is shown in Figure 2.47. The buttons change the mouth from a smile to a surprised look.

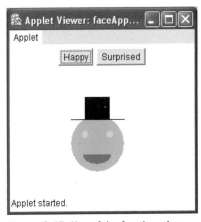

Figure 2.47 Use of the faceApp class

The code for the class is shown below (there is nothing really new in the code, so a detailed explanation is not given):

```java
import java.awt.*;

import java.applet.*;
import java.awt.event.*;

public class faceApp extends Applet implements ActionListener
{
    private boolean isSurprised;
    private Button smileButton = new Button("Happy");
    private Button surprisedButton = new Button("Surprised");

    public void init()
    {
    this.add(smileButton);
    this.add(surprisedButton);
    isSurprised = false;
    smileButton.addActionListener(this);
    surprisedButton.addActionListener(this);
    }

    public void paint(Graphics g)
      {
      // the head
      g.setColor(Color.pink);
      g.fillOval(85, 95, 75, 75);
      // two eyes
      g.setColor(Color.green);
      g.fillOval(100, 115, 10, 10);
      g.fillOval(135, 115, 10, 10);
      // the hat
      g.setColor(Color.black);
      g.drawLine(85, 100, 160, 100);
      g.fillRect(105, 70, 35, 30);
      g.setColor(Color.red);
      if (isSurprised == false)
      {
         // the smile
         g.fillArc(102, 135, 40, 25, 0, -180);
      }
      else
      {
         // the surprised look
         g.fillOval(114, 143, 15, 15);
      }
```

```
        }
    public void actionPerformed(ActionEvent e)
    {
        if(e.getSource() == smileButton)
        {
            isSurprised = false;
            repaint();
        }
        if(e.getSource() == surprisedButton)
        {
            isSurprised = true;
            repaint();
        }
    }
}
```

As well as drawing lines and shapes, it is also possible to create and use a limited number of different text font styles. The **Font** class is part of the AWT and its constructor takes a number of parameters:

Font(*fontname, fontstyle, fontsize*)

◆ The font name can be set to "Serif", "SansSerif", "Monospaced", "Dialog" or "DialogInput".

◆ The font style can be set to Font.PLAIN, Font.BOLD or Font.ITALIC (bold and italic can be combined using a plus sign).

The simple program shown next demonstrates how these fonts can be used:

```
import java.awt.*;
import java.applet.*;
public class fontApp extends Applet
{
    public void paint(Graphics g)
    {
    g.drawString("Standard text", 20, 20);
    Font font1 = new Font("SanSerif", Font.PLAIN, 18);
    Font font2 = new Font("Serif", Font.ITALIC, 28);
    Font font3 = new Font("DialogInput", Font.ITALIC + Font.BOLD, 20);
    g.setFont(font1);
    g.drawString("This is font 1", 20, 60);
    g.setFont(font2);
    g.drawString("This is font 2", 20, 100);
    g.setFont(font3);
    g.drawString("This is font 3", 20, 140);
    }
}
```

This program is shown running in Figure 2.48.

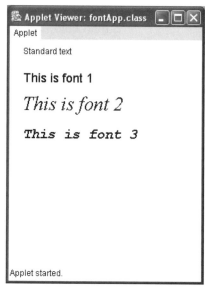

Figure 2.48
Text fonts

3.9 Applet methods

All the applets that have been written so far have an *init()* method. When the applet loads into the web browser this is the method the browser calls. There are other methods that are called by the web browser:

◆ **start()** is used where the applet displays something like an animated image. It is called by the browser immediately after the init() method. It is also called if the user returns to the current HTML page after leaving it.

◆ **stop()** is called by the browser when the user moves off the page containing the applet. It should be used to stop any operations started by the start() method.

◆ **destroy()** is called after the stop() method when the user shuts down the browser. It can be used to release any resources the applet uses.

Chapter summary

This chapter has covered:
◆ Windows programming with the AWT
◆ use of the import statement
◆ implementing a listener to handle events
◆ creating applets and using various components
◆ using layout managers
◆ dialogues, frames and menus
◆ manipulating images, shapes and fonts
◆ applet methods.

4 Two sample programs

In this section, two complete example programs will be created and explained in detail:

◆ the date verifier program introduced in unit 1 (see page 33)
◆ the mobile phone keypad program which simulates the keypad and screen on a mobile phone.

4.1 Date verifier

This program is designed to be part of a larger program which inputs students' details into a school or college database. It could, of course, be used in many other programs that require the input of dates. The design of the program is used as a case study in unit 1. A structure diagram for the complete student-details input program is shown in Figure 2.49.

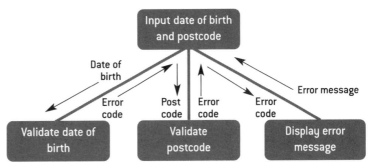

Figure 2.49 Structure chart

The only parts of the program implemented here are the date validation routine and the error code routine. A flowchart showing the steps required to validate a student's date of birth is included in unit 1 — it is shown again in Figure 2.50.

The date validation program will be written as a self-contained *dateChecker* class, which, in line with good object-orientated programming practice could easily be reused in any program. A simple data input applet will also be written to test that the dateChecker class works correctly. The correct format for the date will be dd/mm/yyyy, where:

◆ dd can be in the range 1 to 31
◆ mm can be in the range 1 to 12
◆ yyyy can be in the range 1903 to 1986 (since college students are unlikely to be more that 100 years old and must be over 16).

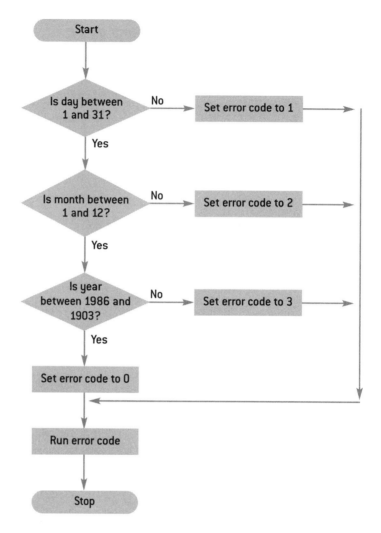

Figure 2.50 Flowchart for the data validation routine

Note that these specifications do not provide complete date validation as they do not take into account the fact that some months have more days than others; so, for example, 31/02/yyyy is an invalid date. The program written here will not check for the number of days in a month as it would make it considerably more complex. However, it could be modified to add this functionality, and some suggestions about how this could be done are given at the end of this section.

As well as checking that the days, months and years are in the correct range, the program also needs to check that the data entered is the correct length (ten characters), that the slashes are in the correct places, and that the values entered are numeric. The different error codes produced and their meanings are shown in Table 2.5.

Table 2.5 *Error codes produced by the dateCheck method*

Error Code	Message
0	Date valid
1	Date not numeric
2	Incorrect number of characters
3	No slash between date parts
4	Invalid number of days
5	Invalid month number
6	Invalid year

The dateChecker class will have just one method, called *dateCheck*. The dateCheck method will be passed a String containing the date as a parameter and will return an integer value indicating whether the date was valid, or if not what the error code was. The date will be entered as a single value into a text field on the applet – input from a text field is always a string value. The UML design diagram for the date checker is shown in Figure 2.51.

dateChecker
dateCheck(String): int

Figure 2.51 *UML class diagram for the dateCheck class*

The class is a little unusual because a constructor is not necessary. The program just starts with the class definition and the definition for the one and only method:

```
class dateChecker
{
    public int dateCheck(String theDate)
    {
```

The program uses a variable to hold the error code. It also has variables to store the various parts of the date: the two slashes, the day, the month and the year:

```
int errorCode;
String slash1;
String slash2;
int theDay;
int theMonth;
int theYear;
```

The first task is to extract the two slashes from the date, using the *substring* method of the String class. The substring method is passed two parameters, which identify which character(s) to pick out of the string. The code needed is:

```
slash1 = theDate.substring(2,3);
slash2 = theDate.substring(5,6);
```

Next comes the first of a quite complex set of 'if' statements. This if...else statement checks the length of the date and that it has two slashes in the correct place:

```
if (theDate.length() != 10)
    {
        errorCode = 2;
    }
    else if (slash1.equals("/") && slash2.equals("/"))
    {
        errorCode = 0;
    }
    else
        {
        errorCode = 3;
        }
    }
```

If the length and the slashes are both correct, the error code variable is set to 0. If not, it is set to the appropriate number.

Exceptions

The next stage is a little more complex and introduces **exceptions** which have not be mentioned before. The basic task is to move the day, month and year into their appropriate integer variables. Converting a string into an integer is easy enough, and the **parseInt()** method of the Integer class has already been introduced.

What does it mean?

*The **parseInt()** method allows a value that is a number, but is contained in a string variable, such as "1", to be converted into an integer and placed in an integer variable.*

However, suppose that one of the date values did not contain a number – perhaps the user had entered an alphabetic character by mistake. If the parseInt() method finds a value in the string that is not a number, it creates ('throws', to use the correct terminology) an exception, which is a type of error. Unless the program contains code to deal with this exception, it will terminate. Properly written programs avoid terminating unexpectedly, as that would lead to loss of data and unhappy users.

The type of exception that is thrown if a parseInt() method finds a value that is not a number is known as a **number format exception**. Therefore, to avoid unexpected program terminations the code needs to catch this exception. Java uses a code block called the **try...catch block** to catch exceptions, the format of which is:

```
try
{
    block of code that might cause an exception
}
    catch (name-of-exception object name)
{
    code to deal with exception
}
```

In the dateCheck method, the try...catch block looks like this:

```
if (errorCode == 0)
{
try
    {
    theDay = Integer.parseInt(theDate.substring(0, 2));
    theMonth = Integer.parseInt(theDate.substring(3, 5));
    theYear = Integer.parseInt(theDate.substring(6, 10));
    }
catch(NumberFormatException e)
    {
    errorCode = 1;
    }
}
```

The code is inside an 'if' block because, if the previous checks have been unsuccessful and the error code already set to something other than 1, this part is unlikely to work anyway. If a NumberFormatException does occur, the only action taken is to set the error code to 1, indicating a non-numeric entry.

The next part of the dateCheck method checks that the day, month and year parts of the date are in the correct ranges. This code is fairly straightforward:

```
if (errorCode == 0)
{
    if (theDay > 31 || theDay < 1)
```

```
        {
            errorCode = 4;
        }
        else if (theMonth > 12 || theMonth < 1)
        {
            errorCode = 5;
        }
        else if (theYear > 1986 || theYear < 1903)
        {
            errorCode = 6;
        }
    }
```

The final part of the method is to return the error code:

```
    return errorCode;
```

The code for the complete program is therefore:

```
class dateChecker
{
    public int dateCheck(String theDate)
    {
        int errorCode;
        String slash1;
        String slash2;
        int theDay = 0;
        int theMonth = 0;
        int theYear = 0;
        slash1 = theDate.substring(2, 3);
        slash2 = theDate.substring(5, 6);
        if (theDate.length() != 10)
        {
            errorCode = 2;
        }
        else if (slash1.equals("/") && slash2.equals("/"))
        {
            errorCode = 0;
        }
        else
        {
            errorCode = 3;
        }
    if (errorCode == 0)
        {
            try
```

```
        {
            theDay = Integer.parseInt(theDate.substring(0, 2));
            theMonth = Integer.parseInt(theDate.substring(3, 5));
            theYear = Integer.parseInt(theDate.substring(6, 10));
        }
        catch(NumberFormatException e)
        {
            errorCode = 1;
        }
    }
    if (errorCode == 0)
    {
        if (theDay > 31 || theDay < 1)
        {
            errorCode = 4;
        }
        else if (theMonth > 12 || theMonth < 1)
        {
            errorCode = 5;
        }
        else if (theYear > 1986 || theYear < 1903)
        {
            errorCode = 6;
        }
    }
    return errorCode;
    }
}
```

The errorClass class

The second class that needs to be created is the *errorClass* class. This, like the dateChecker class, could be used as a general-purpose class to display all the different errors within a whole project. It has only one method – the **errorMsg method** – which, when provided with an error number as an integer parameter, returns the appropriate error message as a string.

In this version of the program the different error messages are stored in a string array. If a program needs to deal with a larger number of error messages, a better solution might be to store the error messages in a text file, which is read into the program. This would make it easier to edit the error messages if changes or additions were needed.

Our program is shown below (there are no features in this program that have not been described before, so no explanation is given):

```
class errorClass
{
    public String errorMsg(int errorCode)
    {
        String theMsg[] = new String[7];
        theMsg[0] = "Date valid";
        theMsg[1] = "Date not numeric";
        theMsg[2] = "Incorrect number of characters";
        theMsg[3] = "No slash between date parts";
        theMsg[4] = "Invalid number of days";
        theMsg[5] = "Invalid month number";
        theMsg[6] = "Invalid year";
        return theMsg[errorCode];
    }
}
```

Running the date checker

Finally an applet must be created to allow dates to be entered. Rather than write the complete program to record student details, a simple 'tester' program will be written. The program is shown running in Figure 2.52.

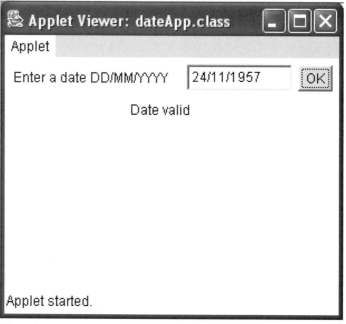

Figure 2.52 The date checker running

This program is straightforward, so no detailed explanation is given. The code for the program is:

```
import java.awt.*;
import java.applet.*;
import java.awt.event.*;
public class dateApp extends Applet implements ActionListener
{
    private Label theLabel = new Label("Enter a date
                                    DD/MM/YYYY");
    private TextField inputDate = new TextField(10);
    private Button okButton = new Button("OK");
    private Label errorLabel = new Label(" ");
    dateChecker myChecker = new dateChecker();
    errorClass myError = new errorClass();
    public void init()
    {
        this.add(theLabel);
        this.add(inputDate);
        this.add(okButton);
        this.add(errorLabel);
        okButton.addActionListener(this);
    }
    public void actionPerformed(ActionEvent e)
    {
        int errorCode;
        String errorText;
        errorCode = myChecker.dateCheck(inputDate.getText());
        errorLabel.setText(myError.errorMsg(errorCode));
    }
}
```

PRACTICAL TASK 2.21

Modify the date checker so that it also tests that the number of days in each month is correct.

One way to do this would to be to set a variable, perhaps called *maxDays*, to the maximum number of days in the month that is passed to the program. So, if the month is 01 (January), maxDays will be set to 31. A Switch/Case construct could be used to set this variable depending on the month. The variable would then be used to test the upper limit of the number of days.

Another problem is leap years. The basic rule is that if a year is divisible by 4 then it is a leap year. You would need to write some code to identify whether this was the case and adjust the upper limit to the number of days in February if it was.

4.2 Mobile phone keypad

This program emulates a mobile phone keypad. As it stands, it does not have any particular purpose other than to demonstrate various Java programming features. However, it could form part of a larger program used to design the software for a mobile phone.

Unlike with the date checker, the layout of the various buttons and text box in this program is quite important. The completed applet is shown in Figure 2.53.

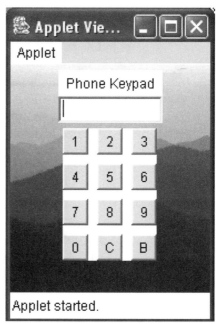

Figure 2.53 Use of the mobile phone
keypad applet

The 'C' button clears the current display, and the 'B' button changes the background picture.

In order to provide a neat layout, two panels are used. The text field and the 'Phone Keypad' text at the top are in a panel which uses the border layout policy (see page 100). The buttons are in a separate panel which uses the grid layout policy (see page 102) – see Figure 2.54.

The first part of the program simply creates a new panel and the text field and label:

```
public class phoneApp extends Applet implements ActionListener
{
    private Panel DisplaySection = new Panel();
    private Label theLabel = new Label ("Phone Keypad",
      Label.CENTER);
    private TextField display = new TextField(10);
```

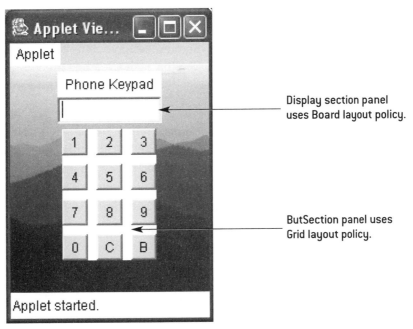

Figure 2.54 Panels used in the keypad applet

The next section creates another panel and the buttons. However, the number buttons are not added as individual buttons. The program could be written with individual buttons, which could be individually added to the panel and have their own action listener. However that is a rather long-winded way of writing the program, because ten action listeners would be required as well as ten 'if' statements to find out which button was pressed. Since each of the buttons performs a very similar task, it is more efficient to use an array of buttons and then use loops to add the buttons, create the action listeners and process the events.

An array of button objects is created in the same way as any other array:

```
private Panel ButSection = new Panel();
private Button [] numButt = new Button [9];
private Button Button0 = new Button ("0");
private Button ButtonC = new Button ("C");
private Button ButtonB = new Button ("B");
private int imageFlag = 0;
```

The buttons 0, C and B work in a different way from the buttons for the numbers 1 to 9, so they are created as individual buttons. The *imageFlag* variable is used to keep track of which background is displayed.

Now to the *init* method. The first few lines set the layout policy for the DisplaySection panel (border layout) and add the label and the text fields in the appropriate places:

```
public void init()
{
    DisplaySection.setLayout(new BorderLayout());
    DisplaySection.add("North", theLabel);
    DisplaySection.add("South",display);
```

Then the layout policy for the button panel is set. This uses grid layout, with four rows and three columns, with 8 pixels between each. The number buttons have been created as an array, so they can be added to the panel using a loop. Each button needs a number on it. The loop counter can provide the number but it must be converted to a string. Action listeners are created for each button at the same time:

```
ButSection.setLayout(new GridLayout(4, 3, 8, 8));
String ButLab;
for (int i = 0; i < 9; i++)
{
    ButLab = "" + (i + 1);
    numButt[i] = new Button(ButLab);
    numButt[i].addActionListener(this);
    ButSection.add(numButt[i]);
}
```

The zero, clear and change background buttons also need to be added to the panel, they also require action listeners, and the two panels need to be added to the applet:

```
ButSection.add(Button0);
ButSection.add(ButtonC);
ButSection.add(ButtonB);
Button0.addActionListener(this);
ButtonC.addActionListener(this);
ButtonB.addActionListener(this);
add(DisplaySection);
add(ButSection);
}
```

The *paint* method is used to display the different backgrounds. The *imageFlag* variable is used to alternate between the two different background images. Additional backgrounds could easily be added:

```
private Image myImage;
public void paint(Graphics g)
{
    if (imageFlag == 0)
    {
        myImage = getImage(getDocumentBase(), "testImage.jpg");
        imageFlag = 1;
    }
    else
```

```
        {
            myImage = getImage(getDocumentBase(), "testImage2.jpg");
            imageFlag = 0;
        }
        g.drawImage(myImage, 0, 0, 180, 200, this);
    }
```

Finally, the action-performed method deals with the actions required when the different buttons are clicked. The current contents of the text field are stored in a String variable, using the *getText* method. If a number button has been clicked, a loop is again used to check each of the buttons in the array to find out which one it was. The loop counter (the variable *i*) will indicate which of the buttons was clicked. However, since the array index runs from zero, 1 must be added to the loop counter and it must be converted to a string before it is added to the current contents of the text field:

```
    String displayText = display.getText();
    for (int i = 0; i< 9; i++)
    {
        if (clickButton.getSource() == numButt[i])
        {
            displayText = displayText + ("" + (i+1));
        }
    }
```

The zero, cancel and background change buttons are dealt with differently. The zero button simply adds a string "0" to the current contents of the displayText variable:

```
    if (clickButton.getSource() == Button0)
    {
        displayText = displayText + "0";
    }
```

The clear button removes the contents of the displayText variable, setting them to a null string:

```
    if (clickButton.getSource() == ButtonC)
    {
        displayText = "";
    }
```

The displayText variable then needs to be used to reset the contents of the text field:

```
    display.setText(displayText);
```

Finally, the B button repaints the applet window so that a different background picture can be displayed:

```
if (clickButton.getSource() == ButtonB)
{
    repaint();
}
```

The complete code for the applet is:

```
import java.awt.*;
import java.applet.*;
import java.awt.event.*;
import java.text.*;
public class phoneApp extends Applet implements ActionListener
{
    private Panel DisplaySection = new Panel();
    private Label theLabel = new Label ("Phone Keypad",
                                        Label.CENTER);
    private TextField display = new TextField(10);
    private Panel ButSection = new Panel();
    private Button [] numButt = new Button [9];
    private Button Button0 = new Button ("0");
    private Button ButtonC = new Button ("C");
    private Button ButtonB = new Button ("B");
    private int imageFlag = 0;

    public void init()
    {
        DisplaySection.setLayout(new BorderLayout());
        DisplaySection.add("North", theLabel);
        DisplaySection.add("South", display);
        ButSection.setLayout(new GridLayout(4, 3, 8, 8));
        String ButLab;
        for (int i = 0; i < 9; i++)
        {
            ButLab = "" + (i + 1);
            numButt[i] = new Button(ButLab);
            numButt[i].addActionListener(this);
            ButSection.add(numButt[i]);
        }
        ButSection.add(Button0);
        ButSection.add(ButtonC);
        ButSection.add(ButtonB);
        Button0.addActionListener(this);
        ButtonC.addActionListener(this);
        ButtonB.addActionListener(this);
        add(DisplaySection);
        add(ButSection);
    }
```

```
      private Image myImage;
      public void paint(Graphics g)
      {
         if (imageFlag == 0)
         {
            myImage = getImage(getDocumentBase(),"testImage.jpg");
            imageFlag = 1;
         }
         else
         {
            myImage = getImage(getDocumentBase(),"testImage2.jpg");
            imageFlag = 0;
         }
         g.drawImage(myImage, 0, 0, 180, 200, this);
      }

      public void actionPerformed(ActionEvent clickButton)
      {
         String displayText = display.getText();
         for (int i = 0; i< 9; i++)
         {
            if (clickButton.getSource() == numButt[i])
            {
               displayText = displayText + ("" + (i+1));
            }
         }
         if (clickButton.getSource() == Button0)
         {
            displayText = displayText + "0";
         }
         if (clickButton.getSource() == ButtonC)
         {
            displayText = "";
         }
         display.setText(displayText);
         if (clickButton.getSource() == ButtonB)
         {
            repaint();
         }
      }
   }
```

Like all applets, this one requires an HTML file to load it into a web browser, and the applet window needs to be set to a small rectangular shape about 180 pixels in width by 200 in height, so the applet looks like a phone keypad with the text field at the top over the buttons. Suitable HTML code is:

```
<html>
<head>
<title>Phone Keypad Example</title>
</head>
<body>
<h1>MyApplet</h1>
<hr>
<p>
<applet code="phoneApp.class" width=180 height=200></applet>
</p>
<hr>
</body>
</html>
```

PRACTICAL TASK 2.22

There are a number of ways in which you could improve this program.

1 Add more background pictures to give the user a wider choice.

2 Add another text field where people's names could be entered and associated with different numbers.

Test software components

Testing software to make sure that it does what it is supposed to do is just as important as writing the programs. This unit covers the testing of programs so that the developer is confident that it is as correct as it can be.

This unit also covers IT health and safety issues.

Outcomes

◆ Prepare for testing

◆ Record the results of tests

◆ Analyse test results

◆ Identify health and safety requirements

1 Prepare for testing

This chapter shows how to identify – from a given specification – what tests are required to carry out functional testing. From this, it explains how to prepare a test plan and how to prepare test data.

The unit specification often refers to a 'tester' and a 'developer or programmer'. In the business world, and more likely in a large company, these may be two separate people. They may even be in different parts of the company. However, as a student, you are likely to be testing your own programs. This means that you should separate in your mind these two roles: your role as a program tester and your role as a programmer.

There are a number of ways in which developers can tackle the testing of their programs.

◆ **White box testing** is logical testing. This depends on knowing the structure or logic of the program code that is used in the software.

◆ **Black box testing** is functional testing. This is carried out without any knowledge of the layout of the code used in the program.

◆ **Top-down testing** checks first that the high-level program modules work. Only then is the detail tested.

◆ **Bottom-up testing** checks first that the low-level program modules work on their own. After this, the low-level modules are linked together at a high level. The program is then tested as a whole.

1.1 White box testing

In the student world, almost all of the initial testing will be white box testing. It is the most common form of testing used by any program developer writing any type of program. It should be used where the developer and tester are the same person. It is also the right way to do it for all but the very largest of programs.

The aim of white box testing is to go through all of the possible paths and lines of code in a program. This is only ever fully done in fairly simple programs. In the business world, it is good professional practice to write **error handling code** for unusual conditions. These are situations that should never occur or occur only very infrequently. However, it is usually very difficult to set up those error conditions. It is therefore not reasonable to test them. It is a balance of cost of testing against the risk of a coding error.

The first step for testing is to write a **test plan**. How to do this is explained in section 1.5. The structures of the test plans for both white and black box testing (see section 1.2) are similar, but the aims of each type of test are different.

1 It starts with simple **valid transactions**.

2 There then follow more complex valid transactions and **error transactions**.

3 Finally, there are one or two valid transactions.

White box testing usually starts with the simplest possible valid functions or transactions. These are passed through the main parts of the program. The aim of this is to answer these questions.

- Do the high-level links from one module to another work?
- Do the main parts of the program do what they are supposed to do?
- Does the program start correctly?
- Does the program end as it should?

The developer then tests more complex – but still valid – functions. This is to cover:

- valid processing in the less frequently used parts of the program
- the more complicated parts of the program.

This is often the most difficult part of the program to debug (see page 179). Errors here may occur only from time to time rather than on a consistent basis.

The final tests are with **error conditions** and with invalid functions and transactions. These check that the error handling routines work in the way that they should. These are left until last because the developer wants the error handler to be called correctly in the code.

The last one or two tests or transactions in any set of test data should always be valid transactions. Programs usually set error flags when they find an invalid transaction. A common programming mistake is not to reset the error flag once the error transaction ends. The error flag should always return to its initial value to show 'no error'. If this is not done, then it can have the effect of rejecting every transaction that follows. A final valid transaction or two makes sure that this has not happened

Program coverage routines

Some development environments have program coverage routines. With this option switched on, it records and then reports on how many times the program ran each part of the code. This gives a report for the developer.

- How well did this set of program tests cover the program?
- Which sections of code never ran?
- Which sections ran repeatedly?

Figure 3.1 shows diagrammatically how program coverage routines can be represented. The left-hand structure chart shows good test coverage – the same amount of testing for each module and each part of a module. The right-hand chart shows poor test coverage – the modules have had different amounts of testing, and the testing within a module is patchy.

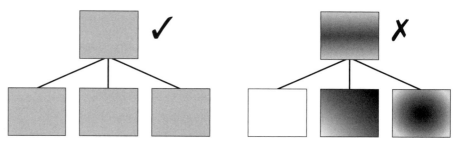

Figure 3.1 Schematic representation of the testing coverage of modules

In the business world, technical management can also use a review of the program coverage report. This report can give them confidence (or not!) on how well and how thoroughly the tester has tested a program.

Check your understanding

1 Note one or more ways in which you could check, before your tests start, that your tests plan to cover all paths through your program.

2 Find out whether your development environment has a program coverage routine. If it has, list how you switch it on and switch it off.

1.2 Black box testing

Black box testing generally happens in the later stages of testing. However, it is also used in these special cases.

◆ The tester is not the same person as the developer.

◆ Several programs are being tested together as part of a system.

◆ The internal program structure is complex.

◆ The internal program structure is unknown. An example of this is where the program or system uses an application development package.

In black box testing, the tester either does not know (or pretends not to know and does not use this knowledge) about the structure of the program. Instead, the tester treats the program as a 'black box' – in other words, its contents are hidden. The tester can see the inputs, and can see the outputs, but cannot see what goes on inside the box – what it is that turns the inputs into the outputs.

The structure of the test plan for black box testing is similar to that for white box testing.

1   It starts with simple valid transactions.

2   There then follow more complex valid transactions and error transactions.

3   Finally, there are one or two valid transactions.

The sequence of the complex and valid transactions varies from white box testing, though. The big difference between black box and white box testing is that in black box testing:

◆   the test cases are created from the *user's* point of view

◆   the emphasis is on testing *what* the program does.

In white box testing:

◆   the test cases are from the *tester's* point of view

◆   the emphasis is on testing *how* the program works.

What does this mean for a black box test?

1   Test cases that the programmer might not have expected may well occur. Black box testing makes sure that the program can handle these unexpected events.

2   A test may cover the same path through a program many times.

3   It is quite probable that more parts of the program will remain untested than for white box testing.

PRACTICAL TASK 3.1

1   For a simple program that you have already designed or written, write a set of white box tests to cover all of its program paths.

2   Write a set of black box tests to cover all of its functions.

3   List those parts of the program that the black box test does not cover. Explain why this is.

4   List those parts of the program that the black box test covers repeatedly. Explain why this is.

Check your understanding

1   When would you use white box testing?

2   When would you use black box testing?

3   What are the advantages of white box testing?

4   What are the advantages of black box testing?

1.3 Top-down and bottom-up testing

◆ **Top-down testing** checks first that the high-level modules fit together. Only then does it plug in the lower-level modules.

◆ **Bottom-up testing** checks first that low-level modules work on their own. After this it links them together into the rest of the program.

The tester uses top-down or bottom-up testing when the program or system under test is too large or complex for the straightforward white and black box testing.

Top-down testing

For top-down testing, a **test harness** lets the developer plug in dummy modules in place of any missing lower-level modules. When the program reaches that point when it is running, it hands over control to the dummy module. Usually, this dummy module just returns typical values from the lower-level module. It does not do any of the lower-level module processing.

What does it mean?

*A **test harness** is a software testing aid that helps developers to do top-down and bottom-up testing. This aid either provides the missing parts of the program or lets the developer plug in a dummy.*

Another way of doing top-down testing is to use the **breakpoint** facility of the development environment. The breakpoint stops the program running at the point at which it is about to enter the missing lower-level module. The tester can then check that the input variables to the missing module have the expected values.

What does it mean?

*A **breakpoint** is a location in a program under test where the program stops running normally and control is given back to the developer. The developer can look at the values of variables, change these values, or go to another point in the program.*

If the variables do have the right values, then the tester can set the output variables for the missing module. These are set to what the lower-level module would have calculated. The tester then starts the program running again.

If the input variables to the missing module did not contain the right values, then the tester halts this test and raises an **error log** (see page 171). This is to record this as an error for the developer to fix.

Bottom-up testing

Bottom-up testing is the opposite of top-down testing. It is typically used to test calculation modules before the rest of the program is written. The tester also uses bottom-up testing for a module where a program can call that module from many places.

A test harness may be used with a simple looping program to replace the higher-level modules, as shown in Figure 3.2.

Top-down testing
• Program code
• Program code
▸ Dummy code for call to missing routine
• Program code
• Program code
▸ Dummy code for call to another missing routine
• Program code
• Program code
Bottom-up testing
• Test harness replaces missing code
• Call to low-level module
▸ Program code under test
• Test harness replaces missing code
• Another call to low-level module
▸ More program code under test
• Test harness replaces missing code

Figure 3.2 Top-down and bottom-up testing

The real lower-level or calculation module is linked in to the test harness. The test-harness test program might just supply a set of input values to the lower-level module. It then also prints or displays the values returned from the lower-level module.

The developer may also use the breakpoint facility of the development environment for bottom-up testing.

1 The tester sets breakpoints at the entry to and exit from the module under test.

2 On entry, the tester sets the input variables to the values that the rest of the program would have set.

3 The tester restarts the program.

4 The module is then tested.

5 When the module hits the breakpoint at its end, the tester checks that the output variables are the expected values. If they are, then the test is a success. If they are not, then an error log is raised.

6 The tester then does the next test with a different set of input variables.

CASE STUDY

Café Theresa

Café Theresa is a chain of coffee shops. It is developing a stock ordering system for its stores. Each store manager orders a stock of food and drink each day for delivery the next day. The new computer system will advise the manager on how much of each product to order. The store managers want to have the right amount of stock. They want enough stock so that they do not turn their customers away through not having the product that is wanted. However, they want to keep their costs low by not throwing away food when it passes its sell-by date. The amount of each product that they sell varies a lot from day to day.

◆ Ice-cream sells well on hot days, and hot soups sell well on cold days.

◆ Premium products sell well during Monday to Friday lunch breaks of local business people.

◆ There is a peak in sales on Saturday afternoons and mid-week evenings when the local football team is playing in the nearby stadium, particularly when they win or play popular opponents.

◆ Croissants sell well in the mornings, while cakes sell better in the afternoons.

A team of three developers is working on the build phase of this project. Lynne has been assigned the roles of project leader and main tester. Her job is to make sure that the system meets the company's business need. She is also testing that the programs do what they are supposed to do.

Jane has the role of senior programmer. Her programs:

◆ manage the input from the screens in the stores

◆ retrieve information from the database

◆ produce displays and reports for the stores.

Kevin is an employee of a specialist software house. He and his software house have a lot of experience in stock control calculations. Lynne employs Kevin just to write the calculation modules. These work out how much of each product to order. This depends on past usage and current and future circumstances.

Lynne decides on this testing strategy for the project:

◆ Jane will use white box testing for her own input and output programs.

◆ Lynne and Jane will use top-down testing for the processing programs.

◆ Kevin will use bottom-up testing for the stock control calculations.

◆ Lynne will use black box testing to test that the complete suite of programs fit together.

1 Why use white box testing for the input and output programs?

2 Why use top-down testing for the processing programs?

3 Why use bottom-up testing for the stock control calculations?

4 Why use black box testing for the complete suite?

5 Do you agree with Lynne's choices? If you do, then justify them. If you do not, then give your reasons.

1.4 The purpose of testing

Testing makes sure that a program really does what it is supposed to do. More broadly, the overall purpose of testing is to make sure that a computer program or system meets the needs of the intended users. For many programs, the purpose of testing is to show that the program:

◆ meets the specification

◆ conforms to site standards

◆ is in line with good programming practice.

This section describes the different forms of testing. In reality, the tester may need to work at a number of different levels for a large complex business system. The programs developed and tested in this course are likely to require just one level of testing.

CASE STUDY

Café Theresa

Café Theresa's development standards say that all batch programs should end with a standard report. This report should give:

◆ the name of the program run

◆ the date and time of the run.

In addition, for each transaction type, the report should give:

◆ how many transactions were input

◆ how many were processed successfully

◆ how many were rejected.

A standard module from their program library produces this report.

1 Why should the tester test for the production of this report?

2 What might be the causes of this being wrong or missing?

In a complex IT environment, there are at least five levels of testing:

◆ **module testing**

◆ **unit** or **program testing**

◆ **system testing**

◆ **customer** or **user testing**

◆ **beta testing.**

Module testing

This checks that just one module, sub-routine, sub-program or part of a program does what it should. The module specification is what the tester compares the module to. The programmer who writes a module usually produces his or her own module test data. Module testing is usually white box testing. The tester makes sure that all the main paths of the module or program run successfully.

Unit or program testing

This is the next step up from module testing. It checks that all the modules of a program fit together correctly. Its purpose is to confirm that the program works in line with the program specification.

1 All the input modules validate and pass data correctly to the processing modules.

2 The processing modules perform their calculation functions according to the specification.

3 The output modules correctly write to the screen, printer, database or other output device.

The team leader or programmer with overall responsibility for the program will usually write the unit test data. This level and later levels of testing are usually black box tested.

System testing

The aim of a system test is to make sure that a suite of programs, such as a payroll or accounting package, meets the computer design specification. This is the final level of testing done by the IT team.

1 It checks that output from one program forms an acceptable input to the next program.

2 It checks that updates to all databases are in line with each other or consistent.

At a large IT site, there may be a **testing quality group** who write the system test data. At smaller sites, the systems analyst or programming team leader may write the system test data.

Customer or user testing

The IT department or the supplier hands over a new or changed system to the customer or user for control-led user testing. This is before the system is used in a real situation. It means putting a copy of real data through the system. The customer or user tester makes sure that the system processes the data in line with the rules of the business.

1 For software developed in-house, user testing checks that the IT department have understood and met the company's business needs.

2 For bought-in software, user testing checks that this company has set up the software correctly for its use. It also confirms that the company has

made the changes in its business processes that are necessary for it to use the new software correctly.

Before using a new system, there is usually a period of **parallel running**. This can be seen as a form of testing, but often it is more about making sure that any changes to the business processes work. The new system takes the place of the old system only when the results from the new are at least as good as from the old system.

What does it mean?

Parallel running is where both the old and new systems are run together 'in parallel'. The tester compares the results from both systems.

It is good practice to have a **cutover** plan. This says what steps the site needs to go through to move from the old system to the new system. This might have:

- development staff on site or on call to fix things quickly if they go wrong
- extra checking of inputs and outputs until everyone is confident that the new system is working
- a management review and escalation process to manage things if they start to go wrong.

What does it mean?

When a new system is first run for real, or put into production running, this is called cutover.

It is good practice also to have a **contingency** plan in place. This is a plan that will only be put into practice if things go wrong, usually only in a big way. If things have gone badly wrong, sometimes the only thing to do is to **fall back**.

What does it mean?

Fall back means to go back to the system, program or program version that ran successfully before the changes were made.

Beta testing

For mass-market PC software, beta testing is the process in which the software vendor runs a controlled programme of testing by potential customers. Volunteer users can download a new application and test it for errors before it is generally released to the market.

Go out and try!

Look on the Internet for a software vendor's beta testing programme.

1 List what the vendor gives to the user.

2 What is the user to give back to the vendor?

3 Who do you think has the better deal from this? Give your reasons.

1.5 Test plan essential features

There are test plans for each level of testing. The first step in developing a test plan is to work out your **test strategy**. For this, the developer needs to answer these questions:

1 What, in general terms, am I trying to test?

2 What tests do I need to do to test that part of the program is working as specified?

3 What shall I use as input test data, both valid and invalid?

4 What output will come from each of the input test cases?

To provide a structure to a test plan, it is best to write down the answers to those questions. This is the test strategy. It often forms the introduction to the test plan. The test plan then consists of a set of test plan sheets, one for each test. An example of a blank test plan is shown in Figure 3.3.

The tester fills in each field in the test plan as shown in Table 3.1.

PRACTICAL TASK 3.2

For this exercise, you should work in pairs. Take a simple program that one of you has developed earlier.

1 On your own, write a test plan introduction. This should answer the four questions given in the topic.

2 On your own, write a test plan. You should complete a set of test plan forms.

3 Compare your test plan introduction with your colleague's.

4 If any of your and your colleague's answers are different, list the different answers and give explanations.

5 Compare your test plan forms with your colleague's.

6 If any of your and your colleague's forms are very different, list the different answers and give explanations.

7 Explain any relationship, or not, between your answers to question 4 and your answers to question 6.

TEST PLAN				
System name: Program name: Module name:			Version no: Tester name:	Page no:
Test no.	Date	Purpose/Type of test	Input/Filename	Expected output/Filename

Figure 3.3 A blank test plan

Table 3.1 Fields in a test plan

Field name	Description	Examples
System name	General description of the project – usually bulk-copied	Café Theresa stock control
Program and module names	The piece of code or system that this test plan covers – usually bulk-copied	Stock-control calculation module
Tester name	The person who prepared the test plan – usually bulk-copied	Sara Student
Version number	The date the test plan was prepared (not the date it was run) – usually bulk-copied	17/9/2004
Test number	Sequential number for this test plan	003
Purpose	What this particular input is testing for	Is month number valid (value too large)?
Type of test	Whether or not this input is valid	No
Input	The precise conditions to be tested	Valid day and year, month number >12
Input values	The input values	Date 01/13/2005; other input fields with valid values
Expected output	The expected result of the transaction	Transaction should be rejected with a meaningful error message stating 'Month invalid: it is >12' There should have been no change to the database.

1.6 Approaches to the design of test data

There are three approaches to the design of test data:

◆ the computing approach
◆ the business approach
◆ the data approach.

The **computing approach** looks in turn at each of the computing functions of a program or system. These are input, processing and output. The test data first checks all of the input functions. It then goes through all the processing functions. The last part of the tests checks all of the output functions. The developer often uses this way of doing things to test a set of batch programs.

In contrast, the **business approach** tests each of the business functions in turn. 'Business' here does not mean that the tester can use this for commercial programs only. As an example, this is how a tester might test a multi-function calculator program using the business approach. First, the tester might test on their own each of these functions: Add, Subtract, Multiply, Divide. After this, the tester might test the more complex mathematical or scientific calculator functions. Finally, the tester might test linking a set of calculator functions together.

The **data approach** is the least common. It first tests all the transactions or functions that read or update a particular table or file. It follows this by testing transactions for the next table or file. The tester often uses this approach if the developer has used a data-driven way of writing a computer system to design the program.

1.7 Choosing data values for testing

It is important to design test data to confirm that a program works in the right way under both normal and exceptional circumstances. To do this, the tester writes test data with three types of value: valid, invalid and boundary.

Valid and invalid test data

Valid test data should run normally through the program. It should produce the right answers that the tester expects. For the first programs that a developer writes, it is most unlikely that this happens on the early test runs. However, as the developer takes out bugs from the program the tester finds that:

◆ fewer valid transactions are rejected
◆ more and more of the expected valid transactions run correctly all the way through the program
◆ there is correct updating of the database or files
◆ the program returns the right output to the user.

The tester looks to make sure that the program throws out **invalid test data** when the program checks if it is valid. With their first few programs, developers are often pleased when early test runs do reject a lot of their invalid test cases. However, it is important to make sure that the program rejects these test cases for the correct reason. If the program's error messages are not very helpful, then this is very difficult to check. An example of a poor error message is 'Invalid input: please re-submit'. The message 'Month invalid: greater than 12' makes it much clearer what is wrong – the error is that the input has failed the test that the month number must be in the range 1 to 12.

Sometimes, invalid data runs all the way through a program or system because it is wrongly taken as valid. This often has strange results. The tester and developer should check these carefully. This might hide a much bigger problem with the program logic.

Boundary conditions

The initial efforts of the tester are to make sure the program is correctly processing clearly valid transactions and rejecting for the correct reason obviously invalid transactions. Then it is time for the tester to check that **boundary conditions** work properly. In programming terms, what the tester is seeking to do is to make sure that the developer has coded all **relational operators** correctly. For more information on relational operators, see page 12.

◆ Has the developer written 'less than' instead of 'less than or equal to'?

◆ Has the developer written 'greater than or equal to' instead of just 'greater than'?

◆ Does the program go round a loop once too often?

◆ Does the program go round a loop once too few times?

The tester tests for each boundary condition and writes two types of test cases. There is a valid test case that uses the last correct value. This forms a pair with an invalid test case that uses the first wrong value.

Here is an example of testing a date. If the program has a month input, then the tester checks that month 12 is accepted as valid. He or she also checks that month 13 is rejected as invalid. There is something wrong with the program if the two test cases are then both accepted or both rejected.

A subtler test is needed to check for day numbers. Clearly, a day number of 0 or 32 is always invalid. A day number of 1 or 28 or any number in between is always valid. Numbers 29 and 30 are always valid in all months except February. Finally, in some months 31 is valid and in some months 31 is invalid. So, there must be correct code in the program to test for day number based on month number. To cater for February, there should also be code that tests the year number to see whether 29 February is a valid date (in a leap year).

Check your understanding

Explain why 'Invalid input: please re-submit' is a poor error message from the point of view of (a) the user, (b) the developer, and (c) the tester.

PRACTICAL TASK 3.3

1 Write in structured English, or as a flowchart or code, a day validation routine to check whether the day number input is valid depending on the month number input. This should allow 29 February as a valid date.

2 Produce a list of boundary test cases of day numbers and month numbers.

3 Test a colleague's answer to question 1 by taking your boundary test cases and desk checking his or her day validation routine.

4 Write in structured English, or as a flowchart or code, a February day validation routine to check whether the day number input is valid depending on the month number and year number input.

5 Produce a list of boundary test cases of day numbers, month numbers and year numbers.

6 Test a colleague's answer to question 4 by taking your boundary test cases and desk checking his or her February day validation routine.

1.8 Recovery testing

The testing that has been covered so far is for what the developers have written to meet the user's business needs. This assumes that supporting hardware, systems software and site operating procedures work exactly as they should, for all of the time. Unfortunately, this happy state of affairs does not yet exist. It is unlikely to exist in the future. **Recovery testing** is done to make sure that data can be recovered after a hardware or software failure.

Hardware at a basic level is now very reliable. There is now a very high mean time between failure (MTBF) rate of all units. However, the growth in reliability of individual units is about the same as the growth in the total number of units. This growth is needed to manage the size and complexity of today's business. Large IT sites have grown from tens of mainframes or servers that they had around 1990, to tens of thousands of networked smaller servers today. The system designs must allow for some small part of the overall computer network to fail without collapsing the rest.

Operating system software reliability has also improved. This has not been at the same rate as hardware. Here, the trend has been to automated system recovery and speed of return. This has led to higher system availability, rather than a lot fewer system failures.

System failures

Even with automated operating environments, there are still operating problems at a site that can cause a system failure. The power supply might fail, or the state of the computer network causes a server to stop or hang. An air-conditioning problem can cause a system shutdown as it is too hot or too cold. An operator might just switch off or power off a processor or a disk unit.

The test plan and the operating procedures for an overall system should therefore include making sure that data can be recovered after a hardware or software failure. For a complex system, where the individual transactions and their timing cannot easily be reproduced, this would typically involve these tasks:

1 Take a fixed or frozen copy of the data, say every week or month.

2 Record or log every change that the user or system makes to the data. This means the system writes to a journal file or log database a 'before' image. This is what a data block looked like before any data change. It also writes an 'after' image. This is what the data block looked like after the change.

3 Record or log every update transaction. The system links these transactions with the changes made to the database. This is also done through the journal.

4 Merge regularly the changes in the journal file. This is because, often, the same record is changed over and over again.

If the operating system fails, then it is necessary to roll back any changes that are in progress or only partially completed. This is so that the database following this roll back is in a consistent state.

CASE STUDY

Café Theresa

Café Theresa's sales database records from the till each item sold to customers. It also records in a different place the total value of each customer's order for all items sold. If the computer system fails while updating sales records, then it must either have recorded all of a customer order or none of it. It would not be acceptable to have different answers for daily sales for a store by adding up the values from individual order lines and by adding up the order totals.

1 What do you think Café Theresa's management would think of the computer system if it gave different answers for daily store sales? Give your reasons for this.

2 List ways in which you might design the system so that it always gave a consistent answer even if there had been a system failure during update.

To provide more system availability and protection if it is the hardware that fails and a disk is damaged, sometimes a site has **mirrored disks**.

Mirrored disks are where there are two, or more, identical copies of the contents of a disk.

For a disk failure with mirrored disks, this is what happens:

Disk 1 fails.
Computer operations carry on using disk 2.
Disk 1 is repaired or replaced.
All the data on disk 2 is copied on to disk 1.
Disk 1 is brought back into operation.

If disks are *not* mirrored, then this happens:

Disk 1 fails.
Computer operations stop.
Disk 1 is repaired or replaced.
The frozen data is copied on to disk 1.
New data is added to disk 1.
Disk 1 is brought back into operation.
Computer operations start again.

This more complex process is needed so that the disk ends up with the current data with no data loss.

Database management systems

Operating systems and database management systems (DBMSs) such as Oracle often have recovery features as part of the way they work. However, it is important to know the principles of what they are doing. The developer explains the recovery needs to the DBMS expert. The expert sets up the DBMS so that these needs should be met. The tester must test to make sure that the setup has actually met these needs.

For a simple system, often all that has to be done is to put the files into read-only mode once a day. This is usually overnight. All the files are then copied or a **backup** is taken. The daily transactions are often logged. To recover from a failure, the backup is used. This restores the files to where they were the previous night. If needed, the daily transactions are reapplied from the log or journal.

*A **backup** is a copy taken of some or all of the files in a system for recovery purposes. It may be a full backup where the copy is taken of all the files in the system. More usually, it is a partial backup or incremental backup – this is just those files or parts of files that have changed since the previous full backup was made.*

Disaster recovery

The most dramatic form of recovery is disaster recovery. For their most business-critical applications, a company may have a second backup site in some other part of the country. This might be the site that their developers usually use. In the event of a disaster, this development use stops or is greatly restricted. The company may also have a recovery agreement with another disaster recovery site. This is the main business for disaster recovery IT companies. Their business model is that disaster will not strike many of their customer's sites at the same time.

These are the disaster recovery steps. Each day, the first site sends a backup copy of the critical data to the recovery or second site. Sometimes, the first site captures and sends the daily transactions as well. Then disaster strikes the first site. At the recovery site, personnel copy the backups on to the database, and possibly apply the daily transactions too. They switch the network to the second site, restart and operate the systems.

That is an idealised description of the process. There are three major concerns for a disaster recovery or standby site:

◆ What if it does not work when it is needed?

◆ How much does it cost to have the computing power unused or doing lower priority work?

◆ How can the second site be kept to the same technical standard as the primary site?

Mirrored sites are a solution to this. Here, the two sites share computing power and share and often copy databases. If one site fails, then the other site can still process the workload. The amount of computer power is less. Some functions and data may not be available, but the application keeps running.

Go out and try!

1 Search the Internet for PC software that supports recovery.

2 Select one or more of these software products and list what they do.

3 Explain how you would use each of these products to provide the parts of a disaster recovery system for a PC-based system.

1.9 Performance testing

Performance testing is making sure that the program or system meets the response time and availability needs of the user.

In many cases, the program specification does not state explicitly these response time and availability needs. In this case, the developer uses professional judgement on what the user will accept and at what cost.

For a large or complex system, or when it is necessary to meet a specific business need, the performance requirements are explicitly stated. This is often in some detail. The contract between the supplier and the user may also state or refer to the performance needs. Often, there are financial penalties if performance needs are not met.

The users will have an idea of what response times to expect from similar programs they have run in the past. The tester should make sure that the program is not a lot slower than this. Table 3.2 gives examples of what acceptable performance might mean to a user.

Table 3.2 *What is acceptable performance?*

Type of software	Speed	Testing notes
Graphics, especially games	Fast enough that movements appear smooth, not jerky	Test on an adequate computer, not the most powerful available development computer.
Desktop software	Immediate for character display, scrolling and response to input events	A few seconds is OK to 'think' or 'do' something that the user sees as a large amount of work. Examples of this are: • searching through a large database of many thousands of records • recalculating a large complex spreadsheet or other calculation • redrawing a large complex diagram.
Transaction processing	Two or three seconds is acceptable for a display or update transaction	A little longer is OK to search for a long list of records from a very large database and display all those records. Here a good way to do this with a fast response time is to just return the first screen or the first 100 records that meet what the user asks for. A PF key press or one button click sets off another transaction that returns the next screen or the next 100 records.
System utilities	As short a time as possible while still doing the utility function	Whether on a server or a desktop, running system utilities often hits the use of that computer. They may even stop any useful work while the utility runs.

CASE STUDY

System utilities

A server vendor gave away free system utilities with their servers. The company put very little developer time into writing these utilities. They ran very slowly. The vendor saw writing of this necessary software as an overhead to their main business of selling servers.

Later, the vendor changed their marketing policy. They began to sell these utilities at a nominal price. When the sales force tried to sell them, there was no interest from any of the potential buyers, so the sales people asked existing customers what was wrong with the utilities.

None of their customers actually used them, even though they had been free. Instead, they had paid a lot of money to competing software companies for equivalent utilities that ran much faster, were easier to use and had more features.

1 Discuss this case study with others in your group.

2 What lessons can be learned from this?

3 What options does the server vendor now have?

4 Which of these options would you choose? Justify your choice.

In doing performance testing, the tester should try to use full volumes of data. If this is not possible, then the tester should scale the results to what will happen for the maximum expected volume of data.

CASE STUDY

Defrag utility

A defragmentation utility for a desktop computer was designed when the standard disk storage was 2 gigabytes. For a partly full disk, following regular defragmentation, it ran in less than an hour. This was acceptable for most users. Technology quickly moved on, and for a 20-gigabyte computer it takes 13 hours for this utility to complete. So this utility, while it still works correctly, is not suitable for use on today's desktop computers.

1 Find out and write notes to explain what defragmentation involves.

2 How long would you regard as a reasonable maximum run time for this utility? Justify your answer.

3 In what ways could the PC user overcome this problem?

4 Find out and list what each of these ways would cost.

Batch programs

With batch programs, the performance aim is to keep as small as possible the amount of server resource that a program uses. This is because the shared server is heavily used in a many-user site. The aim may also be to meet elapsed clock time needs.

Many businesses do a lot of computer processing overnight. For example, the business need might be that the processing cannot start until their call centre closes at 2200 hours. The warehouse may need the output from the system at 0200 hours. This is so that the warehouse staff can pick the stock and ship the stock to the store for 0800 hours. Another need might be to email or fax sales reports for the previous day to managers around the country by 0700 in the morning.

CASE STUDY

Café Theresa

Café Theresa invested heavily in a new system to change the way one of the head office departments worked. It had a dedicated server which was the most powerful that could be bought of that type. The user department was very happy with the testing on a sample of data. The tests showed that the new system met its functional needs completely.

The department started parallel running. The new system even showed up faults in the old system that had been there for years. However, as more and more data moved across to the new system, the run times slowed. At last, it took nearly 24 hours each day to run the daily batch processing. If they hit a problem that delayed the runs for 6 hours, it took a week to get back up to date.

This could not go on, so this is what Café Theresa had to do.

◆ Stop taking on more data.
◆ Delay putting the system fully live for a long time.
◆ Rewrite much of the system to run more quickly.
◆ Drop some functions they had already built as they just took too long to run.

So, failing to performance test turned what should have been a great success into a near disaster.

1 Discuss why the system went wrong and how the problem could be prevented.

2 List a set of performance needs for this system.

3 How would you set about testing these needs?

4 What could you do when you found the system did not meet them?

Performance testing should be thought about at the time the system is being specified. The systems analyst should ask the user about response time or clock time needs, beyond the good practice described earlier in this section. Here are some examples of what the user might say.

◆ One set of functions is done across the Internet. The company's customers will be waiting for a response and there will be Internet delays to consider.

◆ The company's customer service agents do a second set of functions. This is either face-to-face to the customer or with the customer on the phone.

◆ A third set of functions is online to the company's staff. There is a staff productivity benefit if these run quickly.

◆ Other functions can run in the background. They can run at lower priority. They can accept a delay when the system is busy.

The designer should take these performance needs into account when designing the computer system. Note that the designer should not deliberately slow down lower-priority transactions. However, the designer may decide, for example, to move slow-running but infrequently wanted functions into separate transactions. The user then enjoys fast responses for most of the time. The user knows when there is going to be a slow response.

The tester should pick up those transactions that perform badly in the same way as identifying others that do not conform to good programming practice. The tester should raise an error log. The developer then reviews what is causing the delay.

Sometimes, it is straightforward to see what is going wrong. For example, the program might read every record in a file to find the one it wants. It would be faster to go through an index directly to the record. To code this might be more complex, and the index might not exist for anything else, so the developer will need to consider whether it is worthwhile to create and maintain an index for this program to use.

At other times, it is just not clear what is causing the delay in response time. There may be a more experienced senior programmer who has more technical knowledge and experience who can look for the cause.

Response-time analysis software

Response-time analysis software reports on which modules and which statements within those modules demand the most computing power. Both testers and developers use this software, though in different ways. These analysers also exist for databases. They can help the developer find which database calls take the most time and use the most system resources. Some sites also produce guides showing best practice. This helps the developer in terms of the balance between:

◆ speed of writing
◆ ease of understanding and maintenance
◆ performance.

Benchmarking is measuring how fast something works in relation to some standard. This is done when there is a need to meet tough response times or run times for a system. Computer hardware and software makers also run benchmarks, to show how much faster their new hardware or software is. This comparison can be with their own older products. More often they compare their new product (always favourably!) with the older products of their competitors.

The tester takes into account any specific performance needs stated in the specification when drawing up a **performance test plan**. Recording software is used to measure for each transaction the response time and the amount of system resources used.

A **thread** of transactions is a set of transactions that run one after another. Single-thread is when just one of these sets is run on its own. Each transaction runs on an empty machine without other transactions running. When one transaction finishes, the next transaction starts. This might run immediately. More usually, it is after a delay to simulate user thinking time. Multi-thread is when several of these sets are run at the same time.

An illustration of this is running in a relay race. When a relay team is practising on its own or running just against the stopwatch, then the one team on the race track is like a computer running in single-thread mode. When several teams are competing in a relay race, then the racetrack is like a multi-thread computer.

Testing should first be carried out using just one set (or stream or thread) of transactions running in single-thread mode. The tests are then repeated in multi-thread mode. Many streams of transactions run at the same time, usually with slightly different test values.

When the machine is fully loaded, increasing the number of threads that are running does not increase the number of transactions processed per minute. Sometimes, it even decreases. This is because the system has to spend more time managing the queues of transactions awaiting running. This is the capacity of that machine for that transaction mix.

Go out and try!

You can simulate performance testing on your PC. Do not do this exercise using any form of shared service or you can expect to be banned for misuse from your computing facility.

1 Find a local PC activity such as recalculating a complex spreadsheet or searching a large local database that runs for between 10 and 60 seconds. This must be just on your PC. It should not go across a network or use a server.

2 Time how long it takes to run on its own.

3 Repeat, running two similar activities.

4 Repeat, increasing the number of activities by one each time. What happens when your computer becomes full?

5 Draw graphs of runtime against number of activities.

6 Discuss your findings with those of your colleagues. Are theirs the same? If not, explain why they are not.

1.10 Test-data generation software

For the simplest of programs, the test stream consists of the tester sitting at a PC or terminal. He or she enters each transaction in turn from the test plan. For each, the tester notes down or copies and pastes the responses. There are several disadvantages to this:

(a) mistakes in entry of the transaction

(b) missing transactions

(c) mistakes in recording the response to a transaction

(d) the very time-consuming need to repeat many times a long transaction stream.

Software to generate test data

This is used to simplify, speed up and reduce the errors in the test process. It also often has features to help to create large volumes of data for performance tests.

What this software does is to simulate the user sending a stream of transactions to a system. It then captures the stream of replies that come back from the system. This is how it works.

1 From the test plan, the tester enters into the software the data that he or she would have entered online into the program under test. This is done field by field.

2 The software records the data for this transaction on to its database.

3 The tester then repeats this for each transaction input and response that he or she wants to test.

4 At the end of this process, the software has on its database the complete test plan.

This is in the format and sequence that the program under test expects. The tester can now check that no mistakes have been made in entry of the transactions. If they have, it is easy to correct just the field or transaction that is wrong. Thus, the software removes disadvantages (a) and (b) above.

Testing harnesses

Many test-data generators work with a testing harness. This software takes the generated test data and runs the transactions with this as input. This is instead of the tester having to enter manually all of the transactions. The harness captures the responses of the program to the inputs. It writes these to its database and associates them with the inputs.

The tester now reviews the output from the test. He or she compares it to what is on the test plan. Where there are differences, the tester raises a **test**

error log. This tells the developer what should have happened and what actually happened. The developer uses this to look into and fix the bug – described further on page 180.

It is helpful for the developer if the tester raises only one test error log per problem rather than one per transaction. For example, if all 20 test cases for transaction 32 failed to run, then the tester should raise only one log form for this. This shows how the software removes disadvantage (c) above.

When the developer has looked into the bugs raised on the first test run and believes that most of them have been fixed, the tester runs the test again. In this way, the software removes disadvantage (d) above.

The tester concentrates on those test cases that failed on the previous run. He or she checks that the test cases now produce the correct action and response.

◆ If a test case does work, then the tester signs off the error log for that error as it is now fixed. Note that it does not always produce the correct action; the first bug may have hidden a second bug! Here, the tester will raise another error log for the developer.

◆ If the developer has not properly fixed the first bug, then the tester does not sign it off. The tester sends the original error log back to the developer for the bug to be fixed properly.

Test output comparison

Some test software has an **output comparison** feature. This checks the full output results of one test run with the output results of a previous test run. It then indicates which outputs were the same as previously and which outputs changed, and lists the changed outputs. This is most useful when the tester is near the end of testing, when he or she is confident that most transactions work.

The tester splits the work into four classes:

◆ *No change and correct last time.* There is no need to check, because it still works.

◆ *No change and wrong last time.* The developer still has not fixed this problem, though he or she may have made an attempt to do so.

◆ *Changed and correct last time.* The developer has introduced an error into what was a working transaction, so the tester needs to raise a new error log.

◆ *Changed and wrong last time.* The developer may have fixed this error. The tester needs to look at this in detail. He or she must make sure that it is now doing what the test plan expected.

This output comparison feature is also useful in **regression testing**. This involves testing that things still work as they used to, when minor changes are made to an already working system. There is more information on this in section 3.6.

Test-data creation

There are additional features in the software to help in creating the content of the test data. More features help to copy and change this for many sets of data.

◆ Constant values can be set into specified fields.

◆ Fields can have a constant value, often 1, added to them or taken away from them between one transaction and the next.

◆ Bulk changes can be made to one set of inputs to form another set of inputs.

Check your understanding

This is a group exercise. Take one program that you are writing or have recently written as part of your course. Assume that you do not have test-data generation software.

1 Discuss how you could reduce the effort of generating test data.

2 Discuss how you could improve the quality of your test data.

3 On your own, write some or all of the test data for that program.

4 Compare what you have written with the rest of the group. How much did each of you miss?

5 Agree with the rest of the group how you will divide up the rewriting of the test data.

6 On your own, rewrite the test data with the others' contributions for your part of the test data.

7 Discuss as a group how much the test data has improved by team working.

1.11 Quality control

Most sites have quality control procedures. These put into practice, for that site, the principles described earlier in this unit. To comply with them, a standardised and rigorous approach to testing is required.

Testing is about checking that the program meets both the specification and the business need. It is also about recording that the tester has gone through these checks. With those records, both the tester and colleagues can be confident that the program has been tested. They can know how much the program has been tested.

Check your understanding

In a progress report, a tester states that 'testing is now 90 per cent complete'. That is a rather vague statement! The team leader asks the tester to define what is meant by 90 per cent, and to prove it. For each of the meanings below, state what proof you could give.

1 Ninety per cent of entries in the test plan are written.

2 Ninety per cent of the test plan inputs and outputs are written.

3 Ninety per cent of the test cases are generated.

4 Ninety per cent of transactions have had at least one test run.

5 Ninety per cent of the test plan transactions either work correctly or have an error logged.

6 Ninety per cent of the error logs have been returned.

7 Ninety per cent of the test plan transactions work correctly.

8 For the 10 per cent of test plan transactions that still do not work, 90 per cent of the error logs have been returned.

Which measure do you think is of most value, and why?

Chapter summary

◆ Four types of testing have been considered: white box, black box, and top-down and bottom-up testing.

◆ Five forms of testing have been considered: module, unit, system, customer and beta testing.

◆ Recovery testing is done to make sure that data can be retrieved after a hardware or software failure.

◆ Performance testing makes sure that the program meets the needs of the users.

◆ Software is available to help with testing routines.

2 Record the results of tests

This chapter shows how to use a test plan to carry out a series of tests. It then describes how to record the results of those tests in a test log. It explains how to provide evidence of testing. Examples of this are printed output, screen shots and file output.

◆ The **test plan** is the input to your testing. It says what makes up the input to each of your tests. It then says what you expect to happen as a result of these tests.

◆ The **test log** is the record of what actually happened on each of the tests.

If a program performs just one simple function then it is easy enough to keep trying to run the program until it does that. However, in the real world, even the simplest program does many things. It is therefore important to record what happens on each test. This is so that the developer knows which parts of the program still have errors that need to be fixed. The developer also needs to know which parts of the program already do what he or she expects. Finally, especially if there are deadlines to meet, it is important to know what parts of the program have yet to be tested effectively.

2.1 Test log essential features

A simple test log is shown in Figure 3.4. Some of the information that the developer enters on this is repeated from the test plan (Figure 3.3 on page 153). Table 3.3 explains the purpose of each field in detail.

Table 3.3 *Fields in a simple test log*

Field name	Description	Examples
System name	Brief title of the project (sometimes just the project code or initials) – usually bulk-copied	Café Theresa stock control
Program name	The larger piece of code that this test plan covers – usually bulk-copied	Stock-control calculation program
Module name	The detailed piece of code that this test plan covers – usually bulk-copied	Stock-control minimum-order-quantity calculation module
Version number	Either the version number of the program that is under test or the version number of the relevant test plan – usually bulk-copied	004
Tester name	The person who completed the test log (not necessarily the same person who created the test plan) – usually bulk-copied	Sarah Coder
Test number	Cross-reference to the test number on the test plan (a sequential number for that test plan)	003
Date	The date this test run took place (not the test plan date, which is when the test plan was prepared)	30/9/2004
Actual output and/or filename	The actual result of the test transaction or program run and/or the filename where the results of this test were written	The transaction was rejected with the error message 'Month invalid: it is >12' There was no change to the database.
Comments on discrepancies	A record of discrepancies between actual results and expected results (the differences between what should have happened and what actually happened)	The month should have been accepted as valid. The transaction should have updated the database.

TEST LOG				
System name: Program name: Module name:			Version no: Tester name:	Page no:
Test no.	Date	Actual output/Filename	Comments on discrepancies	

Figure 3.4 A blank test log

PRACTICAL TASK 3.4

For this activity you should work in pairs. First choose a simple program that one of you has recently written.

1 Working on your own, fill in one page of a test plan and one page of a simple test log. Compare your results with your partner's.

2 As a pair, list which parts of your forms you have completed the same and which parts are different. Give your reasons for this.

2.2 Cross-referencing tests

One very important piece of information in testing is the **test number**. This number acts as the cross-reference between the various documents:

◆ the test plan

◆ the test logs that record the runs

◆ test output that is either printed output, screen shots or the output file or files.

For each test, the tester works out and records on the test plan what is the right input and the expected output. He or she assigns a test number to each test case – usually the next number in a sequence. If a program has many different functions, then more than one set of numbers may be used. The tests for credit transactions may be numbered C1, C2, C3, etc., while the tests for debit transactions may be D1, D2, D3, etc. In the same way, if there are several testers then Jane may use test numbers J1, J2, J3, etc. while Kevin uses K1, K2, K3, etc.

In the business world, the number of test cases may run into thousands. However, in the student world, the number will be in tens or at most in the low hundreds. For example, for a small three-module program:

- test cases 1 to 20 test module 1
- test cases 21 to 40 test module 2
- test cases 41 to 60 test module 3
- test cases 61 to 100 test the complete program.

For most programs, there is a need for a testing strategy – that is, an idea of how to tackle the testing. Often, a tester decides to test each module in turn and then test the program as a whole.

An example of how a set of tests might go and how to complete the test log is shown in Figure 3.5.

The tester decides that the first test run is for tests 1 to 20. Unfortunately, the program crashes for each transaction.

Test no.	Date	Actual output	Comments on discrepancies
1 to 20	1/2/04	Program crashed. Output saved in file Crash20040201a.	Not applicable. Error log 1 raised.
1 to 20	2/2/04	All transactions rejected with message 'Transaction number error – must be numeric'.	All but one transaction should have had valid transaction numbers. Error log 2 raised.
1 to 20	3/2/04	Tests 4 & 7 worked correctly as expected. Tests 9 & 14 produced the expected error message. The rest of tests 1 to 8 were rejected. The rest of tests 10 to 20 produced the wrong error messages.	Error logs 3, 4 & 5 raised for tests 1 to 8. Error logs 6 to 11 raised for tests 10 to 20. There are fewer error logs than tests because some tests failed with the same error.
1	4/2/04	Correct record updated message and database changed correctly.	Error log 3 confirmed as now fixed.
2	4/2/04	'Invalid quantity' instead of valid transaction.	Error log 4 fixed, but this was hiding another problem. Error log 12 raised.

Once the developer fixes the program crash, then each transaction is rejected incorrectly.

On the third run, there is a positive test. Some of the tests run as expected. Others either fail when they should have worked or work when they should have failed. The tester produces an **error log** for each of these for later investigation and correction.

Figure 3.5 *Example of a completed test log*

Check your understanding

1 List the disadvantages of not using test numbers to cross-reference tests.

2 By mistake, two different sets of tests for one program were created with the same test numbers. List the problems that this could create.

2.3 Testing in the target environment

The developer normally develops a program in a very different technical environment from the user of the software. The developer has software tools that help him or her to design, write, test and document the program. These tools often:

◆ include debugging and tracing features

◆ are able to stop the program at any point

◆ can change any variable in the program

◆ can change where the program will next execute

◆ have a set of supporting software libraries that are consistent with the code the developer wrote.

To run these powerful tools usually means that the developer has up-to-date system software, running on powerful modern hardware. The developer can rely on having supporting libraries and programs. In contrast, the user will often have only as much as is needed for the job the computer has to do!

For example, an early model Pentium running *Windows 95* can still provide good response times and functionality for all of these activities:

◆ word processing using *Word 95* and spreadsheets using *Excel 95*

◆ presentations using *PowerPoint 95*

◆ email using *Outlook Express 4* and Internet using *Internet Explorer 4*

◆ specialised database programs.

The major constraint of hardware and software from the Windows 95 era is that it is poor at running more than one major program at the same time.

Minimum system requirements

The developer should decide on the typical minimum hardware and software specifications for the application.

◆ If the developer is working on a video editing program, then the user is likely to need a fast processor speed, a large and fast disk drive, good video equipment and fast data transfer around the system.

◆ A high-speed action game has many similar needs. It does not need large and fast disks.

◆ At the other end of the scale, a multi-function calculator, a specialised database program or a PC utility may need less than 10 per cent of any of a modern computer's resources. These programs are ideal for running in many computer environments from Windows 95 onwards.

Even where there is a real need for powerful modern hardware and software to run an application, similar functions may be found in older environments. It may be commercial considerations that have made the older program obsolete.

◆ In the games field, there are programs such as *Sim City* that has developed into *Sim City 2000*, *Sim City 3000* and *Sim City 4*. The underlying theme is still the same, but with better, more powerful graphics and computing.

◆ Many sports games produce a new game for each season. Often the major change is to the data for the simulated players or teams, rather than any major new functions.

There is little functional difference for the average user in most desktop business software. Updated versions bring impressive new functions for 'power users'. They may also increase the volume and size of data that the program can cope with. However, the developer should consider carefully the target audience when trying to set the minimum specification of computer that the new program needs.

◆ Most spreadsheet users are not professional accountants or financial analysts.

◆ Most word processor users are not professional writers producing complex documents all day long.

Testing for different environments

The approach uses the same form of test plans, test logs and error logs as the tester used in functional testing.

First, the tester checks that all the functions of the program work on the developer's hardware and software. Then the tester moves to a more typical modern user environment and repeats the tests. While the program usually still works, some features may work either unacceptably slowly or not at all. The program may even fail to load or crash with a system error message. The tester should record these tests on the test plan and test log and raise error logs if any problems arise.

The tester then tests the program on examples of the rest of the computer hardware and software that they expect the program to run in. The results of these tests are not likely to be functional problems. They are more likely to be that the program needs certain software version levels, minimum hardware requirements and other software for the program to work. Sometimes, the developer needs to change the way in which parts of the code have been written. This is so that the program can use optionally older support software that is available on older computers.

PRACTICAL TASK 3.5

This activity shows how similar functions are delivered by different versions of software for different environments. You should work in pairs or small groups. You will be looking at what *Office* software is installed on several PCs. Pick PCs that are of different ages and specification. For each PC:

1 List the hardware and system software specification.

2 List the name and version number of each item of *Office* software installed.

3 Where different versions of the same applications are installed, compare their functions.

4 List the functional differences between these versions.

5 Estimate what percentage more functions there are in the newer versions.

6 Calculate what percentage more power, by processor speed, amount of memory or some other factor, there is in the newer larger computer.

7 List how often you might use each of these new features. What conclusions can you draw from this?

Chapter summary

The following have been covered:

◆ test log essential features
◆ cross-referencing of tests
◆ testing in the target environment.

3 Analyse test results

This chapter shows how to use the test log to produce a testing report. This analysis of the test results:

◆ specifies the presence or absence of errors
◆ makes proposals for rectifying errors
◆ reports on the success of the test against the original software specification.

3.1 Types of software error

Several forms of error can occur in a computer program. The first – and most serious – is that program does not meet the business needs. Perhaps the program does meet the specification and the specification was at first correct, but now the needs have changed. This may mean changes to the modules, to the sizes of some of the data fields, or even to the structure of the programs.

At the programming level, a correct program is one that conforms to (is in line with) the program's written specification and good computing practice. The program should validate or check input so that it tries to process only valid data. It should also detect and correct errors, and not crash under unexpected conditions.

Compliance with specification and good programming practice

A program specification at most contains the structure of the solution. The developer needs to write code that is in line with that specification. He or she also needs to write code that is in line with good programming practice.

The program should validate input so that it processes only correct values. The program should reject incorrect values with an error message that means something to the user. This error message should also tell the user what needs to be done to correct the error. For example, if the user attempts to enter '32' as the day of the month, then the error message should say something like 'Invalid day: day must be 31 or less'.

For an updating program, the program should explicitly test for valid transactions or values. It should reject them gracefully if they are not correct.

Programming errors

Sometimes a program just does not work. Programmers can make two types of programming error: **logic errors** and **syntax errors**.

> **What does it mean?**
>
> *All languages, both spoken and computer, have rules of grammar and spelling. A syntax error is made when the developer has broken one of these rules.*
>
> *A logic error is made when the program may appear to run successfully, but the results are not what the developer or user expects. There is an error in the 'logic' of the program.*

If the developer makes a syntax error, then the computer is not sure what the developer wants it to do. The computer may detect this when:

- the developer is writing the program
- the program is compiled
- the developer or tester is running it during testing
- the user runs it in production.

For an **interpreted language**, the computer detects a syntax error only in the last two cases.

What does it mean?

*In a visual programming environment, the program is usually **interpreted**. This means that it is converted into what the computer understands only when you run it.*

It is more difficult for the computer development system to help to find out logic errors. Most testing therefore aims to find out and correct logic errors.

Runtime errors

When there is a runtime error, the program works successfully most of the time, but occasionally fails. This is the hardest type of error to sort out. It is difficult to catch in the first place. It is even difficult to make the error happen over and over again. It is often then hard to find out what is causing the problem and it may never be solved. It is sometimes only partly solved by a 'workaround', such that the user does not put the program into the position that causes the error to occur.

CASE STUDY

Café Theresa

Café Theresa's stock control update program is specified to receive two types of transactions to change the stock database.

- Credit transactions add to the quantity and value on the stock database.
- Debit transactions subtract from the quantity and value on the stock database.

The easiest and quickest way to code this program might be to test for a credit transaction and treat anything else as a debit transaction. This might appear to work, but give results that are in error when a new transaction type is introduced.

Better coding would be to test separately for credit and debit transactions. If the transaction

was neither, then the program could report an error message. An even better and more robust solution would be to log the unexpected transaction type to a form of error log and continue processing.

1 List the advantages of just testing for a credit.

2 List the advantages of testing for a credit and a debit and, if neither, reporting an error message.

3 List the advantages of having an error log here.

4 Discuss as a group each of these advantages.

5 Produce, as a group, a set of guidelines for Café Theresa developers stating when they should use each approach.

Look back at the last program you wrote.

1 How many syntax errors did it have?

2 How many compiler runs did it take to find these?

3 How many logic errors did that program have?

4 How many test runs did it take to find the logic errors?

5 What conclusions can you draw from the answers to questions 1 to 4?

3.2 Common causes of runtime errors

There are many ways in which a program can fail at runtime. Here are some examples that happen very often, with suggestions as to what the developer can do to avoid these errors.

Forever loops

The simplest example is of this form:

```
Label: DO X;
DO Y;
GO TO Label;
```

With structured programming, the programmer is unlikely to write code exactly like that, but he or she might write slightly more complex examples.

```
I = 1;
DO WHILE I > 0;
Code;
END;
```

Here, the variable I is always greater than zero and never changes, so the loop never ends. Here is a variation of the same problem:

```
I = 1;
DO WHILE I > 0;
Code;
I = I + 1:
END;
```

In that example, the loop counter changes but still never goes to zero. Here is yet another variation on this:

```
I = 1;
DO WHILE I > 0;
Code;
J = J – 1:
END;
```

In that example, the programmer has used two different variables, I and J, as the loop counter and still the loop never ends.

Illegal file operations

When handling files, there are many ways in which a program can fail, or not produce the expected results. The most simple is the file handling equivalent of 'Web page error 404 – page not found'. This unit uses the terms from database processing of 'row' and 'table', but similar errors apply to file handling with 'record' and 'file'. Here are some of the most common errors that the developer may come across when a table is being read.

- Allow for a 'row not found' status even if it is expected that the row always exists.
- Allow for a 'row not found' status, but processing as if a row had been found. This gives unpredictable results and it is often very difficult to find out what has happened.
- Try to read a row before a database has been opened.
- Try to read a row after a database has been closed.
- Reread the same row, instead of retrieving the next row.

What can a developer do to avoid these pitfalls?

1 When updating a row, make sure that the row does exist.

2 On the other hand, when inserting a new row, make sure that the new row does not already exist.

3 When deleting a row, make sure that the row being deleted exists before trying to delete it. In other words, make sure that the right row is deleted.

Sometimes in a large, highly secure system, physical deletion of some records is not allowed in an online transaction. Any attempt to do so causes a file error exception. The online transaction may only set a 'delete requested' flag. Some later batch process then comes along, performs the necessary security and consistency checks and writes audit records. Only then does the batch process do the physical row deletion.

Dividing by zero

Division by zero is not defined as a mathematical function. If the developer writes code that tries to do this, the computer will throw an exception. Best not to do it!

CASE STUDY

Café Theresa

Café Theresa sells one sandwich at £2, one at £2.50 and one at £3. They sell one coffee at £1.50, one at £2 and one at £2.50. They price teas at £1.80, £2.20 and £2.60 but sell no teas.

1 What is their average price for each product type?

2 Write a well-defined specification for the calculation routine.

Answers

Question 1:

Sandwiches $(2 + 2.50 + 3.00) / 3 = £2.50$

Coffees $(1.50 + 2 + 2.50) / 3 = £2$

Teas $(0 \times 1.80 + 0 \times 2.20 + 0 \times 2.60) / 0 = $ undefined

Question 2:

Incorrect solution:

FOR each product type, add up the quantity sold multiplied by the price of each product.

THEN divide by the total number sold of that product type.

Correct solution:

IF the total number sold is non-zero, THEN

FOR each product type, the average price is calculated by adding up the quantity sold multiplied by the price of each product.

THEN divide by the total number sold of that product type.

ELSE average price is undefined.

3.3 Testing and debugging

There is a difference between testing and debugging.

◆ **Testing** is the process of making sure that a program works in the way everyone expects it to. This includes the user, the people who specified the program, the developer and the tester. Sections 3.1 and 3.2 have shown how to tackle this. The result of these testing activities gives the developer a set of error logs to fix. These show where the program does not work in the way that the tester expected. These error logs do not say *why* the program does not work as it should. The developer uses these as the input to debug the program.

◆ **Debugging** a program is to first find out why a program does not work in the way that the tester, user or developer expected it to work – and then fixing or correcting the program so that it does work as specified and expected.

Debugging

Bugs can be consistent, frequent, occasional or once-only.

◆ If error Y *always* occurs when situation X occurs, the tester describes this as a **consistent bug**.

◆ If error Y *usually* occurs when X occurs, this is a **frequent bug**.

◆ If error Y *sometimes* occurs when X happens, this is an **occasional bug**.

◆ If error Y occurred *just once* when X occurred, it was a **once-only bug**.

The developer should be able to fix consistent and frequent bugs because they can be repeated and cured. This means that the developer or tester can create again and again the situation for the bug. When the developer thinks the bug has been fixed, he or she can set up situation X again and make sure that the correct result now happens, rather than error Y.

Finding occasional and once-only bugs is more difficult. As the developer often cannot repeat the situation that produced the bug, he or she cannot prove that the bug has been fixed. It is often possible to try to fix them only if there is a large amount of evidence.

Note

*The evidence for occasional and once-only errors is usually in the form of a **trace** so the developer has something to look into. A trace identifes the path a transaction takes through a program.*

Debugging first has the developer copying into his or her own environment the bug that the tester has found. This is because sometimes the tester makes a mistake in describing the bug. It could also be that the tester and the developer understand differently what the specification means. The bug may be caused by technically different test and development environments.

Debugging a program is a mixture of logical analysis, experience, technical knowledge and intuition.

How to debug

When a bug report lands on a developer's desk, the bug should be investigated in a logical manner.

◆ In a well-structured program, if there is a fault with the validation of the input fields then the bug is in the relevant input module. If the output format does not look right, the bug is in the output module for that screen or report.

◆ If the program is not well structured, then the fault could be anywhere. It will be very much harder to find.

The developer starts by **desk-checking** the part of the program where he or she thinks the fault lies. This means looking at the code on the screen 'at the desk'. The developer tries to follow the path through the code that this error takes. Sometimes, it is then clear where the bug lies. If it is not, then it is time for the developer to call on help from the development environment.

The developer reruns the program under the control of the development environment. He or she sets **breakpoints** and **traces** at the part of the program where things may be going wrong. When the program reaches these points, the developer can:

◆ display and change the values of variables

◆ change the path through the program

◆ look in much more detail at what the program does while it runs.

Experience often plays a large part in debugging. Once the experienced developer has found the easier bugs, he or she can think back to when a problem like this was last seen. Some developers keep a notebook of unusual testing problems and what caused them. The notes can be consulted when a bug is elusive.

Figure 3.6 shows part of an error message produced from a website to a commercial user when the site had gone through testing and was in production. This error message did not mean anything to the user. It probably did not even mean much to the maintenance developers who received this message attached to a bug report!

Fault (4) : Cast from type 'DBNull' to type 'String' is not valid.

Description: An unhandled exception occurred during the execution of the current web request. Please review the stack trace for more information about the error and where it originated in the code.

Exception Details: System.Exception: Fault (4) : Cast from type 'DBNull' to type 'String' is not valid.

Source Error:

```
An unhandled exception was generated during the execution of the
current web request. Information regarding the origin and location
of the exception can be identified using the exception stack trace
```

Stack Trace:

```
[Exception: Fault (4) : Cast from type 'DBNull' to type 'String' is not valid.]
_30.fbAirport.ActiveTo(fbUser user) +338
_30.sda.Page_Load(Object sender, EventArgs e) +242
System.Web.UI.Control.OnLoad(EventArgs e) +67
```

Figure 3.6 Example of a poor error message

Intuition or luck occasionally plays a part in finding a difficult bug. Typical problems where this might happen are:

◆ missing language punctuation, such as full stops, semi-colons or comment markers

◆ duplicated language punctuation, such as brackets

◆ wrongly spelt variables

◆ a variable with the wrong initial value set

◆ a variable with no initial value set.

Some developers have the intuition to find bugs caused by this sort of error very quickly. They are often in great demand by their colleagues to look at their code to find difficult bugs and to see whether they can spot the problem quickly.

PRACTICAL TASK 3.7

Look back at the last program you wrote and tested.

1 List each bug that you found during testing.

2 Classify each of those bugs as either consistent, frequent, occasional or once-only.

3 Classify each bug that you found as simple, medium or difficult to find and fix.

4 What can you say about the type of bug and how easy or not it was to find and fix?

CASE STUDY

Minimum system requirements

A developer might use a *Windows XP*-based computer with a large amount of memory. The program is meant to run on all machines running *Windows 95* and later version of *Windows* with a limited amount of memory. If there is something wrong with the way the program uses memory, then it may fail to run on an older and/or smaller computer, while on a large modern computer it runs happily but inefficiently.

◆ As a group, discuss how you might work out what the minimum system requirements are for a program you are writing.

3.4 Test plans, test logs, test results and tests reports

It is important for you to understand what each of these four pieces of documentation is and what each is used for (see Figure 3.7).

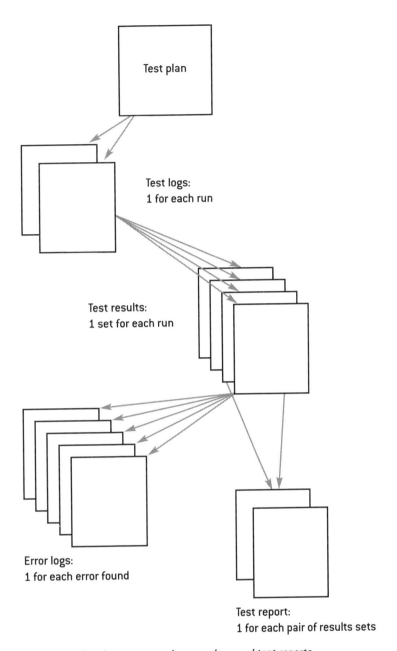

Figure 3.7 Test logs, test results, error logs and test reports

◆ The purpose of a **test plan** is to identify what parts of the program functions to test, how to test them and the expected results. The tester writes this before any test runs take place. It is a static document. At a big site, it is often signed off by all working with this program as a plan for a thorough test.

◆ The tester records on **test logs** what actually happens on each test run. The aim is for the final test run to record successfully that all parts of the program perform as expected. However, in both the student and business environments, time-scales sometimes overtake the developer. The test logs are a way to record how far the testing has gone at the end of the project. The program might not be fully correct, but may be good enough to regard as finished.

◆ The tester records one entry on the **error log** for each error found. This says what should happen and what actually did happen. The error log is then given to the developer to start the debugging process. When the bug has been corrected, the developer completes the error log. This is returned to the tester who then checks that the bug really has been fixed.

◆ **Test results** are the computer output from each test run. They are used directly at first to check that the actual results are the same as the expected results.

◆ **Testing software** is available to compare two sets of test results. This produces a **test report** on the differences between the two sets. This test report is used in the later stages of testing, when almost all the program works and there are only a few bugs left to fix. The tester uses this software to look at the differences between one test run and the previous run. What the tester is expecting is that the bugs that should have been fixed in this run now produce the expected answers. The tester also wants to be certain that the parts of the program that worked on the previous run still work now! The bug fixes should not have introduced any new bugs.

Check your understanding

This activity is to make sure you understand the process for the forms that go with testing. The group should divide into pairs. Each pair chooses to pretend to test a very simple program. One student plays the tester and one plays the developer. They then switch roles and repeat.

1 The tester creates the test plan for the program.

2 The tester and the developer agree and 'sign off' the test plan.

3 The tester pretends to run a test. He or she creates a set of 'test results'.

4 The tester raises a test log and one or more error logs.

5 The developer looks at the error log, fills in the rest of the error log and gives it back to the tester.

6 Repeat steps 3 to 5.

7 The tester and developer now switch roles and repeat steps 1 to 6.

List what you have learned from this exercise. What improvements can you suggest?

3.5 Testing and software quality and maintenance

Both the developer and tester need to know what quality of program the user needs before they start their work. If the program is a simple game to keep the developer amused, or a utility to help make a computer task easier, then the program only has to be good enough. If the program does not work under some conditions, then this is only a problem for the developer, who can perhaps achieve the necessary results in another way.

Sometimes, **speed of development** is a high priority compared with program quality. A business may suffer a lot if the deadline for delivery of a new program is not met. In this case, it may be acceptable that an early delivery date is more important than time spent on development and testing. This certainly leads to a lower quality program or system. This is only acceptable if the cost of this quality loss is much less than the benefit from fast delivery.

For some types of program or system, though, the developer and tester should not compromise on program quality.

◆ **Safety-critical systems** should be fail-safe. The tester must be able to show and document that the system continues to work safely at all times and in all situations. Some businesses that this applies to are nuclear, medical, airline engineering and railway signalling.

◆ **Mission-critical systems** exist in most businesses. A business may have just one or two systems without which it cannot work properly. Before making large changes to these systems, the changes must be rigorously tested. There must be a fall-back plan in place in case things do go wrong.

◆ **High-volume desktop software** is an example of a type of software in which a bug might have a small impact but on a larger number of people. If a company sells high-volume desktop software and it fails to test it enough, then it annoys many thousands of users. This poor reputation spreads rapidly to other products that the company makes. It quickly leads to a great loss of business to the company. This is one of the reasons why small IT companies can bring to market new software very much more quickly than the large companies with a large user base.

For many selling organisations, the IT system that supports telephone sales is the most critical system. For a retailer, the till or point-of-sale system is the most critical. Without this, they cannot sell goods or take money from their customers, For an airline, the most critical system is the passenger check-in system, not telephone sales. This is because a check-in system failure at once drives their customers away to other competing airlines. If the telephone sales system does not work then there are still several ways to carry on selling tickets to the customer, such as through the Internet or travel agents.

There are some types of system where maintenance and its ease or speed is the most important element of quality.

◆ *Multi-lingual systems*. These should allow easy introduction and change of language-dependent features. This is because it is known that frequent changes are needed to introduce new languages or to improve on the existing message wording.

◆ *Long-life systems*. Some systems may cost so much to either build or implement that it is not cost-effective to redevelop them very often. Code in these systems should be designed for ease of maintenance since, without this, the total cost of ownership will be even higher.

◆ *Systems for a fast changing business.* The business systems to support a sales or marketing part of a business are likely to change faster than those to support engineering or finance. This is because the way the sales or marketing part of the business works usually changes much faster. If the software developer knows that frequent speedy change is likely, then it is good to design that system for ease of maintenance.

PRACTICAL TASK 3.8

1 As a group, list different sorts of computer program.

2 Working on your own, give a rating of needed software quality, in the range 1 to 10, to each of these programs.

3 Working on your own, give a rating of speed of development needed, in the range 1 to 10, to each of these programs

4 Working on your own, give a rating of ideal cost of development, in the range 1 to 10, to each of these programs

5 As a group, discuss your answers to the above rating tasks and calculate the average rating for each program.

6 List where you have answers that differ greatly from the group. Justify your reasons for giving different ratings.

3.6 Regression testing

Regression testing was first introduced on page 167. This section describes how to reuse well thought-out test plans and test data for repeat testing after fixing errors or making maintenance changes. This form of testing is to make sure that new bugs are not introduced into a working program when the developer makes a change to it. The reason for the change can be:

◆ the program does more things

◆ maintenance (continuing to do the same things as the user makes minor changes to the way of doing things)
◆ fixing a problem.

A regression test runs a test against both the old and new versions of a program. The tester makes sure that they still produce the same answers. This checking is done either manually or by using testing software. Both methods identify where there are changed results.

The tester then goes through the changed records to see whether what has changed is what was expected. If it is not, then the tester raises an error log to have the problem fixed. The tester also needs to check that any of the outputs that were expected to change with the new version of the software did actually change.

In the business world, what happens in practice is that a regression test plan and test data may be produced as part of delivery of the original system. It is formed from a subset of the full data used to originally test the system. As new features are introduced into the system, the tester adds a few test transactions for these new features to the regression test plan and test data.

PRACTICAL TASK 3.9

Draw up a list of situations when you would *not* use a regression test when you change an existing program.

3.7 Version control

This section describes the purpose of version control procedures when developing, testing, amending and maintaining software and documentation with reference to quality assurance.

If the developer is writing a program that will not be upgraded there may be no need for **version control**.

CASE STUDY

Café Theresa

Café Theresa organises sales areas by county. They needed a new sales area reporting program. Their IT department wrote this report, it was tested and went into live running. However, they found that it was producing several total lines for each county.

The developer looked into this bug and found that the stores database had inconsistent names for counties. For example, the store in Preston had a county of 'Lancashire', the Blackburn store had a county of 'Lancs', while the Blackpool store had a county of 'Lanc'. A program was needed to change the contents of the 'county' field. The user wanted the abbreviation 'Lancs' to replace 'Lancashire' or 'Lanc' (and the incorrect 'Lancaster') whenever they appeared in the county field. The developer wrote the code to do this and fixed any bugs as they were found during testing. When the program was complete and approved, it was run just once in production to correct the database.

1   What else should this database correction program do as well as changing the Lancs county names?

2   What other changes should the developer make and to which part of the system to stop this problem happening again.

The staff in an IT organisation and elsewhere need version control for several reasons.

◆ *The developer*. During development, changes can be made that are wrong. The developer wants then to return (fall back) to the previous version.

◆ *The developer and the maintenance programmer*. Both need to be able to identify when new features were added or bugs sorted out.

◆ *The tester and the developer*. Both need to identify which version of the program produced which set of test results.

◆ *The person responsible for documentation*. It is essential to produce documentation that is in line with a certain version of the program.

◆ *The users*. They want to know what the version that they are using does. They also need to know what changes a new version of the program brings and how to use these features. Programs that run under Windows usually provide their version number to the user from the *About* button on the Help main menu.

When a developer releases or promotes a new version of a program into production, the use of a version number can make sure that the production program is the right one. The developer may be working on new features for the *next* version, or be trying to fix some minor bugs in an older version. These versions would not be put into production.

Version control systems can have up to three sets of numbers.

CASE STUDY

Version coding

The text of this unit was first written using Word version 9.0.3821.

◆ The first number indicates the major version of the program. The vendor will often use it in their technical marketing, although there may be a more user-friendly or marketing version of the name. So *Word* version 6 for the PC went with *Windows 3.1*, *Word 7* was better known as *Word 95*, *Word 8* was *Word 97*, and *Word 9* was marketed as *Word 2000*. The vendor will sometimes give a new product version a code name and decide on the marketing name close to production release. This may change only every two years or so.

◆ The vendor uses the second number to show new features of technical value but not large enough to need marketing. For example, the *Oracle* database went from 7.1 to 7.2 to 7.3 before moving to 8.0 and then 8.1.

◆ The final number has two uses. For the vendor and user technical support, it shows in production the exact set of code that the user is running. In development, it lets the developer to know the status of the code.

1 List the marketing names and version numbers of *Excel*.

2 List the marketing names and version numbers of Windows.

For the developer, version numbering is often automatic. The development environment will often identify versions by a sequential number, or by a date, or a combination of both of these. The developer will often want to use versions together with **program status**.

What does it mean?

Program status means what state a program version is in and who can use that version:

◆ production – *release for use by customers*

◆ testing – *for testers to use for levels of testing*

◆ development – *for use only by the developer*

◆ special – *a version that has been developed for a special need.*

Once a new version of a program is in production, there is still a need to keep securely all versions of the program that any customer might use. However, there is a high maintenance cost in keeping old program versions and their documentation. Most vendors therefore have a policy whereby they stop actively supporting older program versions at a suitable time after their new program versions are available. This time is often 18–24 months. They may leave their technical support program knowledge base available, but will not look at any bugs that users find. This sometimes leads to conflict between vendor and user. Why?

◆ The newest version of the program may not work for that user.

◆ The user may have no need for the newer features of the program.

◆ The user may not have been affected by the bugs that the new version corrects.

◆ The new version of the program may need a higher equipment specification than the user has installed.

◆ User priorities are elsewhere and so the user does not have the IT effort available to make the changes.

◆ The vendor might charge for the move to the new version, sometimes a lot of money, and the user does not see the benefit for this cost.

The technical support maintenance programmers who work for the vendor may make changes based on many production versions. They need to keep under control all of these changed versions while they test minor changes. Once this testing is successfully completed, these minor changes need to be released to the users. This is often in the form of **patches**. The user can download them from the vendor's website. Patches are small pieces of code that include only changes to another version.

The developer may be controlling several versions of the same program. Often, when a program moves into systems testing and beta testing, the developer starts to work on the next major version of the program. The system testing needs minor changes to one version, while major changes are going on in parallel to another version. For some programs, there may be different versions that run on different technologies, but deliver the same function.

Go out and try!

Search for a program that has many versions. You could do this by using the Internet or by using your site software library and documentation. *Windows*, *Word* or *Excel* are examples. For your chosen program, list the main differences between the versions.

Chapter summary

The following have been covered:

◆ types of software error

◆ causes of common runtime errors

◆ testing and debugging

◆ test plans, test logs, test results and test reports, and the relationship between them

◆ software quality and maintenance

◆ regression testing

◆ version control.

4 Identify health and safety requirements

This chapter explains how to maintain a safe working environment for the user and others. It stresses the use of **safe working practices** at all times. It is important to operate equipment in line with suppliers', manufacturers' and workplace needs. It describes how to use and maintain equipment, materials and accessories to a safe standard. To head off problems, it tells how to use reporting procedures to report any hazards.

4.1 Good working environment

Three major factors lead to a good working environment for computer work:

◆ frequent breaks away from the computer

◆ correct positioning of screens, chairs and keyboards

◆ adequate lighting and ventilation.

Frequent breaks away from the computer have a number of good effects (see Figure 3.8).

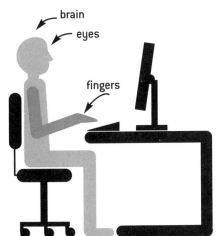

brain
eyes
fingers

Figure 3.8 The major bodily strain points for computer users

◆ The first benefit is for the **eyes**. Looking at a computer screen for a long time means that the eyes are focused at the same distance during that time. Normal office or college work has variation between close work in reading a document or a book and long-distance work such as looking towards a colleague or teacher or across the room. Leaving the screen allows your eyes to exercise.

◆ Other parts of the body to benefit from a break away from the screen include your **muscles**. While at the keyboard, your **fingers** are working very hard but the rest of your body hardly moves at all. This means that the muscles associated with your fingers have too much strain, while the rest of your body has no exercise at all. A break away from the screen allows your fingers to have a rest while the rest of your body starts to move a bit.

◆ Another last part of your body to benefit from a break from the computer is your **brain**. There is usually a lot of concentration when a user is busy at the keyboard. While this is good for short periods, with most people there is a great loss of concentration after between 30 minutes and 2 hours. This means loss of productivity in a business environment. In a learning environment, it means a loss of effectiveness. The amount of this effect depends on the person and the type of work. A break and perhaps a brief talk to a colleague means the brain can relax for a short time. It then becomes much more effective again.

The **physical environment** – such as computer screens, chair and keyboard – has to be correct if a computer user is to be at his or her most effective.

It is often difficult to position a computer, its screen and keyboard in exactly the right position. This is because the rest of the furniture is usually there first and the **computer screen** is put where it can then fit. What is the best position for a computer screen?

◆ If possible, position it side-on to any nearby window, to minimise **reflections** on the screen.

◆ Often there is a wall or physical screen behind the computer. This can provide the right level of **light contrast**.

◆ The computer screen should not be at the same height as the user's eyes, but at a *slight angle*. This is also to prevent **glare**.

◆ The screen should *swivel* and *tilt* to make it easier for the user to adjust it to prevent glare.

What features does the ideal **computer chair** have?

◆ An *adjustable back* will help to prevent back strain and provide a comfortable support while working.

◆ An *adjustable height* will allow the user to view the screen at a slight angle and to comfortably use the keyboard and mouse. If one person only ever uses a chair then the screen height could be changed to do this. However, in most cases, there are many users, so the chair height needs to be changeable.

◆ *Armrests* are usually provided as an aid to use of the keyboard. They are useful during user thinking time and while waiting during a long response time.

◆ Easily movable *feet* (e.g. on castors) can make it easier to have frequent breaks away from the computer.

The computer **keyboard** has been developed from the 'QWERTY' typewriter, but with a lot of improvements for computer usage. The first computer keyboards were similar to typewriters, but today's ergonomic keyboards are a great improvement.

Adequate **lighting** and **ventilation** is important for the most effective use of a computer system. Lighting should:

◆ be good enough to read non-computer documents easily

◆ not give glare against the computer screen

◆ provide enough contrast between the computer screen and its office background.

Ventilation should have enough airflow to:

◆ keep the computing equipment at temperatures within their operating specification

◆ provide a comfortable working environment for the computer user

◆ meet at least the minimum requirements of the **Offices, Shops and Railway Premises Act** or similar legislation (for example a temperature of at least 16 degrees Celcius from an hour after the normal work start time)

◆ not be so hot as to reduce the computer user's productivity.

Check your understanding

1 List the features that are common to the typewriter and today's ergonomic keyboard.

2 List the new features of the modern keyboard compared to the typewriter.

3 Explain the benefits or reasons for introduction for each of the new features.

4.2 Health and safety precautions

Under normal operating conditions, computers are one of the safest items of equipment that can be used. There are, however, some health and safety precautions that all users should follow – see Figure 3.9.

Figure 3.9 Hazards!

Electrical hazards

The necessary electrical precautions are similar to those when using any electrical or electronic item.

1 Make sure that all power cables are safely secured.

2 Do not overload a power point with lots of plugs or extension points.

3 Do not probe the inside of computer equipment. The user should leave this to a qualified computer technician.

4 Do not spill liquid or food into a computer or any other equipment.

5 Do not block any vents in the equipment – they are there for cooling purposes.

Failure to follow these precautions can lead to various failures, such as:

◆ temporary failure of the equipment

◆ permanent failure of part of the equipment, leading to replacement of the failed part

◆ complete failure of that computer

◆ smoke and fire – in an extreme case spreading beyond the failing computer.

Tripping hazards

How do tripping hazards arise? Most personal computers have lots of wires attached to them, such as power cables to the computer, monitor, printer and many other attached devices. There are also data cables between the computer and all of its attached devices.

Many computers also have a network connection. At home, this is through a modem attached to a telephone line. In an office, college or school, the network connection is likely to be a local-area network (LAN).

Any of these wires could present a tripping hazard, especially as they have to be firmly attached at both ends to make good connections. It is therefore important not to have loose cables lying about. They should be carefully secured, bundled together and not run across the floor where the users or others could trip on them.

Weight hazards

Attempting to carry heavy items presents a weight hazard. Computers in the 1960s were so large that it seemed that the computer room had been built around them. Computers today have shrunk so that one technician can usually lift, handle and install them. Large monitors can still be awkward, however, so special care should be taken with them.

All people must follow standard good practice rules for lifting heavy objects. This is particularly true for PC system boxes and monitors.

Computer equipment is fragile. Circuit boards in particular are easily damaged by knocking or vibration. Dropping a piece of electronic equipment is very likely to break it or make it unreliable.

Before moving a piece of equipment:

◆ *switch off and unplug*

◆ *remove all attached cables between devices*

◆ *temporarily secure these detached cables so they do not become a tripping hazard.*

Look at the area around where your computers are.

1 On your own, list any hazards that you find there. If there are none, make some up.

2 In a group, discuss these hazards.

3 Produce a list of the hazards, with what needs to be done to fix the hazard, how much this might cost, in time or money, and the risk if the hazard is not fixed.

4.3 Injuries

Three common injuries arise when using computers in a bad working environment:

◆ repetitive strain injury

◆ eye strain

◆ bad posture.

Repetitive strain injury (RSI) is a generic term that covers a range of musculoskeletal disorders. It can affect the hands, wrists, fingers and arms when a computer is used a lot with a bad way of working. Relief comes with a reduction in the use of the computer and a better way of working, such as:

◆ resting the hands when not using the keyboard

◆ placing the keyboard and mouse at the right distance

◆ using a chair and keyboard at the right height.

There are a number of bad working practices that can lead to **eye strain**:

◆ The screen may not be at the right distance from the user's eyes.

◆ There may be reflected glare from the sun or lights when the screen is not in the right position.

◆ Flicker from the screen can occur if it has not been configured correctly.

◆ The display may be blurred if the screen is set to use too high a resolution. For example, do not expect a 15-inch monitor to handle better than 1024 by 768 pixels.

◆ Failure to use glasses when prescribed for computer work can cause eye strain. Businesses are required to provide eye tests for employees who are frequent computer users.

Bad posture when using a computer can lead to pain in the back, neck, shoulders or arms. There are many causes.

◆ The user, the keyboard and the screen may not be in a line.

◆ The user may be sitting at an angle on to the screen and keyboard.

◆ There may be no footrest.

◆ The user may be sitting at the wrong height for the keyboard.

◆ The user may be sitting at the wrong distance from the keyboard.

If the user has a chair that has an adjustable height and can easily move, this helps him or her to change posture to a more comfortable one. The user should also swivel and tilt the screen to where it is comfortable. The law requires that all modern screens can do this.

4.4 Cleaning

In general, IT equipment should be cleaned and treated in a similar way to other electronic office equipment. However, there are some extra guidelines that the user should follow.

◆ Screens should be cleaned with anti-static wipes so that there is no grease on them.

◆ Particles of food and dust should be removed from keyboards so that they don't interfere with the electrical contacts betweens the keys.

◆ Occasionally, a wired mouse should be opened up and any dust removed from the mouse ball. This removes one cause of jerky mouse movements.

◆ When there is a paper jam in a printer, the cleaner should take care to remove all damaged parts of the sheet of paper before putting the printer back online.

◆ Do not attempt to clean inside the PC system unit. The user should only dust the outer casing to reduce the amount of dust that might be drawn into the PC.

Go out and try!

Do this only if your site allows it.

1 Clean each of the parts of a PC that you have access to.
2 Produce a status report on how clean, or otherwise, each part of your PC was.
3 In a group, compare your reports to see whether there is a pattern.
4 As a group, recommend whether there should be any change to your site's cleaning practices.

4.5 Ergonomics

Ergonomics, when used with computers, is about making the physical computer environment as easy and healthy to use as possible. There is no one right ergonomic design. This is because all people are different. Some are short and some are tall. Some have long arms and some have short arms.

People have different uses for their computer and so different ergonomic factors become important. Table 3.4 shows examples of the top ergonomic priority item for each type of use.

Table 3.4 *Ergonomic priorities*	
Type of use	**Priority**
Word processing	Keyboard/mouse
Surfing the Internet	Mouse
Graphic design	Mouse
Data entry	Numeric keypad or keyboard
Games	Keyboard/mouse/game peripheral

Note

The International Ergonomics Association has produced this definition.

'Ergonomics (or human factors) is the scientific discipline concerned with the understanding of interactions among humans and other elements of a system, and the profession that applies theory, principles, data and methods to design in order to optimise human well-being and overall system performance.'

Go out and try!

This is a group activity using one PC.

1 For each of you in turn, position yourselves most comfortably at the PC.
2 Measure the height of the chair, the distance from the keyboard and the angle to the horizontal between the screen and the eyes.
3 Discuss why each of you has different results.
4 Return to the PC. What does it feel like when you use the PC furniture set more appropriately for someone else?

4.6 Legislation

Over the last 40 years, many laws have been introduced to improve heath and safety at work. It is the law that the employer must ensure safety at work for all employees. Employees also have to do their part as well. They must not put themselves or their colleagues in danger.

There are four main Acts or Regulations that affect the computer world in the UK.

The Health & Safety at Work Act 1974

The Health & Safety at Work Act is the main piece of law in work safety. Under it, the employer has to take reasonable steps to ensure the health, safety and welfare of employees at work. If they don't, then they are breaking the law. An employee may also sue the employer for personal injury.

An employer has to assess the level of risk compared to the cost of eliminating that risk. This is to show whether the employer's action, or lack of it, is *reasonable*. The employer's responsibility is usually to provide:

◆ safe plant and machinery

◆ safe premises

◆ a safe system of work

◆ competent, suitably trained and supervised staff.

Some groups of employees may need more care and supervision than others. Examples of these groups are disabled workers, pregnant workers and illiterate workers. The employer must consult on safety matters with employees, either:

◆ directly

◆ or through an elected health and safety representative

◆ or through a trade-union appointed safety representative.

An employer should have a written code of safety conduct, rules regarding safety training and supervision, and rules on safety procedures. There must be a health and safety policy in place.

Electrical regulations

The electrical regulations that affect computer work are the **Electricity at Work Regulations 1989**. An employer must assess the risks involved in all work activities involving electricity. This includes PCs, computers and those devices that are attached to them. The laws even cover home electrical appliances used at work, such as kettles. All this electrical equipment must be properly maintained.

Working with VDUs

The **Health & Safety (Display Screen Equipment) Regulations 1992** are the rules that control working with VDUs. These are usually known as the **Display Screen Regulations**. The purpose of these laws was to do something to prevent injuries such as RSI, fatigue and eye problems in the use of computer equipment.

These laws say that an employer must look at each workstation and surrounding work environment. The employer must make sure that the workplace meets the specified ergonomic requirements. The employer must provide to the employee:

◆ eyesight tests for frequent users on request

◆ breaks from using the computer

◆ health and safety information about the equipment.

Hazardous substances or COSHH regulations

The use of hazardous substances can put people's health at risk. To prevent this risk, the COSHH regulations control their use.

Note

COSHH stands for the Control of Substances Hazardous to Health Regulations 2002.

COSHH requires employers to control exposures to hazardous substances. This is to protect both employees and others who may be exposed from work activities.

Hazardous substances are anything that can harm the health of an employee when working with them if the substances are not properly controlled. An example of this control is the use of adequate ventilation. Hazardous substances are found in nearly all workplaces – factories, shops, mines, farms and offices. They may be:

◆ substances used directly in work activities such as glues, paints and cleaning agents

◆ substances generated during work activities such as fumes from soldering and welding

◆ substances that are naturally occurring such as grain dust, blood and bacteria.

For almost all commercial chemicals, the presence or absence of a warning label will show whether COSHH is relevant. For example, household washing-up liquid does not have a warning label. Bleach does have a warning label. So when used at work, COSHH applies to bleach but not to washing-up liquid.

Government advice for employers is to comply with COSHH in the following ways.

◆ Work out what hazardous substances are used in the workplace. Find out the risks to health from using these substances.

◆ Decide what precautions are needed before starting work with hazardous substances.

◆ Prevent people from being exposed to hazardous substances. Where this is not reasonably practicable, the employer must control the exposure.

◆ Make sure that control measures are used and maintained properly. Make sure that safety procedures are followed.

◆ If required, monitor exposure of employees to hazardous substances.

◆ Carry out health surveillance where an assessment has shown that this is necessary or where COSHH has specific requirements.

◆ If required, prepare plans and procedures to deal with accidents, incidents and emergencies.

◆ Make sure employees are properly informed, trained and supervised.

Almost all the things that go with a computer are not hazardous substances. Laser printer toner and typing correction fluid are the only hazardous substances most computer and office users see near the computer.

Go out and try!

1 Look in your kitchen cupboard or in the cleaning department of a supermarket.

2 List those products that are hazardous substances.

3 List the type of hazard that they are, such as irritant.

4 What safety procedures would you follow at home when using each of these products?

5 Compare and discuss your answers with your colleagues.

4.7 Fire doors, exits and reporting

It would be rare for there to be a fire either in a computer room or in an office containing PCs. However, standard office fire rules must be followed. This will keep to a minimum the effect of any fire.

In the event of a fire, the most important things to do are:

◆ start to move everyone to a place of safety

◆ report the fire to the fire brigade

◆ only then, if appropriate, tackle the fire.

Fire doors are the normal first line of defence in preventing a fire from spreading through a building. They should open in the direction of the exit from the building. Fire doors should be kept closed at all times except when someone is walking through them. They must never be wedged open. If a technician is moving bulky equipment through them, then they should have a colleague help them in opening the doors. Fire doors must protect all dedicated fire exit staircases.

Green signs showing an icon of a running man, a rectangle representing a door and an arrow identify **fire exits** (see Figure 3.10). Where appropriate this sign should be lit with an emergency light. This is so that the way to the exit can still be seen, even if the fire has already destroyed the electric power cables and there is no lighting.

Figure 3.10 The standard fire exit sign, always in green

So that they can be used in an emergency, fire doors and exits must always be kept clear and unblocked. Where they lead to the outside, it is acceptable for security purposes to have them open only from the inside, preferably with a bar push rather than a handle. For internal fire doors and exits, it is best that there should be no locking.

Reporting a fire

As part of their health and safety policies, all organisations must make it clear how to report a fire. For a small organisation, this may be as simple as calling the fire service on 999. The caller must know the full address of where the fire has broken out. The person taking the call at the fire brigade may be at the other end of the county. He or she might not have local geographic knowledge either of your town or of the buildings on your site. If the caller just says that there is a fire in classroom 5 at the County College, then the brigade does not necessarily know the details of the town, the street address, the campus or the location within the campus.

For large organisations, there may be special procedures. These may be to call first the organisation's switchboard or to report the fire to a control centre.

Reporting a fire hazard

Most organisations are required to have a Health and Safety committee as described earlier. Part of their responsibility is to react to fire hazards. They should consider what to do to eliminate or minimise the risk of fires. There is often a procedure for drawing hazards to their attention. The hazard should be monitored until it is fixed.

Go out and try!

This is a group exercise to review the fire safety of your building.

1 Follow one or more fire exits from your room. Do all the fire doors open outwards, are they normally closed, and are they indicated with a green sign? Record any that do not conform to these rules.

2 Look at the lifts in your building. What fire precautions do they have?

3 Look at the staircases in your building. What fire precautions do they have?

4 Investigate the assembly instructions for your building in case of a fire.

5 Investigate the fire reporting instructions for your building.

6 Find out the full reporting address of your building in the case of a fire.

7 Discuss this fire safety as a group.

Write a personal report on the fire safety of your building. You should say what things are already good and what could be improved.

4.8 Fire extinguishers

There are four classes of fire extinguishers, A, B, C and D, each meant for a different type of fire. Class A and B fire extinguishers also have a number that serves as a guide for the amount of fire the extinguisher can handle. The higher the number, the more fire-fighting power there is.

◆ *Class A extinguishers* are for fires in ordinary combustible materials such as paper, wood, cardboard and most plastics. The number on class A extinguishers shows the amount of *water* it holds and the amount of fire it can put out.

◆ *Class B extinguishers* are for fires in flammable or combustible liquids such as gasoline, kerosene, grease and oil. The number on class B extinguishers shows approximately how many square feet of fire it can put out.

◆ *Class C extinguishers* are for fires in electrical equipment, such as appliances, wiring, circuit breakers and outlets. Never use water to put out a class C fire. The risk of electrical shock is far too great. There is no number on a class C extinguisher. The class C means the extinguishing agent does not conduct electricity.

◆ *Class D extinguishers* are commonly found in a chemical laboratory. They are for fires that involve combustible metals, such as magnesium, titanium, potassium and sodium. There is no number on a class D extinguisher. They do not have a multi-purpose rating. They are meant for class D fires only.

Obviously, some fires may involve a combination of these classifications.

Water extinguishers or air-pressurised water (APW) extinguishers are suitable for class A fires only. They must never be used on grease fires, electrical fires or class D fires. This is because the flames will spread and make the fire bigger. Water extinguishers are filled with water and pressurised with oxygen. They should be used to fight a fire only when one is certain it contains ordinary combustible materials only.

Dry chemical extinguishers come in a variety of types. They are suitable for a combination of class A, B and C fires. They are filled with foam or powder and pressurized with nitrogen. Dry chemical extinguishers have an advantage over carbon dioxide (CO_2) extinguishers in that they leave a non-flammable substance on the extinguished material, reducing the likelihood of re-ignition.

◆ *BC.* This is the normal type of dry chemical extinguisher. It is filled with sodium bicarbonate or potassium bicarbonate. The BC variety leaves a mildly corrosive residue. This must be cleaned at once to prevent any damage to materials.

◆ *ABC.* This is the multi-purpose dry chemical extinguisher. The ABC type is filled with monoammonium phosphate. This is a yellow powder that leaves a sticky residue. This may be damaging to an electrical appliance such as a computer.

Carbon dioxide extinguishers are used for class B and C fires. They contain CO_2, which is a non-flammable gas. They are highly pressurised. The pressure is so great that it is not uncommon for bits of dry ice to shoot out the nozzle. They do not work very well on class A fires because they may not be able to displace enough oxygen to put the fire out. This causes the fire to re-ignite. CO_2 extinguishers have an advantage over dry chemical extinguishers in that they do not leave a harmful residue. This means that they are a good choice for an electrical fire on a computer or other electronic device.

Check your understanding

1 If your PC starts to smoulder, what type of fire extinguisher should you use to put the fire out?

2 If a wastebin containing only paper catches fire, what type of extinguisher should you use to put the fire out?

Go out and try!

1 Find out where the fire extinguishers for your building are located.

2 What types of extinguisher are they?

3 What sort of fire is each one designed to tackle?

4 Investigate your local procedures for notifying colleagues and the fire brigade of a fire.

Chapter summary

The following have been covered:

◆ the importance of a good working environment
◆ essential health and safety precautions
◆ common injuries
◆ cleaning
◆ ergonomics
◆ legislation
◆ fire doors, fire extinguishers and exits
◆ the reporting of hazards in the workplace.

Unit 4

Website design

This unit covers the basic principles to enable you to create and maintain a set of web pages. Assessment will be by means of a set assignment.

Outcomes

◆ Describe and apply the basics of web page development

◆ Undertake user requirements analysis

◆ Use appropriate development tools to implement web pages

◆ Test websites

◆ Use graphics software to create and manipulate images on web pages

◆ Publish and maintain web pages

1 Describe and apply the basics of web page development

Most of this unit covers the skills and techniques that you need to create and publish a website. This chapter provides you with some underpinning knowledge. Without this, some aspects of web design will seem very puzzling. It is easy to assume that the process of designing and creating a website is very similar to desktop publishing, but you will discover that there are many important differences.

In particular, you need to be aware of:

◆ the technical issues and limitations in creating a website

◆ the constraints imposed by the screens and settings that website visitors use

◆ the variations in browsers.

1.1 Screen resolutions and colour depths

A screen displays many dots of colour, known as **pixels** (derived from 'picture cells'). The number of pixels that can be displayed – expressed as width × height – is known as the **screen resolution**. It is usually possible to change the screen resolution, although there will be a maximum resolution for each screen.

PRACTICAL TASK 4.1

Find out the resolution on a screen that you are using. If you are using Microsoft Windows, select *Settings* and *Control Panel* in the Start menu. Select *Display*, and in the dialogue box click on the *Settings* tab (see Figure 4.1).

Use the slider to change the screen resolution. As you move the slider, you will see the resolutions that your screen can support.

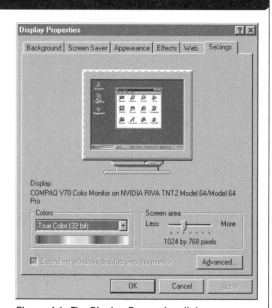

Figure 4.1 The Display Properties dialogue

Typical resolutions are 1280×960 ('high resolution'), 1024×768, 800×600 and 640×480 ('low resolution'). Note that they all maintain the ratio of 4:3. The 640 pixels width is rarely used these days.

Your choice of screen resolution will depend on the physical dimensions of the screen. For example, it is difficult to read text on a small screen set at high resolution. This is particularly significant for small laptop screens. A user with visual impairment might also choose a lower screen resolution to give enlarged images and text.

Designing websites for different screen resolutions

Websites should be designed to be viewable at all resolutions.

Scroll bars allow the user to reach the parts of a web page that are not displayed. But users are normally reluctant to use the horizontal scroll bar if a page is wider than the screen. For this reason, many commercial websites are still designed for 800 pixels width resolution. Other sites are designed on the assumption that most users have at least 1024 pixels width resolution.

Resizable web pages

The size of a **browser window** can be changed by the user, and it does not have to fill the whole screen. When a screen is set comfortably at a high resolution, many viewers take advantage of the extra space to display several windows at the same time. So they may well keep the browser window at a smaller size within the overall window.

This means that, even when used on a high-resolution setting, the actual display area of a web page cannot be predicted with certainty.

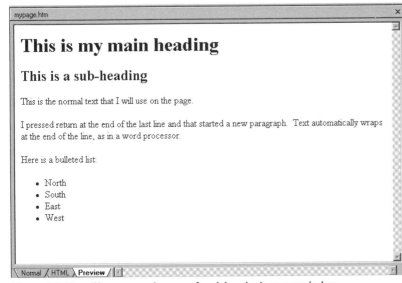

Figure 4.2 The effect on a web page of resizing the browser window

One solution to this problem is to design web pages that are **resizable**. Indeed, when you create a web page it is normally resizable unless you force it to fit into a fixed width. When the window is resized the text wraps around and images can be repositioned (see Figure 4.2). Many designers do not like working with resizable web pages because they cannot control the final appearance of the pages.

Colour depth

Figure 4.1 shows a control to alter the colours. The options are:

- true colour (32-bit)
- high colour (16-bit)
- 256 colours (8-bit)
- 16 colours.

True colour uses 32 bits (4 bytes) of memory to store the data about each pixel. Most screens today offer 32-bit colour. But when you design a web page you have to consider the needs of users who may be using lower colour settings.

1.2 Speed of Internet connection

Users connect with the Internet using either a **dial-up modem** or a **high-speed broadband** connection. The speed of the connection directly affects the time it takes for a page to be downloaded from a **webserver** to the user's system. If a broadband connection is shared by many users on a network, the actual download speeds may be much slower than expected.

Web pages should be designed bearing in mind the needs of the users with the slowest connections. The typical dial-up modem runs at a speed of 56 kilobits per second (kbps), which is equivalent to 7 kilobytes per second. This is the maximum speed that can be achieved by the modem, depending on the amount of traffic through the Internet service provider's servers and, in practice, many dial-up connections can be much slower.

When you download a web page you first of all download the actual page, which is a simple text file. The browser then interprets the code on the page, and downloads any images that are required. The images are stored as separate files on the server.

A typical simple web page may be 10 kilobytes in size and can download in a couple of seconds. The images on it can then take considerably longer to download. The process of requesting the image files itself adds extra time to the waiting period.

1.3 Web browsers

A browser is a piece of software which is used to view pages on the WWW. The most commonly used browser is Microsoft *Internet Explorer*, but other browsers, such as Netscape *Navigator*, are also used (see Figure 4.3).

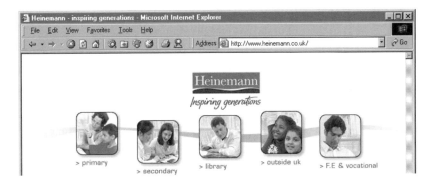

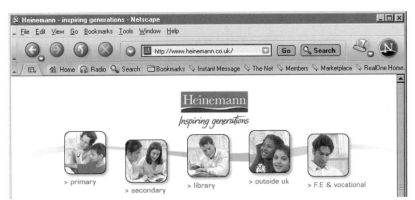

Figure 4.3 Internet Explorer *and* Netscape *web browsers*

Web pages are stored as files written in **hypertext markup language** (**HTML**). The HTML code is interpreted by the browser and used to generate a web page on the visitor's screen.

A browser does a number of tasks.

1 It sends a request for a page to the webserver where the website is stored. The request identifies the page by its uniform resource locator (**URL**) – often referred to as its 'web address'. The HTML code for that page is then transmitted over the Internet.

2 It interprets the HTML code and displays the web page.

3 It sends requests to the webserver for additional files that are referred to in the HTML code for the page. These could be for graphics or sounds. Each image or sound is transmitted as a separate file.

4 When the user clicks on a **hyperlink**, it sends a new page request to the webserver.

Browsers have been updated to match the developments in HTML, but it is important to realise that not all users use the latest versions. Web pages can appear differently in different browsers and in different versions of the same browser.

1.4 Hypertext markup language (HTML)

When you download a web page into a browser, the HTML code is transferred to your computer. This is referred to as the **source code**. HTML code is always stored and transmitted in a simple text file (an **ASCII** file). It usually has a filename with .htm or .html as its file extension – for example, homepage.htm.

In *Internet Explorer* you can view the source code by selecting *View + Source*. This usually opens up *Notepad* and displays the code (see Figure 4.4). *Notepad* is a text editor, and is the simplest means of viewing and creating text files. If you use a different browser, then you should also be able to view the source code from the *View* menu.

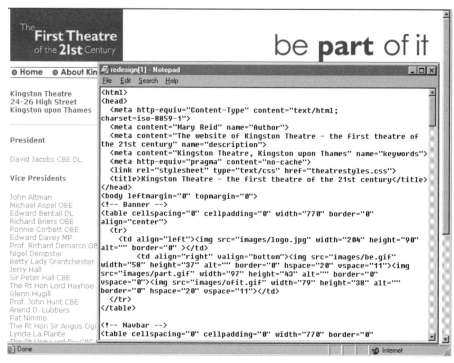

Figure 4.4 HTML source code displayed in Notepad

Checking the files used on a web page

If you scan through an HTML file, you will see references to other files that must be downloaded to complete the page. For example, you may see something like this:

```
<IMG src="http://www.thisismydomain.co.uk/pic.jpg" width=
          100 height=80 border=0 alt="My picture">
```

This tells the browser that it needs to download the picture stored as pic.jpg from the site www.thisismydomain.co.uk. You may also spot some links to other files that may be used, such as video or sound, or files that contain program code.

Web authoring software

Many websites are created using specialist web authoring software packages. These let you create a web page in much the same way as you would create a document in a word processing or desktop publishing package. The web authoring software then generates the HTML for you. You are free to look at the HTML code at any time, and to change or add to it directly. But it is perfectly possible to create a straightforward website, that meets its purpose, without knowing any HTML.

Macromedia *Dreamweaver* and Microsoft *FrontPage* are examples of web authoring software packages.

However, professional web developers often work directly with HTML. Some of the advanced features of websites can be created only in this way.

HTML editors

If you are a beginner then you are strongly advised not to use an HTML editor, but to use web authoring software instead. However, if you already have some skills with web authoring you may like to try writing HTML directly. You can do this in one of three ways:

1 *Use a simple text editor*. You can write HTML in a text editor such as *Notepad*. Each time you want to view the page you will have to save it, with the file extension .htm or .html. You can then view the layout of the page by loading it into your browser.

2 *Use the HTML editor in web authoring software*. Most packages allow you to edit the HTML code, and then switch to the page layout option to see what it looks like. This is the best way to experiment with HTML.

3 *Use a specialist HTML editor*. There are a number of packages on the market which make it easy to write HTML code quickly and accurately. These include Macromedia *Homesite*, *CoffeeCup HTML Editor* and *HTML-Kit*.

1.5 Pixels

Just like screen resolution, every image is measured in pixels. When you are preparing an image for use on a web page you should always be aware of its dimensions in pixels. Some graphical software offers you the choice of measuring the image in centimetres or pixels – always choose pixels.

You will also see that you can adjust many aspects of the layout of a page by referring to the size of components in pixels, such as:

◆ the thickness of borders and lines

◆ the width of cells in tables

◆ the margins around a page

◆ the spacing around an object

◆ the width and height of frames.

1.6 Graphics file formats

All images have to be prepared for web use, before they are inserted into a web page. Images are prepared by reducing them to the appropriate size, and by **compressing** them into one of the standard WWW formats.

When we use a computer graphic, we can refer to its size in two senses:

1 *The* **memory** *needed to store the image.* Most computer graphics use a very large amount of memory. For example, a photograph taken with a digital camera will be 2MB (megabytes) or more. On a slow connection, a picture this size could take half an hour or more to download from the Internet!

2 *The* **dimensions** *of the image measured in pixels.* It is important that an image created for a web page is exactly the right size for the space it is going to occupy. That ensures that it has no more pixels than it really needs.

Because of the memory requirements, all images used on websites are stored in a compressed format. Compression reduces significantly the amount of memory needed to store an image of given dimensions.

Two compressed formats are commonly used on the WWW:

◆ **JPEG** (usually shortened to JPG) is used mainly for photographs.

◆ **GIF** is used for most other images, but it is limited to 256 different colours.

Creating an image in a graphics package

There are many ways of finding or creating images to use on a website. You can use a simple package like Microsoft *Paint* or a more sophisticated one like Adobe *Illustrator*. As you will be saving it in GIF format, you should use only the preset colours that are offered to you. Once you have designed the image, you should reduce the dimensions (number of pixels) to the exact ones needed on the web page.

Figure 4.5 shows a simple image of a sprig of heather created as a **bitmap image** in *Paint*. *Image + Attributes* was used to set the page at 100 pixels by

100 pixels. The image was then reduced to 25 per cent of its width and height, by using *Image + Stretch and Skew*, before being saved in GIF format. The image can now be used as a small icon or bullet.

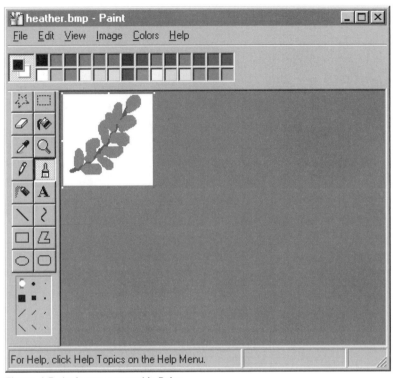

Figure 4.5 An image created in Paint

Using a photograph

You can either take a photograph with a digital camera or scan in a photo print. This will normally be stored as a bitmap image (.bmp), which is a non-compressed pixel format. You can then load it into a photo manipulation package, such as Microsoft *Photo Editor*.

Once again, reduce the dimensions to the number of pixels needed on the web page. Then save the photo as a JPG.

If you take a photo from a photo CD that was supplied when a film was developed, the images will normally be in JPG format already. You will normally need to reduce the dimensions of the photo, to something between 100 and 300 pixels wide. Save the image as a JPG again.

Figure 4.6 shows a photo loaded into Microsoft *Photo Editor* from a CD. The dimensions of the image are being changed using *Image + Resize*. The units should be displayed in pixels.

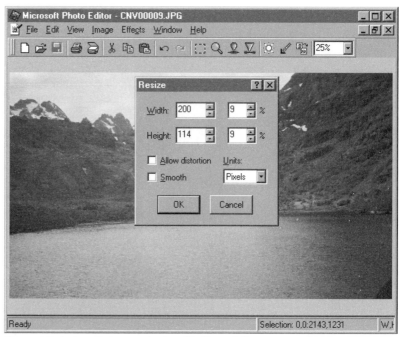

Figure 4.6 A photo being manipulated in Photo Editor

Obtaining an image from the WWW

You should never simply copy images on existing websites as the images will probably be protected by **copyright**. But fortunately, there are many sources of copyright-free images online. In many cases, the creators do ask you to acknowledge the source of any image you use. A search through a search engine will produce a bewildering choice, but you might like to start with www.freefoto.com and the portal site www.freegraphics.com.

1.7 Copyright issues

Writing, music, films and works of art are described as **intellectual property**, and the creators (or their employers) normally own the copyright to their work. This means that no one else may copy, print, perform or film work without the copyright owner's permission. In Britain, normally copyright extends for 50 years after the creator's death, and the rights extend to their heirs.

For many years, it was not clear whether copyright extended to software products. The **Copyright, Designs and Patents Act 1988** states that software (including websites) should be treated in the same way as all other intellectual property.

The copyright of a website belongs to the organisation that commissions it, not to the web designer.

Collecting and presenting information on websites

All content on a website should fall into one of these three categories:

◆ material created within the organisation

◆ material used with the permission of the copyright owner

◆ material that is free from copyright.

Permission must be sought before using text, photographs, images, videos, music and other sounds that have originated elsewhere. This applies whether they are found on a website or in books or recordings. Software used on websites, such as scripts in Java, Visual Basic and other languages, as well as Flash animations, are also covered by copyright. The copyright holders will usually charge for permission to use their materials.

In general, it is wisest to assume that any material published in any format, including on the WWW, is covered by copyright, unless it explicitly states that it is copyright-free. Copyright-free material is not necessarily cost-free, but on the WWW there are many sources of copyright-free materials which can be downloaded and used at no charge.

There are several other terms used for software and other materials in relation to their copyright status.

◆ **Shareware** is software that has been copyrighted by the originator, but is sold (or given) to users with permission to copy it and to share with others. Sometimes, the conditions of use prevent the shareware from being used for commercial purposes. Shareware may be offered free on an evaluation basis, but with payment required for continuing use. Many scripts are offered as shareware.

◆ **Open-source software** is software that can be distributed without restrictions, so that all users can view and modify the code. Open-source software is not necessarily free of charge. Originally, open source was known as free software – in the sense of 'free to share' rather than 'at no cost'.

◆ **Public domain** materials are items that are completely free of copyright and can be used by anyone.

Go out and try! Find sources of copyright-free, no-cost materials on the WWW that can be used legally on a website. You could look for images, photos, animations, literature, articles and music.

1.8 Example of web page development

This section is an introduction to creating a simple web page. Chapter 3 describes some more advanced techniques that you can use to enable you to develop a complete functioning website.

In a unit of this size, it is not possible to provide comprehensive instruction on web page design, but there are many books and online tutorials that can supplement your reading.

Selecting an appropriate web authoring package

Web authoring packages, or web page generating software, provide facilities that are very similar to desktop publishing (DTP) packages, but geared to the specific demands of the WWW. These packages give you a WYSIWYG (what you see is what you get) environment in which to develop web pages.

As you construct a web page in authoring software, the package generates the HTML source code. This code can be edited directly and can also be enhanced with **scripts** for dynamic effects.

There are a number of useful web authoring packages available, such as Microsoft *FrontPage* and Macromedia *Dreamweaver*. Another simple web authoring package, Netscape *Composer*, can be downloaded free with the browser, Netscape *Navigator*. These packages provide you with a complete environment which helps to automate the process of linking pages together to form a complete website.

Most of these packages provide useful page **templates** that can be used to lay out the content. A beginner can use any of these, although to gain a real understanding of how web pages are built it is better to start with a blank page.

Web authoring packages often provide **wizards** that can be used to create complete sites, with built-in themed graphics and page layouts. Although some of the results can be quite pleasing, they are rather limiting. Websites produced in this way are sometimes difficult to modify and update, and they do look very similar to each other.

Finally, the templates and wizards in web authoring packages are very useful for creating quick design **prototypes** of sites, even if the final site is developed using more refined techniques.

In this section, all the case studies are based on Microsoft *FrontPage 2000*. Similar features will be found in later versions of *FrontPage*, and in other web authoring packages.

PRACTICAL TASK 4.2

When you launch Microsoft *FrontPage*, it usually opens with a blank page. If anything else is displayed instead, then click on *Page* in the *Views* bar (see Figure 4.7 – the left-hand side of the window).

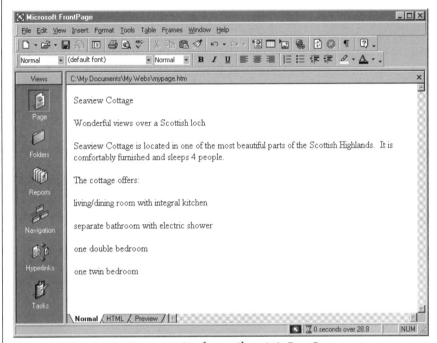

Figure 4.7 Entering text in page editor (normal) mode in FrontPage

Type in some text, as you would in a word processor, and then save the page, giving it a suitable name. All standard web pages are saved with either .htm or .html as the filename extension.

Notice that the text wraps at the end of lines, just as it does in a word processor. Also, as in most word processors, pressing *Enter* starts a new paragraph, whereas pressing *Shift + Enter* starts a new line omitting the paragraph spacing.

FrontPage, like most web authoring packages, will allow you to display the page in three modes:

◆ normal (page editor)
◆ HTML
◆ preview.

You create the page in the **Normal mode**, and then you can check what it will look like when displayed by a browser in the **Preview mode**. At this stage, they will look very similar, but differences will emerge as you use more advanced features.

A web authoring environment includes a page editor and an HTML editor. As the page is developed in the page editor, the HTML code is being generated in the background. Web designers can work in either editor and can easily switch between them.

The environment also provides a means of viewing the page in a browser. Some provide a built-in preview mode, which gives an immediate impression of how the page will be displayed. Some website design environments allow you to specify a standard browser that can be used for previewing the pages. However, there are some differences in the way different browsers (and different versions of the same browser) do interpret HTML code, so it is important to check web pages in a range of standard browsers before they are published.

Understanding the HTML

The HTML code for a page could look like this:

```
<html>
<head>
<meta http-equiv="Content-Language" content="en-gb">
<meta http-equiv="Content-Type" content="text/html;
    charset=windows-1252">
<meta name="GENERATOR" content="Microsoft FrontPage 4.0">
<meta name="ProgId" content="FrontPage.Editor.Document">
<title>New Page 1</title>
</head>
<body>
<p>Seaview Cottage</p>
<p>Wonderful views over a Scottish loch</p>
<p>Seaview Cottage is located in one of the most beautiful parts
    of the Scottish Highlands.  It is comfortably furnished
    and sleeps 4 people.</p>
<p>The cottage offers:</p>
<p>living/dining room with integral kitchen</p>
<p>separate bathroom with electric shower</p>
<p>one double bedroom </p>
<p>one twin bedroom</p>
</body>
</html>
```

The markup codes placed between triangular brackets are called **tags**. Tags are *not* case-sensitive (they can be in lower- or upper-case). Most tags come in pairs – the start tag (e.g. <p>) and the end tag (e.g. </p>).

This is the overall structure of the HTML code:

```
<html>
<head>
</head>
```

```
<body>
</body>
</html>
```

Lines of text placed between the head tags are hidden from the visitor, but can be used very powerfully, as we will see later.

◆ **<p>** and **</p>** mark the beginning and end of a paragraph.

◆ ** ** is an abbreviation for non-breaking space and is the code for a normal space character.

◆ **
** (not shown here) marks a line break.

If you press the *Tab* (indent) key on the keyboard it simply adds a fixed number of non-breaking spaces to the text.

Using heading and paragraph styles

The page editor allows the designer to highlight text and apply styles from a style list (see Figure 4.8). This list is similar to the style list found in word processing packages, but it is initially limited to a fixed set of styles. The list will always include 'Normal' (or default), headings 1 to 6, plus bulleted and numbered list styles.

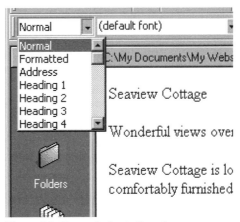

Figure 4.8 The style list in FrontPage

PRACTICAL TASK 4.3

In Normal mode, you can use pre-set styles with any of the text. The style list is found at the left end of the **formatting toolbar**, and the drop-down list displays the styles available (as in Figure 4.8).

1 Highlight the lines of text in turn and apply the Heading 1, Heading 2 and bulleted list styles from the style list as in Figure 4.9 ('Normal' is the default style for the page).

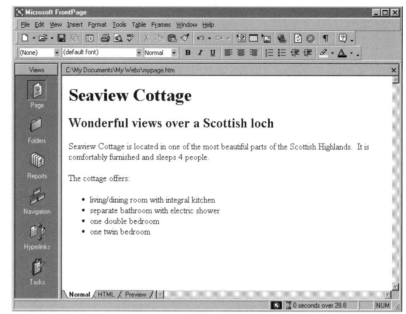

Figure 4.9 Headings and bulleted styles applied to the text

2 Check the HTML code to see what effect this has had.

3 In Normal mode, try replacing the bulleted list style with the numbered list style, and then check the HTML code again.

You may be tempted to use the other options in the formatting toolbar, and introduce other fonts, but try to resist this for the moment.

The HTML code for the body of the page uses a different tag for each style:

```
<body>
<h1>Seaview Cottage</h1>
<h2>Wonderful views over a Scottish loch</h2>
<p>Seaview Cottage is located in one of the most beautiful parts of
   the Scottish Highlands.  It is comfortably furnished
   and sleeps 4 people.</p>
<p>The cottage offers:</p>
<ul>
   <li>living/dining room with integral kitchen</li>
   <li>separate bathroom with electric shower</li>
   <li>one double bedroom </li>
   <li>one twin bedroom</li>
</ul>
</body>
```

◆ **<h1>**, **<h2>** etc. are the tags for headings 1, 2, ... in the style list.

◆ **<ul>** marks the beginning of an unordered (i.e. unnumbered) list.

◆ **<li>** is a list item.

All tags, such as <p>, use the 'Normal' (default) style from the style list, except those that have been specially defined.

Methods for formatting the text

There are several ways of formatting the text on a web page.

1 Using text formatting options on the formatting toolbar.

2 Using design themes.

3 Creating user-defined styles.

It is useful to know about all three methods, although the last method is by far the best.

A visitor's browser will be able to display a font only if it is already resident on the visitor's computer. So although a Web designer may want to use an attractive but obscure font for a heading, the visitor will be able to see the characters displayed in that font only if it is already 'on board'. If they do not have the required font then the browser will display the text in the **default font** for that browser. On a Microsoft Windows system the default font is usually Times New Roman, but the visitor can change the default font.

In web authoring packages it is possible to highlight some text and use the formatting toolbar to format it, making a selection from fonts, font styles, text alignment and colours. Unfortunately, if this method is used, every single paragraph and heading on every page of a website has to be individually formatted. This is a tedious process and some text can easily be overlooked. Worse still, if the web designer decides at some point to change the formatting – for example, to use a different colour for the main text – then every single instance has to be laboriously changed.

Figure 4.10 shows a formatted page. This is the HTML code for the body of the page:

```
<body>
<h1><font face="Tahoma" color="#0000FF" size="7">
    Seaview Cottage</font></h1>
<h2><font face="Tahoma" color="#008000">
    Wonderful views over a Scottish loch</font></h2>
<p><font face="Arial" color="#0000FF">
    Seaview Cottage is located in one of the most beautiful parts of
    the Scottish Highlands.  It is comfortably furnished and
    sleeps 4 people.</font></p>
<p><font face="Arial" color="#0000FF">
    The cottage offers: </font></p>
<ul>
```

```
<li><font face="Arial" color="#FF0000">
    living/dining room with integral kitchen</font></li>
<li><font face="Arial" color="#FF0000">
    separate bathroom with electric shower</font></li>
<li><font face="Arial" color="#FF0000">
    one double bedroom </font></li>
<li><font face="Arial" color="#FF0000">
    one twin bedroom </font></li>
</ul>
</body>
```

◆ **<font>** includes all the font properties that apply up to the next </font> tag.

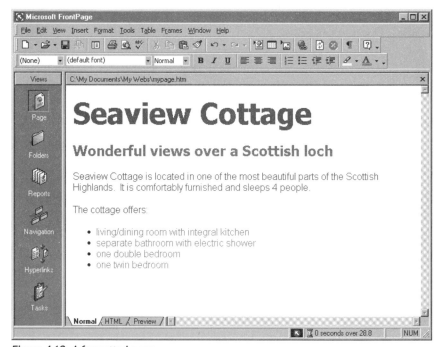

Figure 4.10 A formatted page

Using design themes

FrontPage and other web authoring packages provide predesigned themes that can be applied across a website. These themes initially look pleasing, so they are very popular, especially on personal websites. They do appear again and again on the WWW, so it is not advisable to use them, unmodified, for serious web development.

However, most elements within a theme can be modified, and this technique can be used to give an acceptable and distinctive appearance to a simple site.

When a theme is used, the HTML may not appear to change much. For example, in *FrontPage* a theme is simply referenced by a tag in the head like this:

```
<meta name="Microsoft Theme" content="sumipntg 011">
```

However, this is a bit misleading because *FrontPage* does insert formatting codes when the page is uploaded to the webserver.

PRACTICAL TASK 4.4

1 Open the page you created.

2 If you have already applied text formatting to the page, select *Edit + Select All* then *Format + Remove Formatting*.

3 In *FrontPage*, select *Format + Themes*. Browse through the themes and select one. You will be impressed by the immediate improvement to all your pages (see Figure 4.9).

You can go back to the Themes dialogue to change a theme at any time. You can also modify any of the elements of a theme by clicking on *Modify* in the Themes dialogue.

Figure 4.11 Using a FrontPage theme

Creating user-defined styles

FrontPage themes are useful for personal or very simple sites, but they should not be used for professional websites. Instead, you can define the styles for each of the styles that you use from the style list.

This process adds to the HTML code a list of the styles that you have defined. A list of user-defined styles is known as a **style sheet**.

PRACTICAL TASK 4.5

1 Open the page you were working on. If you have already applied a theme to the page, select *Format + Themes* and choose *No theme* from the list of themes. It should now look like Figure 4.9 again.

2 Select *Format + Style*. In the Style dialogue box (see Figure 4.12), select the h1 (heading 1) tag from the Styles list. Click on *Modify*.

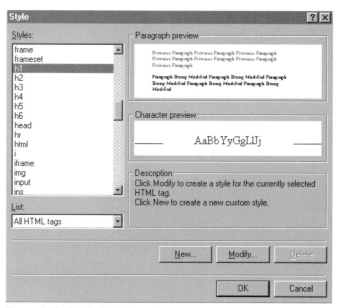

Figure 4.12 The Style dialogue box

3 In the Modify Style dialogue (see Figure 4.13), click on *Format*, then select *Font*.

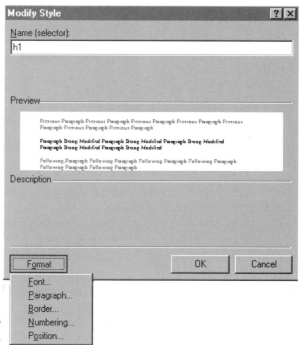

Figure 4.13 Modifying a style

4 In the Font dialogue box (see Figure 4.14), select from the font options that you want for h1, then click on *OK*.

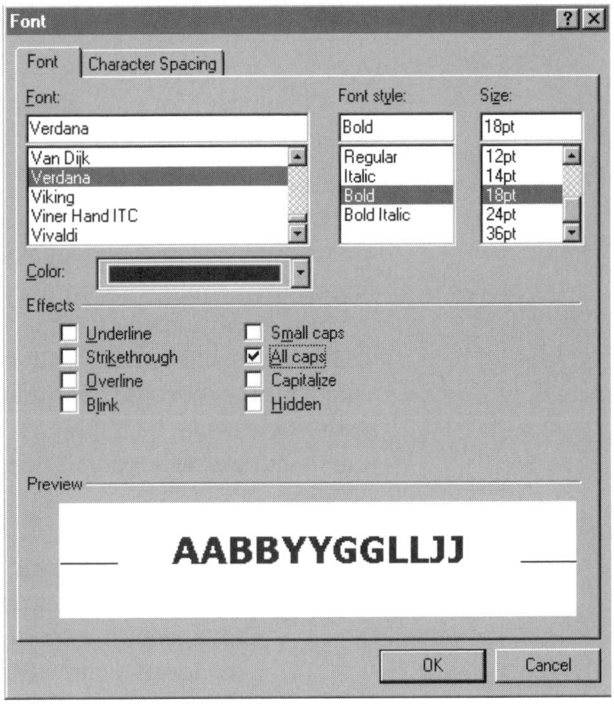

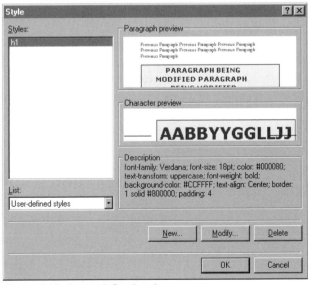

Figure 4.14 The Font style dialogue box

5 Back in the Modify Style dialogue, click on *Format*, then explore the other formatting options open to you.

6 When you have defined one style, you will observe h1 listed as a user-defined style (see Figure 4.15).

Figure 4.15 A user-defined style

> **7** To define another style, click on *List:* and select *All HTML tags*. Find the tag you want to define and repeat the process. Don't forget to format the styles for p and li.

Figure 4.16 on the next page shows a Web page with user-defined styles. The HTML for the page looks like this:

```
<html>
<head>
<meta http-equiv="Content-Language" content="en-gb">
<meta http-equiv="Content-Type" content="text/html;
    charset=windows-1252">
<meta name="GENERATOR" content="Microsoft FrontPage 4.0">
<meta name="ProgId" content="FrontPage.Editor.Document">
<title>New Page 1</title>
<meta name="Microsoft Theme" content="none">
<style>
    <!--
    h1   {font-family: Verdana; font-size: 18pt; color: #000080;
            text-transform: uppercase; font-weight: bold;
            background-color: #CCFFFF; text-align: center;
            border: 1 solid #800000; padding: 4;}
    h2   {font-family: Tahoma; font-size: 14pt; color: #800000;
            text-align: center; font-weight: bold;}
    p {font-family: Arial; font-size: 12pt; color: #000080;}
    li {font-family: Arial; font-size: 12pt; color: #000080;
            text-align: left;  list-style-type: square;}
    -->
</style>
</head>

<body>
<h1>Seaview Cottage</h1>
<h2>Wonderful views over a Scottish loch</h2>
<p>Seaview Cottage is located in one of the most beautiful parts
    of the ScottishHighlands.  It is comfortably furnished
    and sleeps 4 people.</p>
<p>The cottage offers:</p>
<ul>
    <li>living/dining room with integral kitchen</li>
    <li>separate bathroom with electric shower</li>
    <li>one double bedroom </li>
    <li>one twin bedroom</li>
</ul>
</body>

</html>
```

The code between the <style> tags lists the chosen styles for each tag. You can edit this directly in HTML if you like.

A style sheet like this opens up many more possibilities, beyond the scope of this book. They can also be used with any web development software, whereas the themes were specific to *FrontPage*.

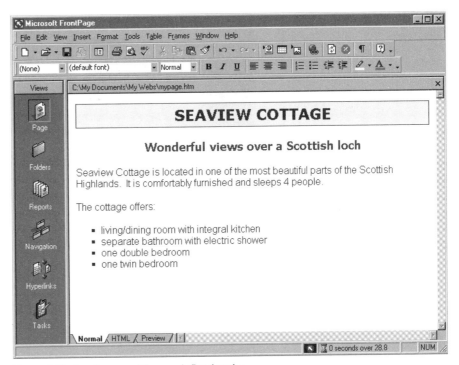

Figure 4.16 A web page with user-defined styles

Adding an image to the page

You can add an image to the page, provided it is already in JPG or GIF format. Some web authoring packages – including *FrontPage* – will convert the images for you, but it is much better to retain control over the process yourself.

Check that each image has the correct dimensions, in pixels, and does not take up too much memory.

PRACTICAL TASK 4.6

1 Open the page you are working on. In Normal view, click at the position on the page where you want to place an image.

2 Select *Insert + Picture + From File*. Find the prepared image and insert it (see Figure 4.17).

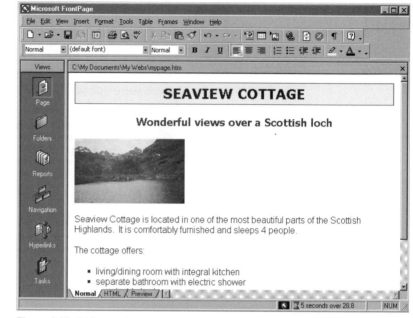

Figure 4.17 Adding a photo to a page

Adding a horizontal line and a background colour

A **horizontal line** can be added to the page, usually using the Insert menu on the web authoring package. The tag for this is simply **<hr>**, for horizontal rule, and there is no end tag in this case. The colour of the line can be set up in a style sheet, so will apply to all the lines you insert.

The colour of the **background** can be changed. This can often be done through a Page Properties dialogue, but in general it is better to do it through the Style dialogue.

Most web authoring packages offer a palette of colours. The HTML adds the 'bgcolor' attribute to the <body> tag:

    <body bgcolor="#FFFF00">

◆ **bgcolor** gives the background colour, with the value expressed either as a six-digit hexadecimal code (e.g. "#FFFF00"), or as an RGB code (e.g. "rgb(255, 255, 0)"), or as a standard colour word (e.g. "yellow").

PRACTICAL TASK 4.7

1 In *FrontPage*, use *Insert + Horizontal Line* to add a standard grey line that extends across the page.

2 Use *Format + Style* to change the colour of any lines you insert. Select the <hr> tag. Use the *Border* option and select the *Shading* tab. The Foreground colour will give the colour of the line.

3 To change the colour of the background on a page, select *Format + Style*, then select the body tag. Again, use the *Border* option and select the *Shading* tab.

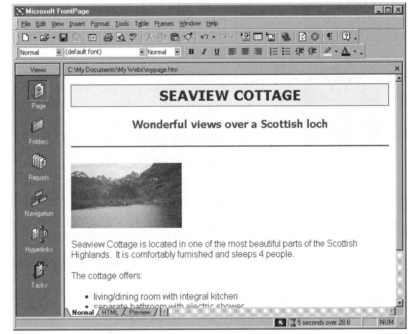

Figure 4.18 Background and a horizontal line inserted

Chapter summary

◆ The appearance of a web page is affected by the screen resolution, colour depth and the size of the browser window on the visitor's system. The speed of the Internet connection determines the time taken for the page to appear.

◆ Web pages are coded in HTML, and you can create pages using an HTML editor or by using web authoring software which generates the code for you.

◆ Images should be prepared for use on websites, by reducing the dimensions to those needed on screen, and by compressing the image.

◆ Most material used on websites is subject to copyright legislation.

◆ Web authoring packages provide a page editor, plus templates, wizards and design themes to help you create pages. A style sheet can be used to define the styles used on a web page.

2 Undertake user requirements analysis

As with any other software project, the development of a website must be taken through the usual stages of analysis, design, implementation and evaluation (review). **User interfaces**, which are of particular importance for websites, are usually developed with **user-centred design** methods.

What does it mean?

*User-centred design is an approach to the design and implementation of software, especially the user interface, that involves the user at every stage of the project. At the design stage, a **prototype** is created which is reviewed by the user and alternative designs developed in response.*

The term 'user' is a bit ambiguous in this situation. It can refer to both the client who commissions the website, and the end user who visits it. In practice, both are involved, although the client is the main 'user' who is considered. At the final stages of evaluation, typical site visitors can also be asked to assess the site.

The design process usually follows this pattern:

◆ user requirements analysis, which leads to a **design specification**
◆ prototyping and implementation
◆ evaluation against the specification
◆ technical testing and publishing.

In the first of these stages the designer must establish – possibly by means of interviews with the client – the purpose of the website and the target audience. The designer then creates a design for the project for approval. This chapter looks in detail at the first stage, with some final comments on the other stages.

2.1 Functions of websites

The first task within user requirements analysis is to establish the purpose and function of the proposed website.

Websites can be developed for a variety of purposes, and many sites have more than one purpose. Here are some possibilities:

◆ *To inform*. All websites provide some information, which is one reason why the Internet became known as the information superhighway.
◆ *To promote and sell*. Websites can be used to promote products and services to visitors.
◆ *To interact*. Websites can easily offer interactivity, allowing the visitor to send information and ideas back to the organisation and engage in dialogue.

e-Commerce is the term used to describe sites that offer online sales.

Types of website

Websites can be developed by a number of different types of organisation. Each will have their own combinations of purposes.

- Educational organisations create websites to inform and interact. One of the earliest uses of the Internet was by universities to circulate academic papers.
- Governmental and other public service organisations create websites to inform the public, and increasingly to provide a space where citizens can interact with decision makers.
- Commercial organisations use websites to promote themselves and also to offer online selling.
- Community organisations use websites to inform people and to interact. Some communities of people with a common interest exist entirely within the WWW.

Using a website to inform

Websites are an ideal means of providing information, so it is not surprising that some of the most visited sites are those that specialise in giving information to the general public.

External communications are those directed primarily at people outside the organisation.

Information sites include the traditional media such as newspapers and magazines, which have developed their own online versions, and television and radio channels. While it is possible to listen to radio and watch television over the Internet, these sites have taken on a life of their own, exploiting the specific qualities of the new medium.

CASE STUDY

BBCi

BBCi (www.bbc.co.uk) has become a channel in its own right and does not simply repeat material broadcast by the BBC. In addition to live radio and streaming video, it provides interactive features such as webchats and message boards, as well as up-to-date information on a huge variety of subjects. It is the most visited website in the UK.

You might like to look at BBC – iCan (www.bbc.co.uk/ican) which offers information and guidance for you to start a campaign, or join an existing one, about something that concerns you.

Figure 4.19 BBCi's logo

Many public services have sites, such as the well-used NHS-Direct (www.nhsdirect.nhs.uk), which specialise in communicating information to members of the public.

There are also a few online organisations that have built huge databases of articles and external links, which they then provide as a service to visitors. One example is About (www.about.com).

You may wonder how an organisation can afford to provide a free information service. You will usually find that these sites are sponsored by other businesses, and the advertisements they have paid for will appear in **banners** and **pop-up screens**. Some information sites, such as the government's DirectGov, are paid for out of public taxation.

Using a website to promote and sell

Many websites promote a service or product but without actually offering online sales. For example, most rock bands have websites that promote the band and their music, although visitors may not be able to buy albums directly from the site.

Many tourist attractions use the Internet to give people information about location and opening times and to encourage people to attend. Similarly, hotels often provide basic information even though you may have to phone to book a room.

CASE STUDY

Disneyland Paris

Disneyland Paris uses its website (www.disneylandparis.com) to show what it offers and to encourage people to visit (see Figure 4.20).

Try to find a few other leisure attractions that market their services on the Web. Here are some hints:

◆ schools, colleges and universities

◆ charities

◆ political parties

◆ churches and other religious organisations

◆ theatres and cinemas.

All these organisations are trying to persuade the visitor to do something in response and are not simply providing interesting information.

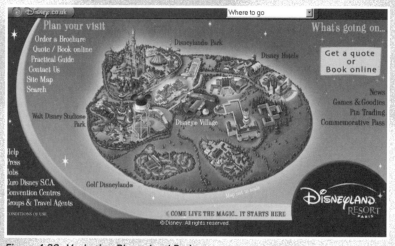

Figure 4.20 Marketing Disneyland Paris

Some promotional sites also offer online sales, and start to develop an e-commerce angle. The dividing line between promotion and e-commerce sites is not precise – the category depends on the *main* purpose of the site.

As the Internet has grown, so more and more businesses have emerged that exist only on the WWW. There are many examples of online banks, shops, travel agencies and insurance companies. These companies sell goods and services directly to the customer.

Customers normally pay for products online with a credit or debit card, and they need to be reassured that their payments will be safe. Online payments are usually routed through a **secure server** which **encrypts** all the data.

What does it mean?

*Data is **encrypted** when it is converted into a secret code. Encrypted data is decrypted when it is converted back to ordinary text.*

Goods have to be sent to the customer either by post or using a distribution company, and successful online businesses usually guarantee delivery in 24 hours or a few days.

CASE STUDY

Amazon, the online bookstore

Amazon describe themselves in this way:

'**Who We Are** Amazon.co.uk is the trading name for Amazon.com International Sales Inc. and Amazon.com International Auctions Inc. Both companies are subsidiaries of Amazon.com – a leading online retailer of products that inform, educate and inspire. The Amazon group has stores in the United States, Germany, France, Japan and Canada. Amazon.co.uk (see Figure 4.21) has its origins in an independent online

Figure 4.21 Amazon's e-commerce site for the UK

store – Bookpages – which was established in 1996, and subsequently acquired by Amazon.com in early 1998.

'What We Do Amazon.co.uk offers a catalogue of more than 1.5 million books, thousands of CDs, DVDs and videos, a wide range of software and PC & video games and a great selection of children's products in Toys & Kids! The site also hosts online auctions and brings independent buyers and sellers together in zShops, our online marketplace. In addition, customers have access to a variety of other resources including customer reviews, e-mail personal recommendations and gift certificates.'

◆ Use your usual **search engine** (e.g. Google) to find other e-commerce websites. Can you work out which types of business mainly have gone in for e-commerce? What types of business are rarely to be found on the WWW?

Some Internet businesses offer services which avoid the need to deliver goods. For example, online banking has grown very rapidly, and customers can view their balance, make payments and generally manage their accounts at any time of the day. Similarly, travel companies can send documents, such as ticket confirmations, by email and may not need to use the post at all.

In addition, many high-street chains now have online e-commerce operations as well. Large supermarkets offer a home shopping service which can be very helpful for people who are housebound, have young children, or lead busy lives.

Go out and try!

Use a search engine or **portal sites** to find a wide range of websites developed for organisations.

For each site you visit, write down:
◆ the URL and name of the organisation
◆ the purpose of the site
◆ the type of site
◆ a brief description of the content.

2.2 The target audience

User analysis for a website includes an assessment of the target audience. The intended audience may be the public in general, or it may be targeted at specified age bands (children, the elderly), communities of interest (members of a club, people who enjoy a leisure activity, researchers, political and pressure groups), geographical communities, shoppers, travellers, etc. Most sites are built with a typical visitor in mind.

One particular consideration is whether the site is intended for internal use only – by members of a company or organisation – or is intended to reach the general public.

Using an intranet

One way of restricting access to a website is to create an intranet. An intranet (note the spelling) is a closed system that has many of the features of the Internet but which is accessible only *within* an organisation.

An intranet is created on the organisation's own network system and can be accessed by users who log on to stations on the network. It will normally include email services and an internal 'website'. Strictly speaking we should not really refer to the pages as a 'website' as it does not appear on the WWW.

An intranet can hold confidential information that should not normally appear outside the organisation, as well as day-to-day administrative arrangements.

By definition, members of the public do not normally have access to intranets, but you may find that you have an intranet at your place of study.

Many employees travel around the country on business or work from home. They also need access to the company's intranet. The organisation may make it possible for them to access the intranet over an Internet connection, using an ID and password system to gain access. This is sometimes known as an **extranet**.

2.3 House style

The house style of an organisation is a key factor in determining the visual design of a website. Most organisations have a style guide which lays down the correct use of company logos, and specifies the colours, fonts, etc. to be used on all publications – including letters to the public. This ensures that the organisation's communications with the public have a consistent look and feel to them.

Most organisations want to carry the style guidelines through to their website. This can usually be achieved although there are sometimes some constraints on the use of specific fonts or exact colour matching.

2.4 Page layouts

There are several ways of controlling the layout of text and images, although it is not always easy to arrange items on the page where you would like them to be.

Using the picture properties

If you click on an image in the page editor view, you can usually display the image (picture) properties either by right-clicking or by selecting from the main menu. The alignment of the image can be set as 'right', left', 'top', etc. –

these are in relation to the text (see Figures 4.22 and 4.23). You can also set a border, or create horizontal or vertical spacing around the image.

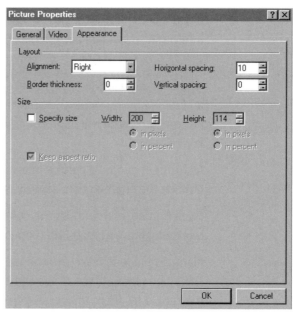

Figure 4.22 Setting the picture properties in FrontPage

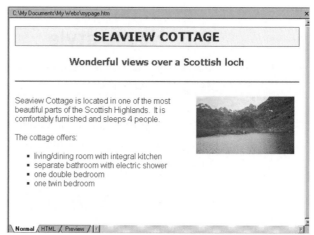

Figure 4.23 Using picture properties to lay out a page (compare this with Figure 4.18 on page 229)

Using a table

Tables can be created on a web page, just as they can in a word processor. But although a table can be used to display data in boxes in the traditional way, tables are more commonly used on web pages as a way of arranging text and images on screen. Often the tables are created without borders, so when the page is viewed in page preview the dividing lines are not visible. You can specify many of the properties of a table by clicking on it, then right-clicking or selecting the table properties from the main menu.

Using frames

The display in a browser can be split into two or more frames, each of which holds a separate web page (see Figure 4.24). This technique is often used so that constant information is shown in one frame while the contents of another frame may change. For example, a main navigation bar can be displayed in a narrow frame at the top or side of a page, with the main page contents varying according to which link has been selected.

Figure 4.24 Three common frame configurations

Note

*A **frame page** is a separate web page which will not be visible to the visitor. Instead it describes the structure of the frames in the window and assigns initial pages to the frames.*

2.5 Maintenance and future development

A website should always be designed with maintenance in mind. A community site that is run by volunteers should not aim to update the site on a daily basis, as that is unlikely to be sustainable. So, the site should be designed to look interesting without necessarily carrying immediate news.

On the other hand, an organisation might have ambitious plans for a site that will be updated several times a day. The organisation has to ensure that enough staff are trained to provide material and to upload pages, and that **fall-back options** are in place in case of staff absence.

Many large sites use **content management systems**, which allow non-technical staff to prepare web pages by simply copying text and images from elsewhere on their computers. These systems are often based on databases, which generate web pages automatically on demand, drawing on the data held in the database.

Major websites are usually redesigned every year or two, to take advantage of the progress of technology and the addition of new features to browsers. If old material is still going to be accessible from the site, there is sometimes a problem creating a new design that incorporates old material. Again, the use of a database that holds the raw content can solve this problem as the page design is handled separately from the content.

2.6 The essentials of designing a website

Based on the analysis, the designer draws up a **design specification** which is agreed with the client. The design requirements of a website can be broken down into three areas:

◆ content

◆ visual design

◆ technical design.

The **content** of a site covers all the information that it will contain, together with any interactive features. Certain information is essential:

◆ *How to contact the organisation.* This information should always be provided somewhere on the site. It may be offered through an online form, or an email address may be given.

◆ *Basic details about the organisation.* Visitors need to know something about the activities of the organisation.

◆ *Privacy policy* (if personal data is collected from the visitor). This is a statement about how the organisation will handle any information given to them by a visitor. This is necessary to comply with the Data Protection Act and to give the visitor the confidence to do business with the organisation.

The content part of the design specification should describe certain other features in outline.

◆ *The information that should be provided.* This should include text, visual information (charts, photographs, video, etc.) and sound (music, etc.)

◆ *The main categories of information.* These will identify the headings that will appear in the main navigation bar.

◆ *The style of language appropriate to the subject matter.* Business sites will tend to use more formal language than sites devoted to leisure interests. The age of expected visitors is also relevant.

As a general rule, visitors should not be overwhelmed with information that they do not want. **Links** can be given to allow visitors to **navigate** to more in-depth coverage of a topic.

What does it mean?

Navigation refers to the way a visitor finds his or her way around a website, using links provided on the pages. Text or images can act as navigation links, and image links are often called 'buttons'. Some of the most important links may be positioned together in a navigation bar.

The **visual design** of the site should specify:

◆ *overall impression* – it could be businesslike, friendly, busy, formal, casual

◆ *required components* – such as company logo or corporate colours

◆ *colour scheme* – background, text and spot colours

◆ *appearance of text* – consistent text styles, length of paragraphs

◆ *use of images* – for information, as decoration, or to create a mood or style

◆ *use of animation and video* – appropriate use to entertain and inform

◆ *layout* – of the '**home page**' and of subsequent pages.

What does it mean?

*Most websites open at an organisation's **home page**. This will set the scene for the visitor and provide essential links to the content of other pages.*

A website should use all its visual elements *consistently*. The main navigation bar should be accessible throughout the site, and should appear in the same position on each page.

The **technical design** concentrates on a number of usability issues.

◆ *Navigation*. Links are chosen for the main navigation bar, and a linking structure for all other pages.

◆ *Use of search tools*. List boxes, keyword search boxes and site maps can help the visitor to navigate.

◆ *Download speed*. A web page should download to the visitor's computer within an acceptable time. The page itself as well as all the images on it have to be downloaded individually from the webserver, so altogether they should not usually take longer than one minute to download using the slowest communication link. Larger files can be made available provided the visitor is warned about their size.

◆ *Browser compatibility*. A web page can change in appearance when viewed with different browsers. The designer will try to minimise these variations through his or her knowledge of the characteristics of each browser type.

◆ *Maintenance*. The site should be straightforward to maintain – that is, to update the content. The frequency of maintenance will depend on the purpose of the site.

Navigation issues

Internal links allow the visitor to find his or her way around the site. Unless the site is very small, you cannot provide links from any one page to *all* the other pages, so you have to design a **navigation structure**. You must consider how the pages are related to each other and work out what pages a visitor might want to see next.

Visitors can be divided into two types: those who are looking for specific information, and those who just want to browse. A site must provide links to suit both.

The website may naturally fall into a number of main sections, and links to the first page in each section should be given in the main navigation bar. This is an example of **linking by structure**. The structure of a website can often be represented in a tree diagram (see Figure 4.25). Here, a page is the **parent** to each of the pages below it in the structure, and is the **child** of any page above it. The child pages of the home page are particularly important, as they will always appear in the main navigation bar.

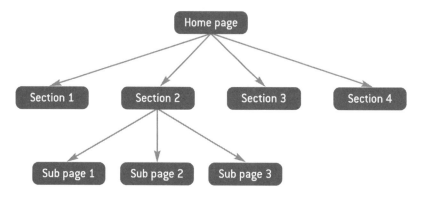

Figure 4.25 Tree diagram showing the structure of a website

CASE STUDY

Supermarket websites

Tesco (www.tesco.com) uses a strong structure to link its pages. The main navigation bar is shown as a series of tabs along the top of the screen and it appears on every page. In Figure 4.26, the shopping link has been selected and the first page of this section is displayed. The secondary navigation bar is down the left side of the screen and shows the links within the shopping section. The secondary bar is displayed on every page in the shopping section.

Visit www.tesco.com to see this for yourself. Also visit the websites of Tesco's main competitor supermarkets (use your favourite search engine) and look for common features they might have. Do their home pages provide clear links to what a typical visitor (or shopper) will be looking for?

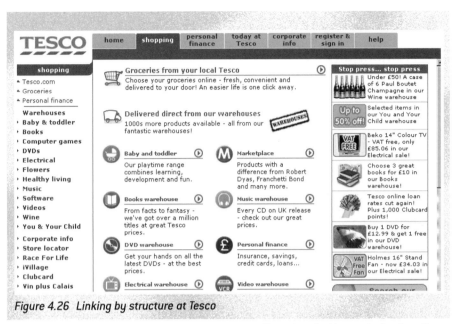

Figure 4.26 *Linking by structure at Tesco*

Reproduced with permission from Tesco

The WWW also allows visitors to browse to any page they like and in any order they like, so it is sometimes helpful to provide links to other pages that cover similar topics. This is called **linking by theme**. The diagram representing this type of linking will look like a random and rather messy network (see Figure 4.27). However, linking by theme helps the visitor who just wants to surf.

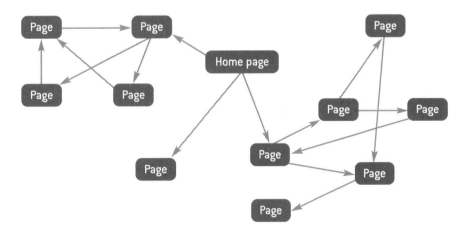

Figure 4.27 *The random look of a diagram representing linking by theme*

Many sites use a *combination* of linking by structure and linking by theme. Often a selection from the main navigation bar on the home page leads to a page that holds both the main navigation bar and a secondary navigation bar. The page also holds thematic links to other pages elsewhere on the site that contain content that might also be of interest to anyone who visits that page.

CASE STUDY

Combining linking styles

The page shown is from a community site, which features news, events and comments about the local area. It has a main navigation bar along the top, but it also has some thematic links in the right-hand column. These link to other news stories about crime and policing.

Check other news sites, such as online newspapers or TV channels, to see whether they use a combination of linking by structure and linking by theme.

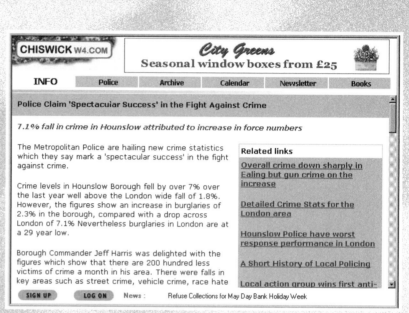

Figure 4.28 *Linking by theme as well as by structure on a community website*

A navigation bar can be placed anywhere on a web page. The main navigation bar is often placed horizontally across the top of the page, or alternatively vertically down the left side.

◆ If the main navigation bar is horizontal, then a secondary navigation bar can be placed immediately above or below it. Alternatively, the second bar could be placed vertically in this case.

◆ If the main navigation bar is vertical, it is quite difficult to place a secondary navigation bar alongside it. One solution to this problem is to use an **expanding navigation bar**. When an item is clicked a space opens up below the item revealing the secondary links.

Both horizontal and vertical navigation bars can be designed in **menu style**. When the mouse clicks or passes over the item, a drop-down menu reveals the secondary links.

A large site may need a handful of pages that contain little more than links to other pages. An **index** will list links to all the pages of a certain type. If the content of a site is managed by a database, then these indexes may be generated automatically. A **site map** is an index listing every page on the site.

Go out and try!

In *FrontPage* you might like to explore the facilities offered by the **Table of Contents** function. This can be used to generate both complete site maps and individual indexes.

Note

The 'three-click rule' is a good guideline to follow. A visitor should be able to find any piece of information being sought on a site with no more than three clicks of the mouse. That can be quite a challenge on a large site, but can be achieved with a combination of navigation bars, indexes and thematic links.

Prototyping and implementation

A **prototype** is a cut-down version of the site which can be used as the basis for a design review with the client.

The first prototype – known as a **storyboard** – is created on paper to match the design specification. The storyboard is usually sketched by hand. It should indicate:

◆ the layout of the home page and other pages
◆ the links on the main navigation bar
◆ the user of colour for background and text
◆ the use of images for information and decoration.

When the storyboard is reviewed with the client, discussion will often highlight aspects of the design specification that were overlooked or not specified clearly enough. At this stage, the client will often be inspired with new ideas for the site, and these can also be incorporated into the design specification.

The designer next creates a **computer-based prototype**, based on the agreed storyboard, using web design software. The design is then subject to review and amendment, and this is repeated until the client is satisfied. The prototype will normally consist of the home page plus a small number of sample pages (which may simply be in outline).

Once the client has approved the prototype, the remaining pages can then be fully implemented. The finished site must be subjected to a final review with the client against the original specification. At this stage any errors that emerge can be dealt with.

Technical testing and publishing

The website goes live at the moment when it is published – that is, when it is uploaded to a webserver and becomes accessible to visitors. Before that happens, the site should be subjected to thorough technical testing.

> # Chapter summary
>
> ◆ A design specification for a website identifies the type, function and target audience of the site. It should list the contents of the site, and describe the visual design, which is often determined by the house style of the organisation.
>
> ◆ The style and structure of navigation within a site should be covered by the technical aspects of the design.
>
> ◆ Page layout can be controlled using picture properties, tables or frames.
>
> ◆ Prototypes are used to demonstrate the design to the client.

3 Use appropriate development tools to implement web pages

3.1 Site management software

You need to be able to use appropriate software to manage the development of a site. It will be an advantage to learn how to use the software at this stage.

A website consists of pages that are linked together. A number of single pages can be created in a web authoring package, and the hyperlinks can be added manually. Alternatively, the website management tools that are built in to most web authoring packages can be used to automate some of the processes.

Site management software

The site management tools in web authoring packages do vary, but they often enable the designer to:

◆ manage the folders and files for a site

◆ view and modify the navigation structure of a site

◆ create and maintain navigation bars automatically

◆ check all the hyperlinks

◆ create a site map

◆ create a design theme for a site

◆ publish the site to a server

◆ manage a website project.

Setting up a website

All websites include one page with a filename **index.htm** (or index.html). This is the first page that any visitor will download. When a URL such as http://www.yahoo.com is entered into the address box of a browser, the browser actually searches for the index page, which in this case is http://www.yahoo.com/index.htm. On many sites, the index page holds the home page, although it can sometimes hold instructions for downloading other pages.

Note

A modern browser will add the 'http://' part of the address for you when it detects that 'www' has been entered.

PRACTICAL TASK 4.8

FrontPage provides a number of tools in the Views bar that help you to construct and manage a site. To see how they work, use one of the website templates or wizards to create an instant site. You should not use these whole-site templates for assessment work, but they are a quick way of demonstrating the principles.

In *FrontPage* each website that you create is stored on your system in a separate web folder. FrontPage refers to these as **webs**.

You should close a web folder by selecting *File + Close Web* or by simply exiting from *FrontPage*. To open a web folder, select *File + Open Web*, and select the folder name.

To get started, first close any pages or webs that are open. Select *File + New + Web*, then select *Personal Web*. To the right you will see a text box in which you can specify the location of a new web (see Figure 4.29). The default location for all *FrontPage* webs is in a folder called My Webs. The default name for a web folder is 'mywebnn', but you should change this to a meaningful name, such as 'personal'. *FrontPage* will create the folder for you.

The structure of the site will be created for you. The tools (or views) for developing the site are displayed in the Views bar.

1 Click on the Folders icon in the Views bar. *FrontPage* creates a new web folder and generates five web pages in the Personal website. It also creates _private and images folders specifically for this website.

2 Double-click on index.htm, then view the page in Preview mode. You can now explore the website. It is not finished, of course, but do not edit the pages. Close any open pages before the next steps.

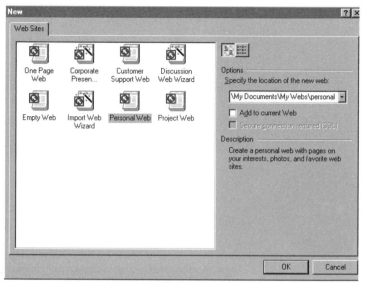

Figure 4.29 Setting up a new web in FrontPage

3 The Reports view on the Views bar lists some statistics about the site which will become more significant as your site grows.

4 You can see how all the pages are linked together by selecting the Navigation view (see Figure 4.30). You can edit any page by clicking on it in Navigation view, and this is usually the most convenient way of accessing pages. The Navigation view can be used to add new pages to your website structure.

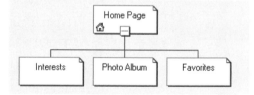

Figure 4.30 Navigation structure of a personal website in Frontpage

5 The Hyperlinks view displays links between pages (see Figure 4.31). Note the direction of the arrows in the diagram. On the left end of an arrow is the page which carries the hyperlink, and on the right end is the page or external website that it links to. Click on the '+' buttons to expand the diagram.

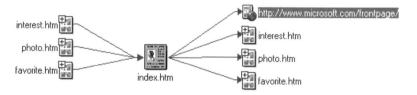

Figure 4.31 The Hyperlinks view of a website in FrontPage

6 The Tasks view allows you to list all the tasks that you have to complete and is a very useful planning tool.

3.2 Creating style templates

Well-designed sites have a consistent look, with the same textual and graphical elements repeated across all the pages. In creating a consistent design, the following design components should be considered:

◆ font type, size, style and colour

◆ background colours and images for page, table and cells

◆ graphic elements such as lines, buttons and images.

As we saw on page 221, the implementation of the visual design can be approached using three distinct methods – text formatting, themes (provided by web authoring packages) and style sheets. Of these, **style sheets** are by far the most flexible. They can also be created in any web development environment, whether you are working directly with HTML or using a full web authoring package.

Style sheets are particularly important for sites that have been designed in a specific house style. The pre-set themes that can be found in web authoring packages are not suitable. The style sheet should be set up at the beginning of the process, not added in later.

Using cascading style sheets (CSS)

You have already created an embedded style sheet, which contained the style definitions between the <head> and </head> tags (see page 226). This method is suitable for styles that apply to one page only.

When you create a full site, you will want to apply the same styles consistently across all the pages. To do this, the best approach is to create an external style sheet document that is then used by all the pages.

A style sheet is a separate page, hidden from the visitor, which is uploaded to the server along with the web pages. It contains a set of definitions for the styles used in the style list. In fact, any tag in the HTML code can have its own style definition.

The style definitions in a style sheet can be applied to all the pages on a site. That means that a simple change to the style sheet can have an effect right across a large site, and in this way visual consistency can be maintained.

A style sheet can be created in a web authoring package or in any simple text editor, such as *Notepad*. Sample style sheets are often provided as well, and these can be a good starting point.

Note

External style sheets are referred to as **cascading style sheets** *and have the file extension '.css'.*

If you are not using web authoring software, then you can simply type in the style sheet code in *Notepad* (or other text editor). Remember to save the file with the filename extension '.css', *not* '.txt'.

PRACTICAL TASK 4.9

In this activity, you will set up a web and create an external style sheet.

1 In *FrontPage*, close any open webs. Select *File + New + Web* and choose the Empty Web template.

2 Specify the name of this web in the *Options* box. In the example shown in Figure 4.32, 'sportsclub' is chosen as the name. Click on *OK*.

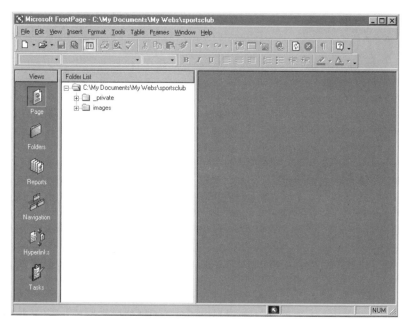

Figure 4.32 A new empty web

3 It is useful to be able to see the list of files while you are working on a page. Click on the *Folder List* button in the top toolbar. You can make the folder list wider or narrower by dragging on its border. You will see that the _private and images folders have been created for you, as in Figure 4.32.

4 Close the blank page called new_page_1.htm.

5 You will now begin to create a style sheet. Select *File + New + Page*. Click on the style sheets tab. Select one of the pre-designed style sheets, such as 'Capsules' (see Figure 4.33).

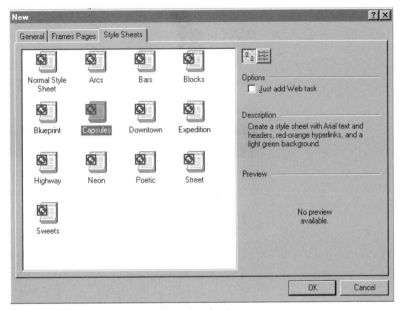

Figure 4.33 Selecting a pre-designed style sheet

6 The style sheet code appears, with a floating toolbar (see Figure 4.34). Have a look at the style definitions, but don't change them for now.

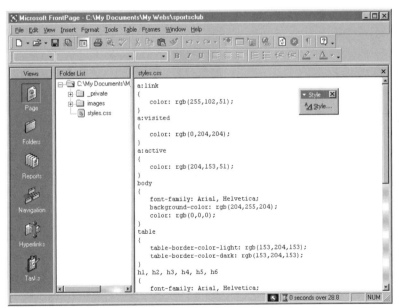

Figure 4.34 A style sheet

7 Save the style sheet as 'styles.css'.

Creating a template

A template is a pre-designed page that can be used as the basis for all the pages in a web. Web authoring packages provide you with a number of templates that you can use, but you can also create your own. These are all stored in a system file and are displayed whenever you create a new page.

If you are working in an HTML editor, then you can simple create a page, linked to a style sheet, and save it with a name like 'mytemplate.htm'.

PRACTICAL TASK 4.10

In the same web as before, you can now create a template that you will use for all the pages in the web.

1   Start by creating a blank new page. To do this, select *File + New + Page*. In the General tab, click on Normal Page. This is the standard page template. You are going to adapt it and then save your own template for this web.

2   On the blank page, type in some basic representative text. Apply the heading styles from the style list. Then add any text that will appear on every page in the web (see Figure 4.35).

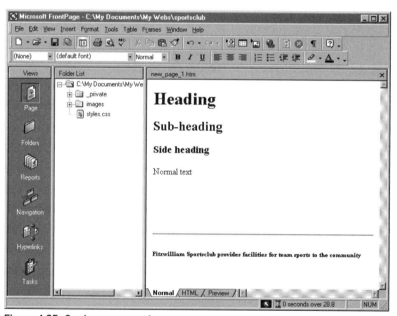

Figure 4.35 Setting up a template

3   Now save this page as a template. Select *File + Save As*. In the Save As dialogue that appears, select *FrontPage Template (*.tem)* in the Save As Type box. Click on *Save*.

4 In the Save As Template dialogue (see Figure 4.36), 'Title' will be the name of the template as it appears in the New Page dialogue. 'Name' is the actual filename (*FrontPage* will add the correct filename extension). 'Description' will also appear on the New Page dialogue.

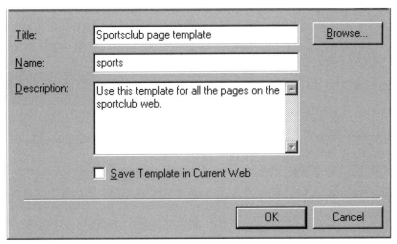

Figure 4.36 The Save As Template dialogue box

5 You now need to create a link to the style sheet from this page. Select *Format + Style Sheet Links*. Click on *Add*, then click on *styles.css* in the file list. Click on *OK*. Back in the Link Style Sheet dialogue (see Figure 4.37), click on *styles.css*, then on *OK*.

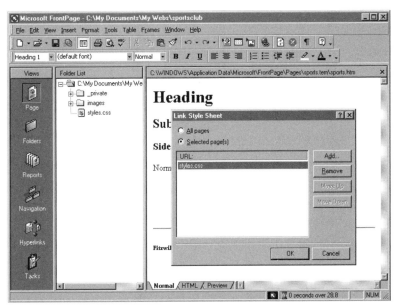

Figure 4.37 Linking a style sheet to a page

6 Click on *Save* to save the template linked to the style sheet. Close the template.

Using a template

When you create a template in a web authoring package, your new template will appear along with the pre-designed ones. Whenever you want to add a new page to your website, you should use this template.

In other environments, you can load up the template page and save it with a new name each time you create a new page.

PRACTICAL TASK 4.11

1   In the same web as before, select *File + New + Page*. Your template will be among the pre-designed ones (see Figure 4.38).

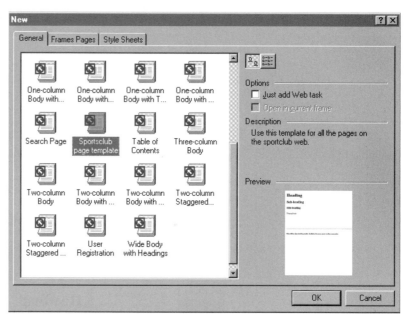

Figure 4.38   Using a template that you have created

2   Select this template. You now have a new page based on the template (see Figure 4.39). This will be the home page for the web. Add suitable text and save this as 'index.htm'.

Choose this template whenever you want to add a new page to this web.

Modifying the style sheet

If you check the HTML for a page created with a template, you will find this line inserted within the head of the page:

```
<link rel="stylesheet" type="text/css" href="styles.css">
```

You can make changes to the style sheet at any time. You will not have to change the template as it is permanently linked to the style sheet.

PRACTICAL TASK 4.12

1 In the same web as before, open the file 'styles.css'.

2 Click on the *Styles* button in the Styles floating toolbar. You can now modify any of the styles in the style sheet. You can also add new style definitions from the list of HTML tags. You will notice three tags called a:link, a:visited and a:active. These format your hyperlinks. Do not change them as you will meet them again later.

3 Save the modified style sheet.

3.3 Embedding images

Images should always be prepared in advance for use on a web page. There is more detailed advice on this later in the unit.

Images viewed on web pages are stored as independent files. This means that when a page is downloaded into a browser, the browser then has to download each of the image files from the server as well. So all the image files that are used on a web page are stored on the server alongside the page files.

It is common practice to store all the images on a website in a folder called 'images'. A web authoring package always provides a means of inserting images on a page, usually from an Insert menu.

PRACTICAL TASK 4.13

1 Open the web that you created before (Figure 4.39).

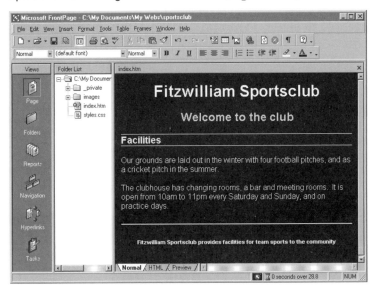

Figure 4.39 A page based on a template and style sheet

2 In *FrontPage*, in Normal mode, place the cursor at the point where you want an image to appear, then use *Insert + Picture + From File*. You will have to click on the folder icon in the dialogue box in order to navigate to the location where the image is stored on your system The image should appear on the page, as in Figure 4.40.

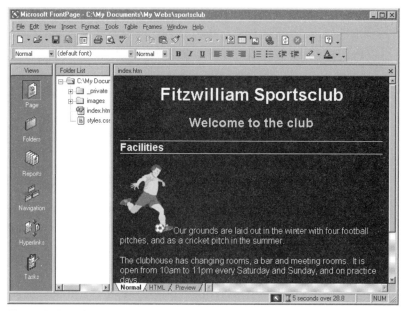

Figure 4.40 *An image inserted on to a page*

3 *FrontPage* has already created an image folder for you. When you next save the web, *FrontPage* prompts you to save the image as well, with the dialogue shown in Figure 4.41. The image should be saved in the images folder. If 'images/' does not appear in the Folder field, click on *Change Folder* and open the images folder.

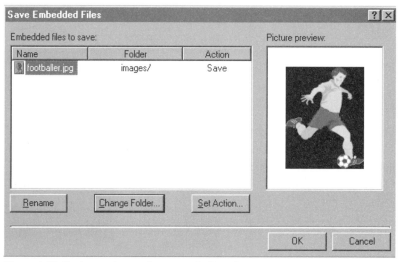

Figure 4.41 *Saving an image for a page in* FrontPage

Note

When you are working in FrontPage, do not use Windows Explorer to copy images directly into the images folder. You have to find them elsewhere, insert them on your page, then allow FrontPage to place them in the images folder.

If you are using another web authoring package, you should create an images folder alongside all your page files. You will probably (depending on the software) be able to place images into the images folder before you insert them into a page.

Changing the image properties

Once an image has been placed on a page, the HTML coding includes an **<img>** tag, such as:

```
<img border=0 src="images/footballer.jpg" width=100
  height=127>
```

Border, source (src), width and height are all **attributes** of the <img> tag. Attributes are HTML's way of listing the properties of the image.

◆ **src** is the filename of the image and its location relative to the page.

◆ **width** and **height** are the dimensions of the image. Altering these values will distort the image but will not change the memory needed.

Images cannot be manipulated as simply as they can in desktop publishing (DTP) packages, but further attributes can be added to the <img> tag. Most web authoring packages provide an image properties dialogue, usually accessed by right-clicking the image in Page Edit mode, and this generates more attributes, such as:

```
<img border=0 src="images/footballer.jpg" alt="A footballer"
  align=right hspace=10 width=100 height=127>
```

See the effect of these in Figure 4.42.

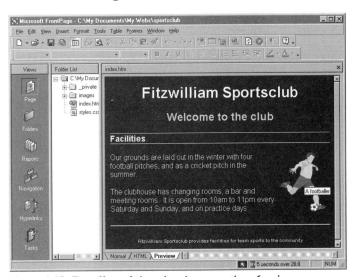

Figure 4.42 The effect of changing the properties of an image

◆ **alt** text appears as a screen label in a browser, when the mouse is held over an image (see Figure 4.42). This acts as a marker if an image is slow to download and it also provides a useful description to the visitor. Alt text is essential to make a site accessible to blind visitors, who will use **text readers** to understand the content.

◆ **align** positions the image relative to the text next to it. The effect depends entirely on where the cursor was placed when the image was inserted.

◆ **border** values greater than zero draw a border around the image, with the given thickness measured in pixels.

◆ **hspace** (horizontal)and **vspace** (vertical) create space around the image.

PRACTICAL TASK 4.14

1 In Normal mode, right-click on the image and select *Picture Properties*. Any changes that you make to the properties of an image will be listed as <img> attributes in the HTML code.

2 In the Picture Properties dialogue box, enter some descriptive text in the Alternative Representations text box. This is the 'alt' text for the image.

3 Next click on the *Appearance* tab. Do not alter the size properties, but experiment with the layout properties. All the values are in pixels. When you have made your selections, view the page in Preview mode.

Using animated GIFs

The GIF format can be used to create short, repeating animated sequences. Many examples of these are displayed on websites, and there are many free sources on the Web. Animated GIFs should be used, if at all, with very great care. The eye is drawn to an animation, especially if it lies on the periphery of vision, and can distract the visitor from the main content.

As a general rule, animated GIFs should be used only to draw attention directly to an item on the page, such as a warning, or to request a visitor to take an action straightaway (e.g. to confirm some input information), or for amusement.

3.4 Using tables

Tables can be created on a web page, just as they can in a word processor. A table can be used for tabulation – to display data in boxes in the traditional way. Tables are, however, more commonly used as a way of arranging text and images on the screen.

Web authoring packages provide dialogues for creating tables, usually from a Table menu. They also allow the designer to set the properties of tables and of individual cells, often by right-clicking on the table or cell in Page Edit mode.

It is useful to see how the HTML handles tables and their properties. The HTML code for a table has this basic structure:

```
<table>
  <tr>
    <td> </td>
    <td> </td>
    <td> </td>
  </tr>
  <tr>
    <td> </td>
    <td> </td>
    <td> </td>
  </tr>
</table>
```

Note the **<table>** opening tag and the closing **</table>** tag. This table consists of two rows each with **<tr>** and **</tr>** tags. Each row has three cells each with a **<td>** tag (for 'table data').

Note

The layout of the code is not important in HTML. What is important is not to forget to insert the closing </table> tag. Some very strange results will be seen without the closing tag.

Text and images can be inserted into any or all of the table cells, to give a layout like the one in Figure 4.43. This is the HTML code for that table:

```
<table width=600 border=1>
  <tr>
    <td>First cell in the top row</td>
    <td>Second cell in the top row</td>
    <td>Third cell in the top row</td>
  </tr>
  <tr>
    <td>First cell in the second row</td>
    <td><img border=0 src="images/car.gif" width=83
                              sheight=30></td>
    <td>Third cell in the second row</td>
  </tr>
</table>
```

The <table> tag can take a number of attributes.

◆ **width** is the width of the whole table, in pixels.

◆ **border** fixes the thickness of the border around the perimeter of the whole table.

First cell in the top row	Second cell in the top row	Third cell in the top row
First cell in the second row		Third cell in the second row.

Figure 4.43 A table with a border

If the border is given the value 0, not only does the outside border disappear but so do the boundaries of the individual cells. This technique can be used to create a page layout in which the text and images are arranged in columns with invisible borders.

Individual cells can be given their own properties, as in:

<td align="center" valign="top">

◆ **align** is the horizontal alignment (the default value is "left").

◆ **valign** is the vertical alignment, in this case placing the contents of the cell at the top (the default value is "middle").

Using tables for layout

Background colours and images can be set up for a whole table or for individual cells. In *FrontPage*, right-click inside the table, then select *Table Properties* or *Cell Properties*.

A group of cells can also be merged together for layout purposes. To merge cells together, highlight them in Normal mode, right-click and select *Merge Cells*.

Using these techniques you can create page layouts with columns, as in Figure 4.44. The HTML for this is:

<td colspan=3 bgcolor="#COCOCO" align="center" valign="top">

◆ **colspan** (column span) identifies the number of columns that a merged cell spans across.

◆ **rowspan** is used when cells in the same column are merged together.

This is a heading

First cell in the second row.   Third cell in the second row.

I can add lots of text to this cell and it will simply expand to take it.

I can add lots of text to this cell and it will simply expand to take it.

This is a good way of laying out a page in three columns.

Figure 4.44 A table has been used to create this layout of heading, text and graphic

Understanding the width of tables and cells

You may want to control the behaviour of tables by fixing the size of various components. The <table> tag can be given a number of size attributes, as in Figure 4.45. The HTML code for this is:

```
<table width=600 border=1 cellspacing=3 cellpadding=5>
```

◆ **width** is the *total* width of the table.

◆ **border** is the width in pixels of the border around the outside of the whole table.

◆ **cell spacing** is the width in pixels between the border and a cell, or between one cell and another, and is shown shaded in Figure 4.45.

◆ **cell padding** is the width of the space inside a cell between the edge of the cell and the text. The limit of this is shown by a dotted line in Figure 4.45, although usually it is invisible on the screen.

Figure 4.45 How the attributes of a table are set

In *FrontPage* you can set all these attributes by right-clicking inside a table in Normal mode, then selecting *Table Properties*.

The width can also be set for an individual cell in a table:

```
<td width=200>
```

or

```
<td width=40%>
```

Here, 'width' means the width of the cell *inside the cell padding*. It can be given in pixels or as a percentage of the total width of the table.

It is necessary to set the cell widths only for one row (any row) in the table, as all the cells in any one column will line up under each other.

PRACTICAL TASK 4.15

1 Open your web, and create a new page with the Sportsclub template. Save the page.

2 Select *Table + Insert + Table*, then enter values in the dialogue box as in Figure 4.46. Note that the width is given in pixels, not as a percentage. Check the HTML code.

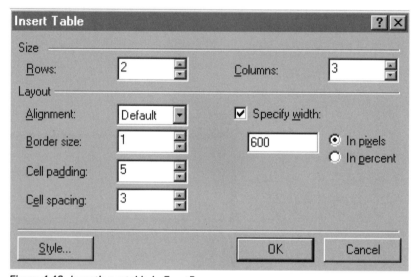

Figure 4.46 Inserting a table in FrontPage

3 In Normal mode, enter some text in each of the cells and place an image in one of the cells. Make sure that the image is a suitable width – preferably no more than 150 pixels wide. Then check the HTML code again.

4 Experiment with the table properties in Normal mode by right-clicking anywhere inside the table, then selecting *Table Properties*. You can add colour to the borders and change their appearance, and you can give the whole table a background colour.

5 You will probably have found that the individual columns varied in width as you entered the text. You can fix the width of each cell to prevent this happening. Right-click on a cell and select *Cell Properties*. Then specify the width as a percentage of the total width of the table – make sure that the percentages in a row add up to 100. You only need to do this across one row of a table, as all the cells in any one column will line up with the one that has a fixed width.

6 You can also fix the width of a whole column by dragging a column border to a new position. This action automatically adds a width attribute into every cell in the table.

7 Use *Cell Properties* to set the background colour for a cell in a table, and to align the text vertically (top, middle or bottom) and horizontally (left, centre, right or justified). Check the HTML to see how these are recorded in the attributes of the cells.

8 To add an extra row or column to a table, click where you want it to go, then select *Table + Insert + Rows or Columns* and make your choices. If you have added a column you should check the widths of the cells again.

9 You can merge all the cells in a row, but note that if you merge the cells where you have set all the width properties, that width data will no longer be valid. For example, you might want to merge all the cells in the top row to give a header that will span all three columns. Highlight the top three cells, right-click and select *Merge Cells*.

Using a table to fix the size of a page

All the web pages you have created so far are resizable. If you change the size of the browser window, the text rearranges itself to fit the window. This can sometimes have unexpected results.

You may want to have greater control over the layout of the page, so that all the elements remain in the same positions relative to each other. You can create a table with exactly one cell. This then holds the complete contents of the page. If the width of the cell is fixed in pixels then its appearance will be much more consistent.

The width of a page can be fixed, and the best width to use is 800 pixels. In practice, the width of the scroll bar to the right of the page uses up some of the screen width, so it is better to set the width at 780 pixels. A table of width 780 pixels can be used as a container for a full page.

When the page is viewed in a higher resolution, the table can either be positioned to the left of the window, leaving space to the right, or it can be positioned in the centre of the window with empty space on each side. Either solution is acceptable, but the preference should be set in the table properties.

PRACTICAL TASK 4.16

1 In *FrontPage*. start a new page. Insert a table 780 pixels wide and aligned to the left. It should have one row and one column. The border of the table should be of zero width. The cell padding and cell spacing can be any value (see Figure 4.47).

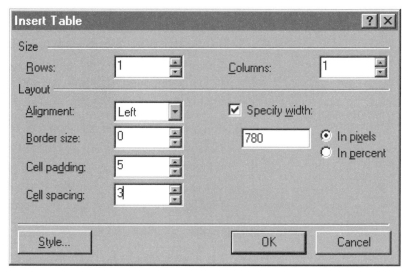

Figure 4.47 The Insert Table dialogue box

2 To see what is happening, use the Table Properties dialogue to give the table a background colour. In Preview mode, you will see that there are still white margins to the top and to the left side of the page.

3 Right click, select *Page Properties*, then click on the *Margins* tab, and set the top and left margins to 0 (see Figure 4.48).

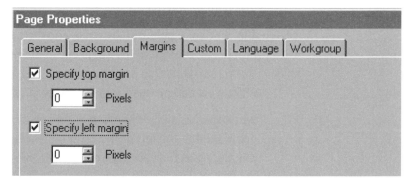

Figure 4.48 The Page Properties dialogue box

4 Although you have aligned the table to the left, you may prefer to align it to the centre. Try it.

You can now treat the single table as the boundary for the whole page. You may want to change the page background so that any extra space showing to the right of the table in higher resolutions matches the table itself, or you may prefer to use a contrasting colour.

Note

Tables can be placed within *the main table, but do make sure that they are not too wide to fit on the page.*

3.5 Using bookmarks

Hyperlinks can be used to link to:

◆ another position on the same page
◆ another page on the same website
◆ another website.

Creating hyperlinks to bookmarks

In a browser, a hyperlink can jump to an invisible bookmark placed elsewhere on a page. Using a page editor, bookmarks can be set anywhere on a page. In the HTML code a bookmark is denoted with the **<a>** tag (standing for 'anchor') which has a name attribute to identify it. In the next example, a heading with the title 'First section' has been bookmarked so that a hyperlink somewhere else on the page can link to it:

```
<h2><a name="First section">First section</a></h2>
```

The text that is to become the hyperlink is then highlighted by the browser and formatted as a link. By default, hyperlinks take on a familiar appearance, with underlined blue text, but that can be changed.

The HTML code for the hyperlink itself uses the **<a>** tag again and looks like this:

```
<p><a href="#First section">Link to first section</a></p>
```

href (standing for 'hyperlink reference') states the location that the hyperlink links to. In this case, '#First section' is the name of the bookmark where it links to, with the # (hash) used to identify it as a bookmark.

Images can also be used as hyperlinks – these are often referred to as **buttons**. The HTML for a graphical hyperlink looks like this:

```
<p><a href="#First section"><img border=0 src=
"images/mybutton.gif" width=120 height=30></a></p>
```

PRACTICAL TASK 4.17

1 Start a new web. For clarity, the examples are created without a style sheet or template, but you may like to add them.

2 Create a new page and enter text similar to that in Figure 4.49, with three distinct sections, each with a subheading. The three lines below the main heading will become hyperlinks to the content further down the page.

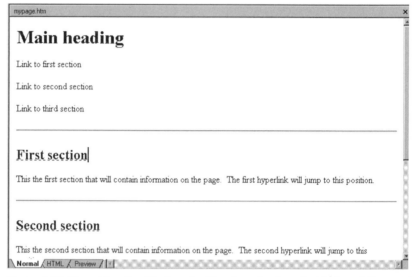

Figure 4.49 The subheading 'First section' has been bookmarked in Page Editor mode

3 To insert a bookmark, highlight the subheading to be bookmarked, then select *Insert + Bookmark*. By default, this gives the bookmark the same name as the subheading. A bookmark is displayed in Normal mode by a dotted underlining (as in Figure 4.49), but is invisible in Preview mode.

4 The hyperlink to a bookmark is inserted by highlighting the text – 'Link to first section' – that will act as the hyperlink, and then selecting *Insert + Hyperlink*. In the dialogue box, the relevant bookmark is selected from the Bookmark list, as in Figure 4.50.

Figure 4.50 Selecting a bookmark that the hyperlink will link to in FrontPage

5 Add the remaining hyperlinks, and then try them out in Preview mode (see Figure 4.51).

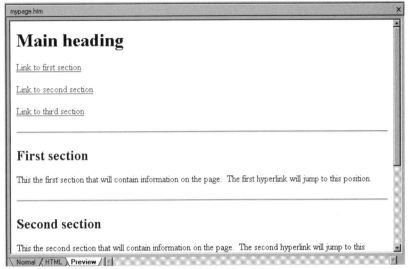

Figure 4.51 Hyperlinks to bookmarks on the same page

6 To make a graphical hyperlink, insert a suitable image, then highlight it and use *Insert + Hyperlink* in exactly the same way as you did with text.

3.6 Using hyperlinks

On the WWW, the links between pages create one vast global network. An individual site will ensure that the visitor explores what the site has to offer by offering internal links to other pages on the same site, and may have external links to other sites.

All web authoring packages allow the designer to convert text or an image into a hyperlink. Usually the Insert or Format menu includes a Hyperlink item which launches a dialogue box. The HTML code for a link to a page called 'news.htm' looks like this:

```
<a href=news.htm>Latest news</a>
```

When an image is used as a button instead of text for a hyperlink, the code will look like this:

```
<a href="news.htm"><img border=0 src="images/newsbutton.gif"
width=120 height=30> Latest news</a>
```

PRACTICAL TASK 4.18

In this activity, you will create a web for a fast-food outlet using *FrontPage*'s site management tools. The home page will give basic information, such as the name, address and telephone number, and details of the delivery service.

A second page will contain the food menu, and a third page will list job vacancies in the company.

The examples are created without a style sheet or template, but you may like to add them.

1 Close any open webs, then select *File + New + Web* and create a new One Page Web. If you cannot see the folder list, click on the *Folder List* button. The index (home) page has been created for you. Double-click on the index page and it will open in Normal view.

2 Simply enter the name and address and any other text, as in Figure 4.52, and save the page.

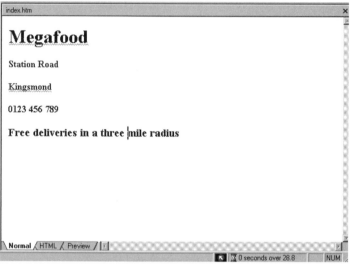

Figure 4.52 *An index page for a site for a fast-food business*

3 Now use *File + New + Page* to create two more pages in Normal view. Save them as 'menu.htm' and 'jobs.htm'. Add a small amount of suitable text to each and re-save them. You can use a table to hold the menu, as in Figure 4.53.

Figure 4.53 *The folder list in* FrontPage, *and a basic page*

Using site management tools to create navigation bars

Site management tools usually assume that the site has a **tree structure**. They can sometimes generate and insert one or more navigation bars on a page on demand. Any additional links must be created individually on the page.

Figure 4.54 shows the Navigation Bar Properties dialogue in *FrontPage*, which offers a number of options. The 'Child pages under Home' option creates the main navigation bar and this can be placed on each page, together with a link to the home page. A secondary navigation bar can be inserted using the 'Same level' option.

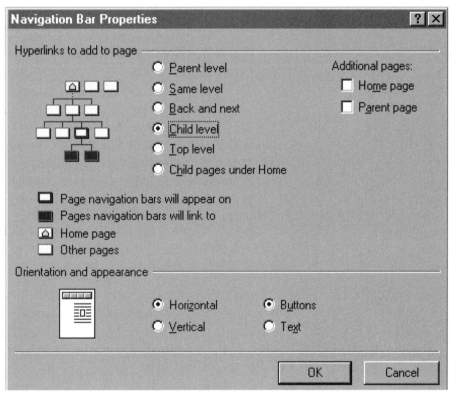

Figure 4.54 Setting the properties of a navigation bar in FrontPage

The navigation bar tool in FrontPage generates HTML code similar to this at the position where the bar is inserted:

```
<!--
webbot bot="Navigation" S-Type="children" S-Orientation=
"horizontal" S-Rendering="graphics" B-Include-Home
B-Include-Up U-Page S-Target
-->
```

This is not standard HTML code. It calls on a procedure – a **webbot** – *that is specific to FrontPage*. The navigation bar tool can create text or image hyperlinks.

PRACTICAL TASK 4.19

1 Open the fast-food site – or, if it is already open, close any pages.

2 Click on the Navigation view. An icon representing the index page will be shown (see Figure 4.55) with the title 'Home Page'. If the folder list is not displayed, click on the *Folder List* button.

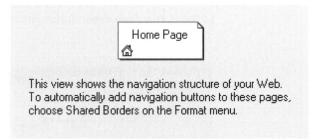

Figure 4.55 Index page for the fast-food website displayed in Navigation view

3 Drag the menu and jobs pages from the folders list on to the diagram to give the navigation structure shown in Figure 4.56. This has defined the relationships between the pages. The index page is the parent to the menu and jobs pages, and the menu page is a child of the index page.

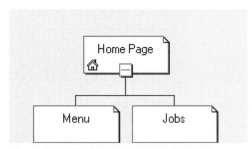

Figure 4.56 Navigation structure for the fast-food website

4 The site management tools can now create the navigation bars on the pages. Open the index page by clicking on its name in the folders list or on the page icon in Navigation view. Place the cursor where you want the navigation bar to appear. Select *Insert + Navigation Bar*, and the Navigation Bar Properties dialogue will appear (Figure 4.54). Under 'Hyperlinks to add to page', select *Child level*. Under 'Orientation and appearance', select *Horizontal* and *Buttons*, as in Figure 4.54.

5 In Preview mode, the page should look similar to Figure 4.57. The buttons do not look very impressive, but they can be transformed by the use of style sheets or themes.

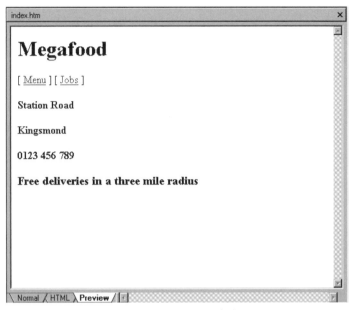

Figure 4.57 A navigation bar created on the index page

6 You now need to add navigation bars to the other two pages. Repeat the process that you used for the home page. This time provide links to pages at the same level as well as to the home page (as an additional page).

When you try out the links in Preview mode you will see that the navigation bar includes a non-functioning button that refers to the page that it is on (see Figure 4.58). This is equivalent to a greyed-out item on a drop-down menu in Windows-based software. It is important to include this non-functioning button as it means that the navigation bar items appear in the same positions on different pages. FrontPage always places the Home button to the left of the others.

Figure 4.58 The Jobs page with a navigation bar

Hyperlinks to other sites

When a hyperlink provides a link to a page on another website, the full URL must be given, like this:

```
<a href="http://news.bbc.co.uk/" target="_blank">BBC News</a>
```

◆ **target** defines the window where the page is opened. The default value is the same page.

◆ **_blank** opens the page in a new browser window.

Links to other sites can be added to any web page. Some sites provide no external links at all, because they do not want the visitor to leave the site once there. On the other hand, some sites contain very many links to other sites; where that is the main purpose it is known as a **portal site**.

Other uses of hyperlinks

A hyperlink can be used to encourage a visitor to send an email to the organisation's address, like this:

```
<a href="mailto://myname@thisismydomain.co.uk">Email me</a>
```

When this hyperlink is clicked, a new email window opens in the visitor's email client software, with the email address already inserted in the 'To:' field.

You can also create a hyperlink that will allow the visitor to download a file from the site. This can be any sort of file – a word processing file, program file etc. The file can be transferred using either hypertext transfer protocol (HTTP) or file transfer protocol (FTP). The HTML code in each case would be like these:

```
<a href="http://thisismydomain.co.uk/mydocument.doc">
    Download the document</a>
<a href="ftp://thisismydomain.co.uk/mydocument.doc">
    Download the document</a>
```

PRACTICAL TASK 4.20

1 Open the fast-food site – or, if it is already open, close any pages.

2 Create an external hyperlink. Add text to link to an external site on one of the pages. Highlight the text and select *Insert + Hyperlink*. In the URL box, enter the full URL of the website, including 'http://'. Alternatively, click on the web browser icon to the right of the URL box, and find the correct page with your browser. When you switch back to *FrontPage* the URL will be entered in the box.

3 Next create an email hyperlink. Enter text inviting people to email the manager. Highlight the text, and then select *Insert + Hyperlink*. Click on the email icon to the right of the URL box. Type in an email address.

4 Use Preview mode to check that these two links work correctly (see Figure 4.59).

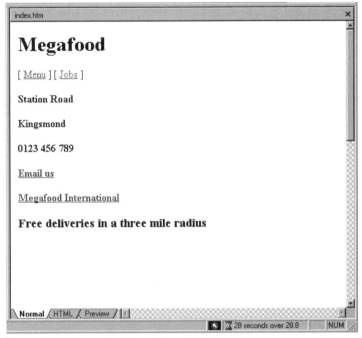

Figure 4.59 External and email hyperlinks

3.7 Creating image maps

A **hotspot** is an area of an image that acts as a hyperlink, and an image that has hotspots on it is known as an **image map**. Image maps can be used as highly graphical navigation bars. They can also be used to help the viewer identify items on a plan or geographical map of an area.

Web authoring packages usually provide an image mapping tool that you can use to develop them. They are a bit tricky to create directly in HTML, but again image mapping tools are available for HTML editors.

PRACTICAL TASK 4.21

You are going to create a map of an area which will show the delivery area for Megafood. This will be placed on the home page.

1 First create an imaginary map in a painting package (such as

Microsoft *Paint*). Alternatively, you could download a map from a website to experiment with.

2 Open the fast-food site you have created. Insert the map on the home page.

3 Click on the image and the Picture toolbar will appear at the bottom of the window. In the Picture bar there are four hotspot buttons, like this:

4 Click on the circular hotspot button. On the map, draw a circle centred on the shop location, as in Figure 4.60.

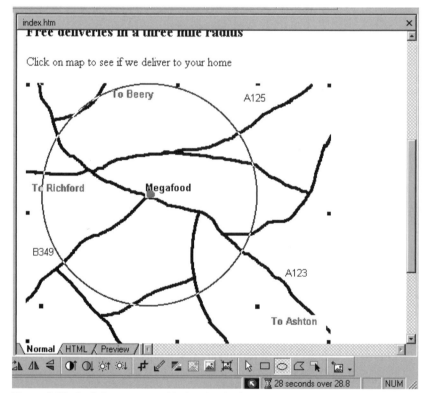

Figure 4.60 Outlining an area with the circular hotspot button

5 When you lift up the mouse button, the Create Hyperlink dialogue appears. From the list, click on the menu page and click *OK*.

6 You can now create hotpots for the areas outside the shop delivery zone. These could link to the websites of other shops, or to a new page that lists other shops.

7 Click on the Preview mode to check that it works correctly. If you click inside the hotspot area, the menu page appears.

3.8 Using metatags and other head tags

The HTML code between the **<head>** tags of a page, such as those below, contains some important information.

```
<head>
<meta http-equiv="Content-Type" content="text/html;
charset=Windows-1252">
<meta name="GENERATOR" content="Microsoft FrontPage 4.0">
<meta name="ProgId" content="FrontPage.Editor.Document">
<title>Menu</title>
</head>
```

These tags provide information about the page that follows, and a number of them are used by **search engines**. These can be edited directly in the HTML code, or web authoring tools can be used instead.

The **<title>** tag gives the title of the page, and this has two important functions. The title usually appears in the browser's title bar. Web authoring packages like *FrontPage* often use the first line of text on the page for the title, but it can be changed to something like:

```
<title>Pizzas, pastas and more to enjoy at Megafood</title>
```

Search engines display the title of a page when they list a site in response to a query, so that is good reason for making it meaningful.

The remaining tags are known as **metatags**. The default ones created by the web authoring package should not be changed. Two further very important ones are the **keyword** and **description** metatags.

◆ The keyword metatag contains a list of keywords that people might use in a search engine, like this:

```
<meta name="keywords" content="Megafood, fast food,
  pizza, pasta">
```

◆ The description metatag contains a description of the site, which may also be quoted by a search engine when it lists a site:

```
<meta name="description" content="Welcome to Megafood –
  where you can find the best fast food in Kingsmond. Pizzas,
  pastas and more.">.
```

3.9 Website development

The style sheet used in the example that follows is one of the samples provided with *FrontPage*, called 'Street'. The effect of this style sheet is shown in Figure 4.61.

Figure 4.61 A page formatted by a style sheet

Each style definition refers to one or more of the HTML tags. This is the **body style** definition in the style sheet:

    body {font-family: Verdana, Arial, Helvetica; background-color:
    rgb(204, 255, 255); color: rgb(0, 0, 102);}

This defines some properties that apply to the whole page between the **<body>** tags. The Normal style that can be selected from the style list is the default style, and this is initially defined by the system settings for the computer. The body style definition sets up the basic style for the page, and a browser will use this as the default style for the page.

◆ **background-color** (note the American spelling of colour) applies to the background of the whole page.

◆ **color** defines the default colour for the text on the page. This is expressed as an RGB (red, green, blue) colour code. Each of the three colour numbers can take a value from 0 (none of that particular colour) to 255 (full colour)

◆ **font-family**, in this case, lists three fonts, although the list can be of any length. The browser works along the list until it finds a font that it can use.

The visitor can view a font only if that font is already resident on the visitor's own system. So although in this case the designer would prefer the visitor to view the text in Verdana, the other two fonts are listed as **fallback** options. Only widely used fonts should be included in a style sheet, but as a precaution two basic fonts can be added to each definition, one font for Windows systems and one for Apple Mac systems.

◆ If the preferred font is a **serif font**, then Times New Roman and Times should be included.

◆ If the preferred font is **sans serif**, then Arial and Helvetica should be added.

The next style definition applies to more than one tag:

    h1, h2, h3, h4, h5, h6 {font-family: Comic Sans MS, Arial, Helvetica;}

The heading 1 style in the style list generates the **<h1>** tag in the HTML code, and so on. This style rule applies to all six heading tags and sets Comic Sans MS as the font for all the headings, with Arial and Helvetica as the fallback options.

The browser has to deal with the seeming contradiction between the font properties for the body and those for the headings. The font defined for the body is the default font and applies throughout the page except where another tag defines it differently. So the Verdana font is used everywhere except in the headings, where Comic Sans is used.

The next style rule defines the colour of one of the headings, and there will be similar rules for all the remaining heading styles:

    h1 {color: rgb(153, 0, 0);}

The <h1> tag has been used in Figure 4.61 for the central text 'Kingsmond Environmental Volunteers'. By default, heading styles are always bold, and the sizes decrease from h1 to h6.

The next style rules define three states that the hyperlinks take. The **<a>** tag is used for both bookmarks and hyperlinks, but these styles affect only the hyperlinks themselves:

    a:link {color: rgb(0, 102, 102);}
    a:visited {color: rgb(0, 153, 153);}
    a:active {color: rgb(255, 102, 0);}

◆ **a:link** is the normal style used for the hyperlink.

◆ **a:visited** is the style used for a hyperlink that has already been followed.

◆ **a:active** is the style used when the mouse button is held down on a hyperlink.

◆ **a:hover** (not used in this example) is the style used when the mouse passes over the hyperlink.

The link to the Kingsmond Herald at the bottom of the window in Figure 4.61 uses the <a> tag, and can take on one of three different colours.

PRACTICAL TASK 4.22

In this activity, you will create a website for a local group. You will use a cascading style sheet to give the page its style and will later add a separate side frame to hold the navigation bar.

It is a good idea to work in 1024 pixels horizontal resolution. The pages will be designed to be viewed at 800 pixels resolution, but by using a wider window in *FrontPage,* you will also be able to see the Views bar and the folder list at the same time as the page itself.

1 Create a new empty web. Select *New + Page*, then select the *Style Sheets* tab. Select the 'Streets' style sheet template and save it as 'mystyles.css'. Create and save a template based on it.

2 Use the template to create a new page and save it as 'home.htm'. Although this will be the home page for the site it will not actually be the first page that is loaded, so is not saved as 'index.htm'.

3 Set up a table to hold the contents of the page. It should be 600 pixels wide, and aligned to the left. Use *Page Properties* to set the page margins to zero. This ensures that the page takes up no more than 600 pixels width.

4 Use *Page Properties* to set the top and left margins to zero.

5 Now add some text and images to the page. Use the styles from the style list, such as heading 1. Include at least one external hyperlink.

Editing style sheets

A pre-designed style sheet can be modified. This can be done by simply amending the text in the style sheet file. In *FrontPage*, the process can be simplified by using the Style dialogues.

A new style sheet could look like this (note the American spellings):

a:link {font-weight: bold; color: gray; text-decoration: none;}

a:visited {font-weight: bold; color: gray; text-decoration: none;}

a:hover {font-weight: bold; color: silver; text-decoration: none;}

body {font-family: Verdana, Arial, Helvetica; font-size: 12pt; background-color: white; color: rgb(0, 102, 51);}

h1 {font-family: Comic Sans MS, Arial, Helvetica; font-size: 20pt; text-align: center; color: white; background-color: rgb(0, 102, 51); border-width: 5pt; border-style: double; border-color: white; padding: 3pt;}

Other style definitions for h2, h3 etc. can be added when needed. Note that a style definition for *a:hover* has been added, and that some of the definitions have been deleted from the earlier code.

The effect of this style sheet can be seen in Figure 4.62. The underlining on the 'Kingsmond Herald' hyperlink has been removed, but the use of a different colour and bold face indicates to the visitor that it is a hyperlink. This is confirmed by its hover state – when the mouse is passed over the link it changes from a dark grey to a light grey.

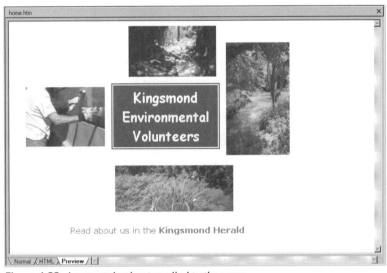

Figure 4.62 A new style sheet applied to the page

Fast and effective hover links can be created using a style sheet and without the use of images. The background, border and padding properties can be used to give a rectangular box around the text, which could change colour in hover mode.

Note

There are many properties that can be applied to tags in style sheet rules. You will need to consult a handbook on cascading style sheets to see them all.

PRACTICAL TASK 4.23

You can change the style sheet by clicking on the *Style* button in the Style floating toolbar. But you can also edit the style sheet directly.

1   In Normal view, first close any pages that are open, then open file 'mystyles.css'. Make changes and save it. A style sheet must be saved before any changes can be observed in a page.

2   If you amend a stylesheet while a page is open, when you switch back to the page you will have to click on the *Refresh* button to reload the page and view the effects of the changes.

3 Now use the Page template to create another page for the website, in which the content should also sit inside a table 600 pixels wide. Do not include any navigation links at this stage.

Creating frames

Frames can be created directly in HTML. The process is quite complex so there is much to be said for using a web authoring package.

Frames are created in a **frame page**, which sets down the sizes and properties of all the frames that are being used (refer back to Figure 4.24 on page 237). The frame page is always loaded first into the browser, so it is usually made the index page for a website. The frame page creates the empty structure and then loads the pages into each of the frames.

PRACTICAL TASK 4.24

Working with the same web as before, you will create a vertical navigation bar which will appear in a frame to the left side of the page. The side page will be 180 pixels wide, so that it will sit alongside the 600 pixels width main pages. The total width of 780 pixels allows for the scrollbar to the right side of a 800 pixels width window.

When using frames, you should not use the Navigation tool in *FrontPage*.

1 Create a new page, using the Page template, and save it as 'side.htm'. Use *Page Properties* to set the page margins to zero.

2 Create a table 180 pixels wide, with one column and one row. The cell padding should be non-zero, so that text is not pushed up against the sides of the frame.

3 Enter an image or some information at the top. Then add links to 'home.htm' and to the other page that you have already created. See Figure 4.63 for an example of how the side page might look.

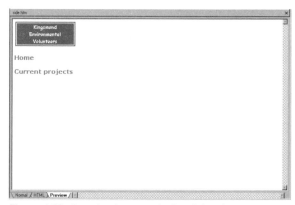

Figure 4.63 A navigation page before it has been integrated into a frame

4 Next the frame page itself will be created. Select *File + New + Page*, then click on the *Frames Pages* tab. Select the Contents template. The frame structure will appear as in Figure 4.64. Save the page as 'index.htm'.

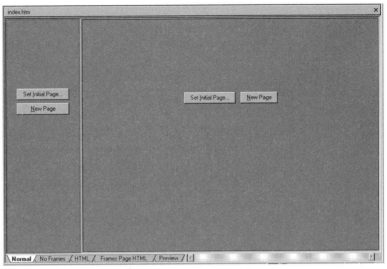

Figure 4.64 The frame structure displayed in FrontPage

5 Right-click anywhere in the left frame, and click on *Frame Properties*. In the dialogue box that appears, set the width to 180 pixels, and both the margins to zero. Under 'Options', you do not want the frame to be resizable, so remove the tick. You also do not want a scroll bar to appear in this frame, so for 'Show scrollbars' select *Never*. The dialogue should now look like Figure 4.65.

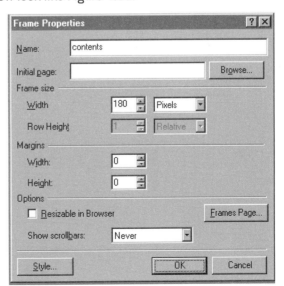

Figure 4.65 The Frame Properties dialogue box

6 In the right frame, simply set the margins to zero.

7 In the left frame, click on *Set Initial Page*, then select 'side.htm'. Similarly, select 'home.htm' for the right frame. Save the frame page again.

8 View the whole frame page by selecting Preview mode (see Figure 4.66).

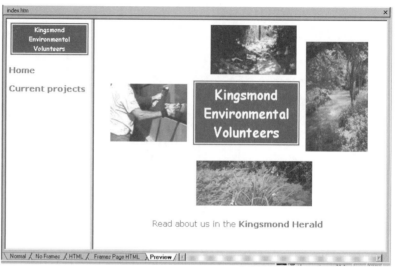

Figure 4.66 A two-frame page

9 The border between the two frames can be removed. Return to Normal mode on the index page, then right-click in the left frame and select *Frame Properties* again. Click on the *Frames Pages* button, and on the *Frames* tab set 'Frame spacing' to zero and make sure that the 'Show borders' box is not ticked.

10 Check the page again in Preview mode. Select the other page in the navigation bar and check that it loads into the main frame, as in Figure 4.67.

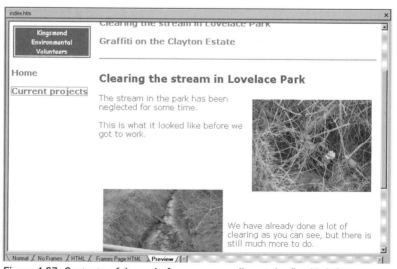

Figure 4.67 Contents of the main frame can scroll past the fixed left frame

Finishing the site

You might like to add an image map (see page 271), identifying the location of all the projects. Metatags (see page 273) should be added before publishing the site.

Chapter summary

You should be able to use web authoring software to:

◆ manage a complete website
◆ create an external style sheet linked to a page template
◆ embed and modify images on a page
◆ use tables and frames for layout
◆ create hyperlinks and navigation bars
◆ create image maps.

---

4 Test websites

4.1 Technical testing

Before a site is published on the WWW, it should be subjected to thorough technical testing, and the tests should all be repeated after the site has been published, along with additional tests. These tests should be constructed to check that the final website matches the original design specification, bearing in mind any amendments that may have been made to the specification during the prototyping stage.

The technical design of a website concentrates on usability issues:

◆ *navigation* – should be tested both before and after publishing
◆ *use of search tools* – best tested after publishing
◆ *download times* – best tested after publishing
◆ *browser compatibility* – should be tested both before and after publishing
◆ *maintenance* – best tested with the client after publishing.

All testing should be carried out in a browser, not in the Preview mode of a web authoring package. The site can be opened in a browser by navigating to the position of the index page on your local drive.

All websites should be fully tested before they go live. They should then be tested again after they have been uploaded to the Internet. Similar tests should also be done whenever a site is updated.

4.2 Style issues

Images

◆ Check that each image occupies the intended space on the screen and is positioned correctly.

◆ Select the properties of each image to check how much memory each uses. Do not forget to include any graphical buttons or bullets that you have used. Calculate the total memory used by all the images on each page. Aim to keep the total to under 60KB per page.

◆ If you want to use a larger image (for example, if you want to offer your visitor the chance to see a full-size photo), you should warn visitors before they link to the page that it will be a slow download.

Layout

◆ Check that each page appears as intended in your usual browser.

◆ Check the whole site on an earlier version of the browser you are using.

◆ Check the whole site on a different browser.

4.3 Verifying links

Before the site is uploaded, the home page should be opened in a browser. These tests should be carried out.

◆ Check that each of the links from the main navigation bar loads the correct page.

◆ Check that the links in the main navigation bar on all other pages behave as expected.

◆ Check all the internal links on each page.

It is important to document the tests carried out on a site as you do them. It is very easy to lose track of the tests you have done, and then to repeat tests unnecessarily, or even leave some out. When you check links you can create a chart like the one in Figure 4.68.

Page: products.htm

Link to:	OK?	Notes
contacts.htm		
home.htm		
cartridges.htm	Bad link	Update this

Figure 4.68 Keep a record of your checking of page links

4.4 Preview in different browsers

Web pages do not appear exactly the same in each browser, mainly because of the slightly different ways in which browsers interpret the HTML code attributes. *Internet Explorer* and *Netscape* are the most used browsers; others, such as *Opera*, are used by smaller numbers of visitors. Older versions of these browsers are still being used.

Your website should first be checked in your resident browser at both 800 and 1024 pixels horizontal screen resolutions. The full width of each page should be visible at 800 pixels without scrolling sideways. The site should also look reasonable when a full-size window is opened at 1024 pixels width.

The site should then be checked in the alternative browsers at both resolutions. If possible, the site should then be checked in the oldest versions of each browser.

Note

The latest versions of both Internet Explorer *and* Netscape *can be downloaded free of charge from their respective websites, which are www.microsoft.com/windows/ie and http://www.netscape.com.*

Changes may have to be made to the pages to ensure that the displays in all cases are as compatible as possible and that any minor differences are acceptable.

4.5 Testing a website after uploading

Immediately after a site has been uploaded to the webserver, it should be tested by entering the URL in a browser.

The full set of technical tests should then be repeated. The most common errors found at this stage occur if a file has not been uploaded, or if one has been uploaded to an incorrect remote directory.

Additional technical testing can be carried out. The designer should:

◆ test each external link to ensure that it loads the correct site

◆ ascertain how long it takes to download each page, including all the images, using the slowest dial-up connections.

Chapter summary

◆ A website should be tested thoroughly both before and after it is published on the World Wide Web.

◆ The testing should check all internal and external links.

◆ Page layout and appearance should be tested in a number of different browsers and with different screen settings.

5 Use graphics software to create and manipulate images on web pages

5.1 Manipulating an image

If you want to prepare images for use on a web page, the best option is to use specialist graphics software. General painting packages, such as Microsoft *Paint*, can be used to create images and also to manipulate existing images. You can then save the images in JPG or GIF format.

Photo manipulation packages such as Microsoft *Photo Editor*, Corel *PhotoHouse* or Adobe *PhotoShop* provide a number of tools that help you to optimise the appearance of photos. They can also be used to work with any ready-drawn bitmap image.

Web authoring software sometimes offers you a limited range of image manipulation tools and these can be used if specialist graphics packages are not available.

PRACTICAL TASK 4.25

You can insert **clipart** on a web page in *FrontPage* just as you can in word processing or desktop publishing documents. You can then use the inbuilt image manipulation tools to change it.

1 Click on the page where you want the clipart to appear. Select *Insert + Picture + Clipart*, then choose the clipart image that you want. It will be inserted on the page.

2 The clipart image will probably have to be changed before it is right for your page (see Figure 4.69). Click on the image, and the Pictures toolbar will appear at the bottom of the window.

Figure 4.69 Clipart inserted on the page, with the Pictures toolbar

3 You can use the buttons on the Pictures toolbar to rotate or flip the image. You can also change the brightness and contrast of the colours.

4 If you want to go back to the original drawing, click on the *Restore* button.

The clipart image will look odd if the background colour of the page is different from the background colour of the GIF. A technique will be explained later for overcoming this by making the background of the GIF transparent.

5.2 Image file size and type

When you download a web page from the Internet, the browser first of all downloads the actual page file. It then downloads all the image files that are used on the page. If there are a lot of images this can take some time, especially on a slow dial-up connection.

Most of the image files that you use in word processing or desktop publishing take up a great deal of memory. The size of the image file can vary from a few kilobytes up to several megabytes.

For example, photos taken with a digital camera are often 2MB or 4MB in size. If you could put these on a website and then tried to download them, they would take many minutes on a slow modem. For this reason, all images on a website are stored in a compressed format which gives much smaller file sizes.

For most pages, try to limit the total memory size of all the images on a page to 60 kilobytes. Larger images can be used if the user is expecting an image-rich site, or if he or she is warned that the page may take a while to download.

You can find out how big an image file is. Click on the images folder in the folder list. Right-click on the image file, and select *Properties*. The Properties dialogue window tells you how big the file is in kilobytes (see Figure 4.70).

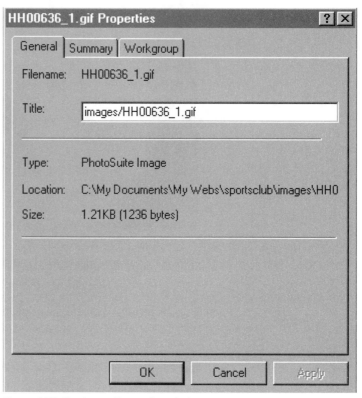

Figure 4.70 The image Properties window

Number of colours

We have already looked at the colour depth of screens. The two image formats that are used on the WWW use differing colour depth.

◆ **JPG** (or JPEG) can use 16- or 24-bit colour values.

◆ **GIF** uses only 8-bit colour values.

The JPG format usually uses 24-bit colour values. That provides over 16 million different colours, which is more than can be distinguished by the human eye. That is why JPGs are used for photographs.

The GIF format uses 8-bit colour values which provides only 256 different colours. GIFs are ideal for simple icons and line drawings.

File compression

The package will offer you some choice over the level of compression for JPGs. A more compressed photo will take up less memory, but will also display less detail. If a dialogue box asks you to chose the quality, select 75 per cent. On the other hand, if you are asked to specify the degree of compression, select 25 per cent. These two choices have exactly the same effect as each other, but unfortunately software packages are not consistent in the way they ask the question.

Manipulating compressed images

Once an image has been saved in a compressed form, GIF or JPG, you should not try to manipulate it any further. If the image is compressed for a second time the quality may suffer noticeably. Always go back to the original version before it was compressed if you want to make any more changes.

You may not have access to the bitmap version of an image but have it only in JPG format (e.g. if you use a photo from a CD). After you have reduced the size, save the image again as a JPG, but this time choose 100 per cent quality or zero per cent compression. If you compress the image a second time the image may become distorted. Check the memory used. If it is too large then experiment with a small amount of compression.

Dimensions of an image

Most photographs should be cropped before being used on a web page. You need to cut out the unnecessary parts of the picture and just focus on the key elements. Photos on a website do not have to conform to any of the standard picture ratios, so can be any shape. If you need to crop a picture do so before you reduce the dimensions.

Note

Images are usually reduced in size before use on a web page. It is not a good idea to enlarge an existing image. Often enlarged images suffer from the 'jaggies', which is the nickname for the jagged edges that you sometimes see on graphics (e.g. Figure 4.71).

Figure 4.71 A case of jaggies in an image that has been enlarged

PRACTICAL TASK 4.26

FrontPage allows you to manipulate images to a certain extent, without using specialist graphics package. You can resize an image directly on the page, but you must resample it to save it again at its new dimensions. This ensures that the image file is no larger than it needs to be.

FrontPage will also convert an image to a GIF or JPG for you automatically when you save it.

1 Resize the clipart image you used before by dragging on the corner handles. If you drag on one of the side handles the image will be squashed in one direction only. If you drag on one of the corner handles the image will get smaller but still keep the same proportions. The image may look a little distorted at this stage.

2 Click on the image, then click on the *Resample* button in the Pictures toolbar. Not only does this reduce the size of the image file but it also improves the appearance of the image (see Figure 4.72). The button looks like this:

Figure 4.72 *The handles have been used to resize the image*

3 Save the page. The Save Embedded Files dialogue window will appear. The name of the images folder should appear under Folder. If the word 'Images' does not appear under Folder, then click on *Change Folder*, and select the images folder.

4 *FrontPage* will convert the image to GIF format and then save the image as a separate file in the images folder.

You can check which image files have been saved by clicking on the images folder in the folders list.

Background images

A background image can be applied to a page instead of a background colour. Backgrounds should be chosen carefully as too much detail can distract the visitor from the text, or even obscure it (see Figure 4.73). All backgrounds are automatically **tiled** – that is, repeated to fill the available space – so quite a small image can be used.

Figure 4.73 Use of an unsuitable background image (tiled)

Web authoring packages usually provide a selection of background images, which are defined in the HTML code like this:

```
<body background="images/ripple.gif">
```

PRACTICAL TASK 4.27

1 To change the background image on a page, select *Format + Style*. Select the body tag, then use the *Border* option and select the *Shading* tab.

2 In the Background Picture box, browse to find a suitable image. You will probably have some background images in your clipart gallery.

Note

The JPG format uses 3 bytes per pixel so takes up more memory than the GIF format. Also, the method of compression is rather different, and beyond the scope of this unit, but the effect is to make GIFs far more economical in terms of memory.

If you do need photorealistic images, or you need to match colours exactly, then you should use the JPG format. Otherwise, experiment with the GIF format to see whether it produces an acceptable image. Web pages download much more quickly if the images are in GIF format.

5.3 Transparency

In Figure 4.72 the telephone image has a black background so fits on the black background of the page. But most clipart and many other images have a white background, so the image can look very odd on the page (see Figure 4.74).

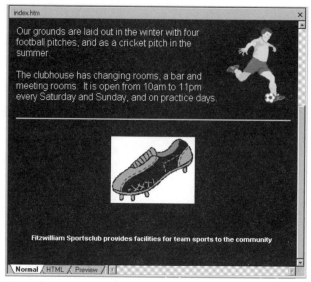

Figure 4.74 The boot image has the wrong colour background

In the GIF format you can make the background of the image **transparent** so that the background colour of the page shows through. You can do this in any full graphics package that generates GIFs. Some web authoring packages allow you to do this to the image directly on the page.

PRACTICAL TASK 4.28

You can experiment with transparency by inserting clipart.

1   Click on the page where you want the clipart to be placed. Select *Insert + Picture + Clipart*, then choose a clipart image that has a different colour background from the background on your page.

2   Click on the image, then click on the *Set Transparent Color* button. You may get a message at this point – if so, click on *OK*. The button looks like this:

3   Click on the background of the image. In the example in Figure 4.74 you would click somewhere in the white area around the boot. The background of the image will become transparent, and show the background colour of the page (see Figure 4.75).

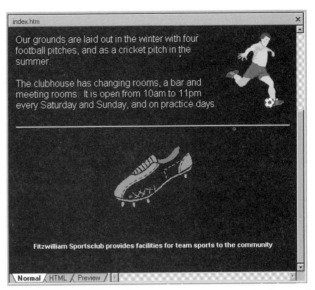

Figure 4.75 The boot image now has a transparent background

4   Save the page and the image as before.

5.4 Colour codes

24-bit colours, as used for JPGs and bitmaps, are stored in RGB (red, green, blue) format. Eight bits are used for each of the three colours, and combinations of these three primary colours give all the possible hues.

The **RGB codes** consist of three numbers, each of which has a value from 0 (none of that colour) to 255 (maximum colour). In a style sheet you will see that colours are expressed like this:

rgb(51, 102, 204)

Thus rgb(51, 102, 204) has some red, more green and a lot of blue, and displays as a strong mid blue.

Black is the complete absence of colour so has the code rgb(0, 0, 0), while white is created by combining all colours and has the code rgb(255, 255, 255). It can be quite tricky working out colour codes for a particular shade from scratch, but colour charts can be found on the WWW. Colours in graphics packages are determined in a similar way.

The **numerical value of a colour** can be expressed in decimal (0 to 255) or hexadecimal (#00 to #FF) numbers. Thus rgb(51, 102, 204) is the same as #3366CC (# is used to denote hexadecimal numbers).

Web safe colour codes

The appearance of colours does vary from screen to screen, even when set at the same colour depth. A limited number of colours have been found to appear clearly and without **dithering** on all screens. These are known as the web safe colours.

In *FrontPage* you may have noticed that only a limited number of colour values are used in the pre-designed style sheets – 0, 51, 102, 153, 204 and 255. The hexadecimal (hex) equivalents are 00, 33, 66, 99, CC and FF. Colours constructed with one of these values for each of the three RGB components make up the web safe colours. Thus rgb(153, 0, 51) is a Web safe colour, whilst rgb(57, 139, 17) is not.

That does not mean that you should never use colours outside the web safe list – indeed photos normally contain many more colours. But if a colour is to be used over a large area – for example, as a background colour – then you should choose from the web safe palette.

Chapter summary

You should be able to use graphics software (including tools within web authoring packages) to:

◆ reduce an image to the correct dimensions
◆ save it in either JPG or GIF compressed formats
◆ create a transparent area on a GIF image
◆ change colours in an image
◆ to select and use web safe colours.

6 Publish and maintain web pages

6.1 Publishing your website

To publish a website on the WWW a designer needs:

◆ access to space on a webserver
◆ a domain name that points to the website on the server
◆ the means to transfer the pages and other files to the webserver.

Webservers and web hosts

A webserver is a computer linked to the Internet which stores one or more websites. A web host is a company that owns one or more webservers, and rents out space on the webservers to others.

All the files and folders that make up a website must be uploaded to a webserver before they can be made available on the Internet. A large commercial organisation may own its own webserver, but the majority of websites are hosted by web hosts.

Most Internet service providers (ISPs) also act as web hosts, and many include a certain amount of web space with their accounts. Typically, the space will be 20Mb to 30Mb in size, and this is more than enough for a quite substantial site. Larger amounts of space can usually be acquired at additional cost.

There are also some specialist web hosting companies. These companies can be found easily by searching for 'web hosts'. Sometimes free space is offered, but this often carries the condition that the site must display some advertising for the host. It may be acceptable to display advertising of this kind on a personal website, but it is not appropriate on a website for a commercial enterprise.

Server-side scripts

Some sites can function properly only if they are hosted on servers that also store additional support software (or **scripts**). In each case, the designer must ensure that the webserver does support the requirements of the website.

Sites developed in *FrontPage* often include special functions that make use of additional software, known as **FrontPage extensions**, stored on the webserver. These are not made available by all webservers; in particular, a number of the major ISPs that include web space in their low-cost packages do not support *FrontPage* extensions.

CGI scripts are used on many webservers. FormMail.pl is a script that is used by many web designers to generate emails from data collected by an online form. The ISP will provide the URL of this script on their server.

Registering a domain name

A domain name, such as 'thisismydomain.co.uk', must be **registered** with one of the registration organisations. All domain names ending with .uk are registered with **Nominet**. There are a number of official registries for .com and other domains. A fee is charged for domain name registration.

Domain names are often registered through ISPs who then carry out the formal registration process on behalf of the organisation or individual. Once the domain name has been registered, the ISP will ensure that the domain name points to the correct web space on their webserver.

A **Whois server** can be searched to find out which domain names are currently registered and which are still available. Again, most ISPs provide a Whois search facility.

Choosing a domain name can be a challenging task, as many millions of names have already been registered. There have been some legal moves to protect commercial names from being registered by individuals who have no connection with the companies, as in the past so-called cyber-squatters have tried to charge well-known organisations large sums to transfer registered domain names to them.

Uploading files to a webserver

When a website has been tested it can be uploaded (published) to the chosen webserver. If the webserver is in-house – that is, owned by the organisation – then the system administrators will provide guidance to users about how to transfer the files to the webserver.

If an external webserver managed by an ISP is used, then all the files and directories will have to be transferred by the designer. This can be done either using the publishing tool built into a web authoring package, or by using file transfer protocol (**FTP**) software. In both cases the following data is needed:

◆ the domain name
◆ the user's name (as registered with the ISP)
◆ the user's password.

FTP shareware software can be downloaded from the Internet. To use it, the user must be online to the Internet. A dialogue window asks for the required data, then locates the web space on the remote server. Figure 4.76 shows a typical layout. The left side shows the files and directories on the home computer (**local system**) and the right side shows the files and directories already on the webserver (**remote system**). The user highlights the files and directories to be uploaded from the left side, then clicks on the right-pointing arrow to transfer them across.

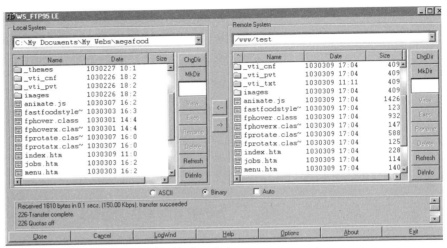

Figure 4.76 FTP software provided by Ipswitch

All the files that make up the site must be transferred, including page files, style sheets, any script files, the images directory and its contents, plus any folders and files that may have been created by the web authoring package.

PRACTICAL TASK 4.29

1 In FrontPage, select *File + Publish Web*. A dialogue box appears as in Figure 4.77.

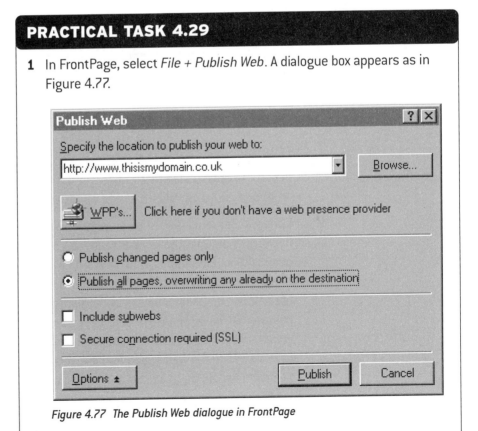

Figure 4.77 The Publish Web dialogue in FrontPage

2 Enter the URL of the domain, then click on 'Publish all pages' (if this is not visible, click on the *Options* button). Click on *Publish*.

3 You will then be asked for your user name and password, as used with your ISP.

An animation records progress, and when the site has been successfully uploaded you will be informed and prompted to view it in your browser.

6.2 Search engines

Search engines are continually crawling through the WWW by following all the links from one site to another. As they do this, they maintain huge indexing databases about the sites. In particular, they note the **keywords** and **descriptions** in the metatags (see page 273), and they also extract keywords from the text on pages. The indexes are then referred to whenever a user enters text in a search engine.

It can take some time for a search engine to discover a new website, but sites can be registered directly with them. Many search engines have UK versions which enable the visitor to restrict the search to UK sites if desired. The most widely used search engines are **Google** (www.google.co.uk), **AllTheWeb** (www.alltheweb.com), **Yahoo!** (uk.yahoo.com) which is powered by Google, **MSN Search** (search.msn.co.uk) and **Ask Jeeves** (www.ask.co.uk).

6.3 Internet security

Unauthorised access to the webserver

In order to upload files to a webserver the designer needs three items of data – the domain name, plus the user name and password for the account.

If the webserver is owned by an organisation and connected to its internal network, then unauthorised access may be possible from within the organisation. Employees who have legitimate access to the server can at times be careless with their user IDs. Even if confidentiality is not breached, user names usually follow a standard pattern within an organisation, and passwords can often be predicted. It can sometimes be easy for an employee who wants to damage the organisation, or who simply wants to play a joke, to gain access to the web space and then change the content. Of course, such behaviour would be traceable and would lead to instant dismissal.

Webservers located within organisations can be protected from external interference by **firewalls**. A webserver owned by an ISP is much more vulnerable. Someone who knows the user name and password for a domain can gain access to the web space from any computer that is connected to the Internet anywhere in the world.

Computer Misuse Act 1990

The Computer Misuse Act makes any unauthorised access ('**hacking**') to a computer system illegal. It defines three offences in increasing order of seriousness.

1 *Unauthorised access to computer material*. The key issues here are whether someone was authorised to access a computer system, and whether the person deliberately did something with the intention of gaining unlawful access. If someone accidentally gains access to a system then he or she is not guilty of an offence, although would be if continuing to explore the system once realising what had happened.

2 *Unauthorised access with intent to commit or facilitate commission of further offences*. This deals with cases where the person intends to commit another crime, such as theft or blackmail, and is gaining unauthorised access in order to do so.

3 *Unauthorised modification of computer material*. This section of the Act outlaws the intentional alteration or deletion of data when the person does not have authority to do so.

Someone who alters a website without authority would be guilty of the third, and most serious, offence.

Secure servers

A webserver may hold database files, containing information collected from the website through an online form. Organisations that collect personal data from customers in this way have to be particularly vigilant in protecting their webservers from unauthorised access. They need to do this:

◆ to comply with the **Data Protection Act**

◆ to reassure customers that personal data about them will be **secure**

◆ to encourage customers to provide credit card details for **online transactions**.

A secure server **encrypts** all the data stored on it (see page 233), so if anyone does gain illegal access he or she will not be able to understand or use the data. Secure servers are used for all financial transactions over the Internet, and increasingly for the collection of other personal data (see Figure 4.78).

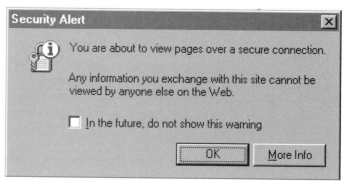

Figure 4.78 Message given when using a secure server

When a website is on a secure server you will see a small **padlock icon** at the bottom of the window as in Figure 4.79.

Figure 4.79 The icon to indicate that a web page is on a secure server

Chapter summary

◆ FTP software, or tools built into web authoring packages, are used to upload a website to a webserver. This process makes the site available on the WWW and is sometimes referred to as publishing a website. Secure servers are used for websites that capture confidential data.

◆ Sites developed in *FrontPage* need to be supported by scripts stored on the webserver.

◆ A domain name can be registered, and pointed to the site on the webserver.

◆ A site can be registered with a search engine, although the engines themselves find sites by crawling the WWW.

◆ Unauthorised access to webservers is covered by the **Computer Misuse Act 1990**.

Index